THE JAZZ ANTHOLOGY

Miles Kington was born in Northern Ireland in 1941, grew up in Northern Wales and was sent to school in Scotland. After reading French and German at Oxford, the very first regular writing job he acquired was as jazz reviewer for *The Times*, which he did for ten years, but he also joined the staff of *Punch* in 1967 and stuck it out there till 1980. He wrote the Moreover column for *The Times* thereafter for seven years, and since 1987 has been writing a daily column for the *Independent*.

He fell in love with the sound of jazz at the age of twelve, and took up the trombone to play this music, but when he found he had embraced the hardest instrument of all he switched to the double bass at university after hearing someone say: 'There isn't a single bass player at Oxford – if someone took it up, he'd make a fortune.' He was a member of the group Instant Sunshine for twenty years, but is still hoping to get into a real jazz group and make that fortune.

MILES KINGTON

The Jazz Anthology

HarperCollins*Publishers*

HarperCollins*Publishers*
77–85 Fulham Palace Road,
Hammersmith, London W6 8JB

This paperback edition 1993
1 3 5 7 9 8 6 4 2

First published in Great Britain by
HarperCollins*Publishers* 1992

ISBN 0 00 638233 9

Set in Linotron Bembo

Printed in Great Britain by
HarperCollinsManufacturing Glasgow

Contents

Acknowledgements

We are grateful to the following authors, owners of copyright, publishers and literary agents who have kindly given permission for material to appear:

Doubleday Publishers for the extract from *Dizzy* by Dizzy Gillespie; Faber and Faber Ltd for extracts from *The McJazz Manuscripts* by Sandy Brown, *Russian Journal* by Andrea Lee and *All What Jazz* by Philip Larkin; Dave Gelly for the extract from *Wire*; HarperCollins Publishers for extracts from *I Remember Jazz* by Al Rose; William Heinemann Ltd for the extracts from *We Called It Music* by Eddie Condon, *Hear Me Talkin' To Ya* by Stan Kenton and *A Girl in Paris* by Shusha Guppy; Hutchinson Publishers for extracts from *Memoirs* by Kingsley Amis; MacGibbon & Kee, an imprint of HarperCollins Publishers, for the extracts from *The Jazz Scene* by Eric Hobsbawm; Pumpkin Productions Inc for extracts from Dick Wellstood's sleeve notes; Quartet Books Ltd for the extracts from *La Tristesse de St Louis* and *Close Enough for Jazz* by Mike Zwerin, *Bix: The Man and the Legend* by Richard Sudhalter and Philip Evans, *Round About Close to Midnight* by Boris Vian (trans. Mike Zwerin) and *All This and Many a Dog* by Jim Godbolt; the University of California Press for the extracts from *Pops Foster: The Autobiography of a New Orleans Jazz Man* by George Foster, with Tom Stoddard; Ian Whitcomb for extracts from *After the Ball*; Women's Press Ltd for extracts from *Mama Said There'd Be Days Like This* by Val Wilmer; Mrs Diana Plomley for extracts from *Desert Island Lists* by Roy Plomley; Institute of Jazz Studies at Rutgers University for extracts from their archives; Hodder & Stoughton Ltd/New English Library Ltd for the extract from *Celebrating Bird* by Gary Giddins; Oxford University Press for extracts from *Jazz Anecdotes* by Bill Crow; Louisiana State University Press for the extract from *Those Swinging Years: The Autobiography of Charlie Barnet* with Stanley Dance; Spellmount Ltd for the extract from *Lester Young* by Dave Gelly; *Punch* for the extract by Paul Desmond; Mark Roman for his article in *Esquire*; David Bolt Associates for the extracts from *Colin Wilson on Music* by Colin Wilson; and Artie Shaw quotations on pages 32–3, 161 and 300 are used by permission of Pathfinder Publishing of California, publishers of *Dialogues in Swing* by Fred Hall.

Every effort has been made to contact the copyright owners of material included in this anthology. In the instances where this has not proved possible, we offer our apologies to those concerned.

Introduction

Ask jazz enthusiasts to tell you their favourite records or musicians, and you will have a hard job stopping them compiling an endless list. But ask them to name a favourite piece of writing about jazz, and you will almost certainly draw a complete blank. I know. I've tried, during the compilation of this anthology, to persuade normally voluble jazz people to suggest examples of jazz writing, and you might have thought, from the resulting silence, that nobody had ever written anything about jazz at all.

This is, however, far from the case. There are hundreds of books about jazz. Many musicians have written, or have had written for them, their life stories. Many a jazz reviewer has pontificated in the pages of many a jazz magazine. But a great deal of this is not the sort of creative writing, or even memorably lively or humorous writing, that you look for in an anthology. What the jazz enthusiast has historically demanded from prose is facts.

I can clearly remember becoming aware of this strange thirst back in 1957. I was sixteen in 1957 and had been sent by my father to spend some of the summer holidays with a family in Paris in order to learn more French. Actually, the family was an elderly widow called Madame Buhler and her middle-aged niece who lived elsewhere, so I had a good deal of freedom to come and go, some of which I used to visit jazz clubs wherever I could find them. My favourite haunt was La Cigale, in Pigalle, where there was a band led by a Caribbean trumpeter called Jacques Butler and a veteran tenor saxophonist called Benny Waters. So veteran was Benny Waters that he had played in the 1920s with King Oliver; to me he seemed like living history, although I realize looking back that it was only thirty years previously that Waters had recorded with Oliver and that this leathery-skinned man, whom I took to be ancient, was merely in his fifties.

Anyway, one night I was there I overheard a British jazz fan talking to Benny Waters, a thing I wasn't brave enough to do, and he was asking Waters what he obviously considered a vital question: could Waters remember, on a session he had recorded with King Oliver in the late 1920s – and here he stabbed at a page in a book he was carrying – could he remember what had been the name of the banjo player?

To the jazz fan, this was a great moment. He was face to face with a man who had actually played on that historic session and could elucidate perhaps, once and for all, the personnel mystery connected with that date. To Benny Waters, it was quite something else; it was one of the stupidest questions he had been asked for a long time, and he burst out laughing. The man persisted. Benny Waters made it plain that he couldn't remember, after all this time, the session, the line-up, the circumstances or anything, and couldn't see any reason for remembering, thirty years on. The conversation never really recovered from this painful start, and died soon afterwards.

More than the followers of most kinds of music, jazz listeners are record collectors and record experts, because recordings are the only tangible evidence of the music they love, and the more they know about records, the more they feel they know about the music. (It is quite extraordinary that jazz, which is created afresh every time it is played and is never the same twice, should be listened to on record at all, which condemns it to being repeated exactly the same, but this is a painful paradox jazz people always ignore.) Jazz is created live, spontaneously, and listened to by most fans repetitively, if not by memory. Musicians on the other hand are generally not great record players or listeners and it is hard to get musicians to nominate records of their own which they like. The British bass player Jeff Clyne once told me that he had been involved in the making of an LP which he thought was quite superb and the best thing since records began. This was so untypical of musicians that I pressed him a little further, only to find that the record had been made two years previously and never released. It was the very lack of release that made him think so fondly of it. The next time I met him it *had* been released.

'Your tremendous record is out now, then,' I said.

'Which one's that?' he said.

I explained.

'Oh, *that* one,' he said. 'Yeah, it was all right, I suppose. Nothing special.'

So to a musician the important thing is that a record should be made, pressed and delivered to the public, like a message sent out. The things that are important to a fan – who played on it, when, what tunes, how many takes – are much less important to a player. Yet so strong is the statistical instinct of jazz fans, what one might call the train-spotting side, that whole books, called discographies, have been published with nothing but lists of the recording dates of musicians through their whole lives, with personnels, dates, places and so on. Discographies can be made of any kind of music, but it seems probable that they were first devised to serve the jazz world. It may seem odd that such a personal, warm, unpredictable music as jazz should be charted in such cold, analytical volumes as discographies, but then a train-spotter's book of train numbers will never hint at the passionate, steamy, smoky experiences which the owner has been through.

Yet when the same Benny Waters came to write his life story, he wrote it as a musician – at the time of writing, Benny Waters is still, amazingly, a very active tenor player in his eighties and could blow away a lot of younger men. His book is called *The Key to a Jazzy Life* and the Foreword gives you some idea of its flavour.

Dear Readers,

I wish that Fletcher Henderson, Jimmie Lunceford, Charlie Johnson, 'Hot Lips' Page, 'Stuff' Smith, Jimmy Archey and many other bands that I've worked with, still existed, then I could verify the dates and so forth . . .

The book is a true story of my life. I hope those who read it will enjoy it.

As far as dates and things, it didn't matter what date it was, as long as I was working, and that, I did all my life. Really, I'm still working at 82 . . .

And among the acknowledgements is: 'To Lily Coleman who has collaborated with me to the redaction of that book and help me with constant dedication.'

That apparently meaningless sentence gains significance if you remember that Waters is based in Paris and that 'redaction' may not exist in English but in French it means 'editing'. The trimmings of the book are in a sort of tremulous Franglais, but the book itself is a wonderfully vigorous flow of anecdote, memory, jumbled travel writing, thoughts on the music, portraits of long forgotten musicians and odd reflections on race, art and food. It doesn't mention that King Oliver session, nor who played banjo on it, but it does, by flowing from memory to memory, build up an unselfconscious picture of a long life in jazz. It has mistakes and strange bits of repetition; it has charm and a kind of magic; it is artless yet very knowing, which are all things you might say about a good jazz solo.

Much of the writing that appeals to me most has the quality of jazz improvisation: personal, unexpected, humorous, warm and flowing. This is especially true of oral history written down, which applies equally to books that set out to be oral history (Bill Crow's *Jazz Anecdotes*, for example) or books that masquerade as autobiographies (such as those by Hampton Hawes or Miles Davis, which were dictated to collaborating writers). Anyone who has mixed even slightly with jazz musicians will know that much of their time is taken up with story-telling, an art in which they excel – sometimes they seem to be lining up to tell stories much as, on stage, they are waiting their turn to take solos. I don't think it is a coincidence that one of the phrases they use to condemn a man who plays solos in which nothing happens is: 'He's not telling a story.'

For a musician live performances are what music is about; a recording session may be important commercially but as a life-enhancing experience it is about as wonderful as a family snapshot session. A recording session provides frozen moments in time, but the jazz life is all about ebb and flow, touring, day and night, travel and staying, audiences and silence. In the Anthology of writing that follows I now realize I have opted for as many extracts reflecting this feeling as I could find. It is not necessarily what most jazz listeners would look for in jazz writing. They would seek, first, hard information (dates, personnel and such); then secondly history (who went where, where the business was); and thirdly, though a long way after, musical information (jazz musicians love talking about the music itself, even if it is something as basic as defining the correct harmonies for a certain song, or discussing which are the best bass strings and where to get them). Fourth, and a long way after everything else, they might seek quality of writing. There is no demand for a good novel about jazz – at least, one's never been written and it has never worried the jazz world. A case could be made out for

The Horn by John Clellon Holmes, which I tremendously enjoyed when it first came out, but every time I have looked at it since it has become more and more dated. Jazz poetry, fiction, short stories . . . none of it has begun to deserve inclusion in an anthology.

Works of jazz history written by self-appointed critics and scholars, who sound like cut-price versions of their classical colleagues, are no more appealing. The best by a long way, musically speaking, is Gunther Schuller, whose continuing history of jazz (after the second volume he is only up to the end of the swing era) is fascinating stuff, especially as he has the courage to throw in lots of written-out musical examples. He also has the courage to change his mind. In his second volume he handsomely apologized for undervaluing Red Nichols and his Five Pennies, saying he had listened again to their records after readers' protests and now realized he was wrong. I would have included in this Anthology his wonderful thumbs-down verdict on the John Kirby Orchestra from the second volume, but feared that he might similarly recant in his third volume.

The autobiographies of Duke Ellington and Charles Mingus should both have yielded wonderful stuff, but it is generally agreed that the only wonder is how both men came to write such shapeless and unfocused books. Miles Davis's autobiography is current and well-known; instead, I have preferred for this collection to take extracts from a similar, earlier and forgotten book by Hampton Hawes called *Raise Up Off Me*, just as scabrous in its details of sex, race and drugs, but perhaps fresher.

In my research I have become extremely fond of some writers who are not perhaps the best-known within the jazz world. The writings left behind by Sandy Brown, the Scottish clarinettist, are among the wisest and wryest ever set down by a musician. I was lucky enough to hear and plunder from a series of BBC Radio 3 talks on the jazz life by poet/pianist Roy Fisher, which otherwise might have been forgotten. And if jazz is often the music of the outsider, it seemed fitting to disinter some rather sharp thoughts on jazz by Colin Wilson, who made his name with *The Outsider*. It would be hard to find anyone more 'outside' in jazz than Valerie Wilmer: where the stereotypical jazz person is black, American, male and heterosexual, she is English, white and lesbian. She is also an extremely gifted writer and photographer, and some of her accounts of the jazz experience are as powerful as anything I have read on the subject.

But the writer who intrigues me more than any other is Mike Zwerin, an American living in Paris. He is now the jazz correspondent for the *Herald Tribune*, but once upon a time as a young man in New York he played trombone with Miles Davis – in fact, he played with the famous Birth of the Cool band in 1949, and is listed on the personnel of the group that was taped at the Royal Roost club, prior to their record session. Unfortunately he had to go back to college and was not present at the historic session, thus stepping out of history at a moment when he might have made it. It sometimes seems that this has marked his career ever since – at various points in his writings you find him looking back longingly at the trombonist he might have become, the niche in jazz he might have won. He probably refuses even to admit the possibility to himself, but instead of being a top trombonist in jazz I think he has become the most original writer on the subject of jazz. His autobiography *Close Enough for Jazz* tells among other things the story of how he inherited the presidency of a steel corporation from his father when all he wanted to do was play jazz. It often reads more like a wild novel than real life. In fact, it's the nearest thing to an outstanding novel ever produced by jazz.

Working on this book has taken me down some strange byways, though it hasn't turned up one particular document I was looking for, a letter from Ronnie Scott. I was once rash enough to say in a review that Ronnie Scott would never be one of the great musicians in jazz. I was subdued a little while later to get a letter from Ronnie in which he said that I would never understand what jazz was about if I didn't realize that no musician ever set out to become great; he set out to have moments of greatness, moments when it all came together and evenings on which he suddenly found himself playing as well as he could, and that was the kind of greatness to which jazz musicians aspired. It must have been about then that I started understanding what jazz was about.

This nostalgic study has also taken my mind back to 1962, the only year in which I ever played jazz for a living for a while. I was about to face my last year at Oxford but, in the last long vacation, found myself playing in a jazz trio in a small night club in the south of Spain. The other two were also students, Nigel Stanger on piano and Mike Hollis on drums, and we played in a small bar belonging to Jesus Tamborero, a very charming property developer who persuaded English people to buy villas he had built which fell down three days after the contract was signed, and who took them to this bar to soften them up for the purchase. Look, he seemed to be saying, I have these three nice English boys playing for me – how could you possibly not trust me?

Because Nigel was (and is) a very good pianist, our fame spread narrowly, and we drew audiences from the local expat community. One night, I remember, I looked up from my double bass and found myself staring at the impassive features of Enoch Powell, who had been brought there by his local hosts and was not, I judged, enjoying himself. Years later I came face to face with him at a *Punch* lunch and mentioned our previous encounter. 'I remember it well,' he said. 'I never forget a face.'

But our most memorable encounter was on the beach behind the bar where one morning, while out swimming, I got talking to a woman with a baby, wandering in a solitary fashion along the shore. She turned out to be American, a retired jazz singer called Stevie Wise. The reason she had retired was to become Lady Listowel, and this baby was presumably the heir to the title borne by her new husband. But in her heyday she had sung, she said, with among others the Count Basie band . . .

Sing with us! we pleaded. And one night she did. She came round to Jesus's little dive, and the woman who had once done a season with Count Basie discussed keys and songs with us, and did several numbers with us. For us it was magic. It may not have been magic for her, as she did not come back, but looking back it seems more like a short story I might have read than something that actually happened.

A great deal of life in jazz does sound like something out of fiction. The more puritan jazz historians and critics complain that too much melodrama is read into jazz, but much of it is present already. I have a record, for instance, by a pianist called Cassino Simpson, about whom not much is known except that he did an above average copy of Earl Hines in the 1930s. He ended up as the accompanist to a singer called Frankie 'Half Pint' Jaxon, whom he attempted to murder one night. He failed, but for his pains was committed to a mental institute where he spent the rest of his life. The record I have bears only the following recording details of time and place: 'Illinois State Hospital, Elgin,

Illinois, 17th May, 1942.' One of the tracks he recorded was a version of 'Tea for Two', taken at tremendous speed, getting faster and ending at a manic tempo halfway through a chorus, abruptly, insanely.

Now, I contend that if you invented a jazz player who a) did what every pianist has dreamt of doing, and tried to kill the singer he was backing; b) got put inside a mental institute; c) was sane enough to make records while inside; d) was mad enough to do the most manic recorded version of 'Tea for Two' ever, well, I contend you would be accused of going over the top. Yet it happened, and provided only a small footnote in jazz history. The jazz addict is constantly imbibing information like this, along with the tunes, the records, the performances, the slang, the reputations, all of which comes to form a kind of international private language, from which you are excluded only by not wanting to pick it up. Without an unspoken background like this, how could three young lads from Oxford have immediately settled on a wavelength with someone from a different background, country and generation?

My intention when starting this book was to illustrate an extraordinary music. I think I have ended up getting to know an extraordinary bunch of people. It has been an exhilarating experience. I hope the reader feels this intimacy and excitement too.

JAZZ IS . . .

Nobody has ever been able to define jazz satisfactorily. This is probably because anyone who was capable of doing so never really wanted to, knowing how much you would have to leave out of the definition. It has been described as the most significant music to be born in the twentieth century, yet in many ways it seems a music miscast. It is a personal and individual music in a collective age; an improvised music in an age of planning; a subversive music in an epoch of state direction. People do not expect to get rich or famous through jazz, and they are usually right. Above all, in an age of mass distribution and commercialization, it is a doggedly private and bloody-minded music. It is also a black-inspired music in a white-dominated world. The amazing thing is that anyone has ever tried to arrive at a definition of jazz at all.

Just in Time

JAZZ MEANS my very life. Jazz can be arranged, can be out of tempo, can be written in any time, arranged in any fashion, use any type of solo or colouration. The prime thing is that it must have the communicative feeling of warmth from the individual musicians . . . There is

more freedom in jazz, more regard for individual emotion. Jazz is a
new way of expressing emotion. I think the human race today may be
going through things it never experienced before, types of nervous
frustration and thwarted emotional development which traditional
music is entirely incapable of not only satisfying, but representing.
That is why I believe jazz is the new music that came along just in time.

Hear Me Talkin' To Ya (1955)
Stan Kenton

In the Club

LESTER YOUNG explained on several occasions that the places
where he could work most effectively were small clubs and dance
halls. Clubs were intimate and relatively quiet and in dance halls the
rhythm of the dancers communicated itself to the musicians and
inspired them. The fact is that jazz of Lester's kind, the purest and
most subtle kind, doesn't actually need a listening audience at all.
What it does need is an atmosphere of relaxation. The musicians play;
people are present. If they want to listen they draw near and attend,
otherwise they can sit at the bar, talk to each other, perhaps get up and
dance. When a master is on the stand, and playing well, they'll listen
anyway because they will fall under the spell of his music. Perhaps this
is an element which jazz has inherited from Africa, where music has
always had a functional, social role. Certainly, the idea that the way to
experience music is by sitting silent and motionless in a seat is peculiar
to Western Europe – and only in comparatively recent times at that.

Lester Young (1984)
Dave Gelly

In the Pub

LIVE MUSIC can draw in crowds and give a welcome boost to bar
sales – providing that the music and the pub are in harmony. Introduce
the wrong type of music to the wrong crowd and the effect could be
catastrophe.

Jazz seems to be one of the safest bets, appealing as it does to a wide spread of ages and sectors. It can be lively and fun or gentle and moody, and fits in well to a variety of venues.

Many major drinks companies have picked up on this and over the past year there has been a deluge of successful jazz events. Often the jazz follower is part of the same socio-economic group as the drinks brand wants to target, so it makes sense to combine the two.

Publican, 28 January 1991

Jazz by Any Other Name

WHATEVER THE origin of the word 'jazz', it has resisted many attempts to change it. Duke Ellington never approved of the word, preferring more dignified terminology. He said:

> By and large, jazz always has been like the kind of man you wouldn't want your daughter to associate with. The *word* 'jazz' has been part of the problem. The word never lost its association with those New Orleans bordellos. In the 1920s I used to try to convince Fletcher Henderson that we ought to call what we were doing 'Negro music'. But it's too late for that now. This music has become so integrated you can't tell one part from the other so far as colour is concerned.

Jazz Anecdotes (1990)
Bill Crow

The Armstrong Definition

WHEN SOME reporter asked him to define jazz, he thought for a minute and said, 'Jazz is what I play for a living.' Like I said, there'll never be another.

With Louis and the Duke (1985)
Barney Bigard

A Black Music for White People

I WOULD like to say, first, that I don't like the term 'stride' any more than I like the term 'jazz'. When I was a kid the old-timers used to call stride piano 'shout piano', an agreeably expressive description, and when once I mentioned stride to Eubie Blake, he replied, 'My God, what won't they call ragtime next?' Terms, terms. Terms make music into a bundle of objects – a box of stride, a pound of Baroque – Lambert played music, not 'stride', just as Bach wrote music, not 'Baroque'. Musicians make music, which critics later label as if to fit it into so many jelly jars. Bastards.

Having demurred thus, may I say that stride is indeed a sort of ragtime, looser than Joplin's 'classic rag', but sharing with it the marchlike structures and oom-pah bass. Conventional wisdom has it that striding is largely a matter of playing a heavy oom-pah in the left hand, but conventional wisdom is mistaken, as usual. Franz Liszt, Scott Joplin, Jelly Roll Morton, Earl Hines, Teddy Wilson, Erroll Garner, and Pauline Alpert all monger a good many oom-pahs, and, whatever their other many virtues, none of them play stride.

The music which has historically been called 'jazz' may be defined as that part of Afro-American music generally acceptable at any given time to the white liberal community. It has been a music, therefore, performed largely by blacks for white audiences. Stride was different. Stride was, as late as 1946, when I used to hear it played in backrooms of bars in Harlem, a music played by blacks for black audiences. Indeed, the very idea of 'striding' refers, it should be said, to movements indigenous to black dance, not to the kind of striding West Point cadets are taught to do. That every single one of the younger stride players is white is a sad commentary on the way young black musicians regard what was once an ethnic black music.

Sleeve note from *Donald Lambert*

Dick Wellstood

Swing is . . .

SWING IS the sum of good time. People with spare time do not swing. If time can be spare, it cannot be good. The possibility of puttering time aside does not exist for someone with good time. You must follow the forward dance. To question it is to go into spare time. Calling time does not swing. *Time* magazine does not swing. Killing time does not swing. One and three do not swing. One and three plod. Two and four swing – the second and fourth beats of the bar, the weak beats push. Generally people called 'hip' swing, or try to, though both 'hip' and 'swing' have been deformed by 'hippy' and 'swinger'. Swing in its good time sense is an instinct. You either have it or you don't. Money does not swing, though what it buys certainly can. Bach swings, Mahler doesn't. Russians do not swing. Generalizations do not swing – I'm sure it's possible to find one swinging Russian. If you are wondering what I'm talking about, you probably don't swing. Black people tend to swing, it is less instinctive for whites. Uncle Toms try to forget how to swing on purpose. People who call themselves 'swingers' swing in spare time. We are talking about good time – the dance of time, a cosmic stance. Gypsies swing. New York Jews can swing if they're also funky.

Funk swings. Funk can be defined as a sort of healthy dirt. Babies are funky. (Babies swing.) Keith Richard swings. (Keith Richard is funky.) Animals are funky. Funk is an attitude towards dirt, towards life-substance. Cunnilingus is funky, but the word isn't. Garlic is funky. Americans get less funky all the time, though they can still swing. A smile swings. Farts are funky. People can be funky without swinging, Lyndon Johnson for example, though you cannot swing without at least a smidgeon of funk. Funk, like swing, can be evil. You often hear swinging soundtracks with violent movies. Hitler was funky, Iago swung. Funky Charles Manson swung. The devil swings hard. (Perhaps God is not funky enough.)

Close Enough for Jazz (1983)

Mike Zwerin

Bluff Your Way Through

JAZZ IS the modern heir to folkery. It all started in an obscure way at an unspecified time in American history and hundreds of books have been written confusing the issue. It is not so long ago that you could dismiss jazz with airy nonchalance or a downright sneer. Now even very highbrow composers allow themselves to be influenced by it, with little marked success, and quite well-bred people know the difference between ragtime and swing.

Men no longer dress up in funny hats in order to play jazz properly. Morning or even mourning dress is more appropriate. Some still make the light-hearted gesture of wearing coloured dinner-jackets or Edwardian costume, but these are mainly English musicians and it is a mere gesture of defiance by those who need something to bolster up their ineptitude.

Jazz musicians no longer smile or look at all pleased when they play – a sure sign that jazz is growing up. After all, nobody would expect a symphony orchestra to look as if it were enjoying itself. The keynote of your approach to jazz should be deadly serious, the deadlier the better, and, as ever, the language must be carefully chosen. Nobody in jazz will misunderstand you if you say the opposite of what you mean. For instance, if you come across a particularly intellectual piece of jazz that might have been written by Schoenberg in a relaxed moment you could describe it as 'crazy'. The proper word for a really good piece of jazz that meets with your approval is 'bad'. A really impressive pianist may be described as 'really blowing'.

A lot of uncouth words you may have picked up in your youth are definitely out of fashion. Words like 'hep', 'hot', 'jam', 'dig' and 'broke' are no longer needed in the jazz world.

There are two kinds of jazz: Traditional, where they all play together and try to outdo each other, and Modern, where each player goes on as if unaware of the existence of the others. You must decide which you support and decry the other on every occasion; or if you can't make up your mind what you like say you prefer 'Mainstream'.

If anyone asks you who you consider the most 'under-rated' jazzman (a favourite adjective, this) you might say Dink Johnson. Or if they ask you who you consider the greatest of all jazzmen you could earn quite a reputation by saying Eddie Condon. They just won't know what to say. The Beethoven of jazz is Charlie Parker.

Bluff Your Way in Music (1966)
Peter Gammond

The Myth of Jazz

WHEN I read, say, Leonard Feather on the subject of jazz improvisation or its musical structure, I find his remarks almost meaningless. Surely all that it is necessary to say about jazz, musically speaking, is that it is based on a regular beat, not very different from march time, or even the kind of beat one often finds in Bach or Vivaldi (as many modern experimenters have shown), but with the addition of syncopation – the accenting of normally unaccented beats and vice versa, the slurring of the last note of one bar into the beginning of the next.

But to say this is rather like saying that the essence of communism is to be found in *Das Kapital*. Clearly it is not. Communism, like jazz, is a mood, a state of mind, a mythology. To define jazz precisely, one must define its state of mind.

The first thing that strikes a newcomer to jazz is that its mythology is so involved with self-destruction. There is Bix Beiderbecke killing himself on corn alcohol; Bessie Smith on gin; Charlie Parker on drugs. The whole legend is bound up with early death, like the myth of romantic poetry. Jazz history is extraordinarily dramatic. It starts with Buddy Bolden blowing his trumpet through the railings of the park to call the people from the rival bandstand. And the person of Bolden contains all the elements of the myth. He rises from the unknown mass of the Negro poor to become the idol of New Orleans; his trumpet is so powerful it can be heard several blocks away. (The myth of power enters here; it is like a gorilla beating its chest and screaming for a mate.) He is proclaimed 'King of the Zulus'; he is seldom seen around without several adoring women clinging to his arms and begging for the privilege of holding his coat – and his trumpet. He leads a fast life and a gay one, then collapses into madness, so that although he lives on well into the great jazz era, he never knows what he started. Finally, there is the mystery of the 'Bolden cylinder', the record of his playing that all jazz fans hope will turn up one day, and that, when it does turn up, will be worth more than the few records of Jean de Rezske that at present repose in a Paris bank vault.

Colin Wilson on Music (1967)
Colin Wilson

Behind the Labels

I DON'T know why the people who write about music feel they have to slap labels on everything. It's the same water-melon mentality that says niggers can fuck and play boogie-woogie better than whites, Jews are rich, Irish are drunkards, Germans are mean, Japanese are mysterious, and Chinese smoke opium. Who cares? There are only two kinds of music – good and bad. The worst thing that can happen to old good music is that it might become dated for a while, but watch out, in ten to twenty years it will come drifting back like bell-bottoms and W. C. Fields movies. A critic once wrote that I was 'the key figure in the current crisis surrounding the funky school of jazz piano'. Shit, there wasn't no crisis. All he meant was that I can get down and I can swing. And if he could have looked deep into my life he would have learned that the reason I play the way I do is that I'm taking the years of being pushed off laps, denied love and holding in my natural instincts when I was a kid, of listening to the beautiful spirituals in my father's church and going in the back doors of clubs to play for white audiences, of getting strung and burned in the streets and locked up in dungeons when I tried to find my way – taking all that natural bitterness and suppressed animal feeling out on the piano. That's why I can swing. There really ain't no secret.

Raise Up Off Me (1972)
Hampton Hawes

The Cry of Jazz

IN THE summer of 1949, I was in New York on vacation from the University of Miami where I was majoring in sailing. No. Actually, sixteen of us were on scholarship to play for dinner in the student cafeteria which was cantilevered over an artificial lake. When we played the way we wanted we sounded like Stan Kenton. The band was called 'Sonny Burnham and his Sunmen'. It was sort of like sailing at that.

In those days I played my horn like a kid skiing down a slalom, with more courage than sense. Falling on my face never occurred to me. One night I climbed up to Minton's, where bebop was born, in Harlem. A lot of white cats considered Minton's too steep a slope, but I never imagined that somebody might not like me because I was white or Jewish. I was absolutely fearless. I walked in, took out my horn and started to play 'Walkin'' with Art Blakey, then known as Abdullah Buhaina, a fearful cat, I was later to learn.

When I noticed Miles Davis standing in a dark corner, I tried harder because Miles was with Bird's band. He came over as I packed up. I sank into a cool slouch. I used to practise cool slouches. We were both wearing shades; no eyes to be seen. 'You got eyes to make a rehearsal tomorrow?' Miles asked me.

'I guess so.' I acted as though I didn't give one shit for his stupid rehearsal.

'Four.' Miles made it clear he couldn't care less if I showed up or not.

Driving home over the Triborough Bridge to the house by the tennis courts, I felt like a batboy who had been offered a try-out with the team.

The next day at four I found myself with a band that would come to be called 'The Birth of the Cool'. Gerry Mulligan, Max Roach, John Lewis, Lee Konitz, Junior Collins, Bill Barber and Al McKibbon played arrangements by Mulligan and Gil Evans, who was musical director.

Miles was . . . cool. Pleasant, relaxed, diffident, it was his first time as leader and he relied on Gil. He must have picked up his famous salty act sometime later because he was sweet as his sound that summer.

It did not seem historic or legendary. A good jazz gig, but there were plenty of them then in New York. We certainly did not have the impression that those two weeks in a Broadway joint called the Royal Roost would give birth to an entire style. It was fun being on a championship team, and when Gene Krupa's entire trumpet section took a front table to hear us I was proud, but my strongest memory of those two weeks is the one we played opposite Count Basie, who then had Wardell Gray on tenor saxophone. Like a later summer spent listening to John Coltrane with Thelonious Monk at the Five Spot, Wardell with Basie is a sound that has never left my head and I will go to my grave with it.

I call that sound that stays in my head 'the Cry'. I seem to remember somebody else once talking about the Cry so if I'm stealing I apologize. Anyway, stealing is the essence of literary love. You cannot patent licks, just shove them out there and hope they are stolen. The Cry is everywhere. The Romanian pan-pipe-player Gheorge Zamfire has it – Zoot Sims, Ray Charles, Bruce Springsteen. Bob Marley had it. The blues are the classical incarnation of the Cry. You could also call it 'the Wail', a direct audial objectification of the soul. You know it when you hear it. Billie Holiday had it, to die. I wonder whether to include Mozart's operas, which might be a bit too structured to fit my definition of the Cry. The Cry must be a bit off, informal, direct, not stifled by structure or commercial considerations. Glenn Gould had it, Trane, Bix, Bird, Hendrix, Prez, Monk. Indian ragas have it, Flamenco singers, Milton Nascimento (all Brazilian singers seem to have it). Jewish cantors, black gospel singers. I could go on but you get the idea. Miles Davis certainly had it.

How would my life have changed had I stayed in New York to pursue the Cry after the summer of 1949 instead of going back to Miami and college like a good boy? A few months later, Miles made that 'historic' *Birth of the Cool* record with Kai Winding on trombone, and I became a footnote to jazz history. Do I have the Cry? Perhaps it is here on a few pages. Will I ever get into the body of the work?

Had I committed myself to jazz at that point I think that today I would be one of the ten best trombonists in the world. I had everything but the conviction. It was an unforgivable crime and I'm still paying for it. Never once, to this day, have I played jazz six nights a week for as long as two weeks running. I've read music with big bands, toured with rock bands, played with jazz bands in which I had a chorus or two a night, but I've never blown, stretched out, stayed in the slot, put my own pots on for as long as two straight weeks. I abused my muse and retribution was pitiless. 'You're an underrated trombone- player,' a customer in an Amsterdam club recently told me. 'It's better than not being rated at all,' I answered. I'm not so sure.

Close Enough for Jazz (1983)
Mike Zwerin

The Marsalis View

I STUDIED classical music because so many black musicians were scared of this big monster on the other side of the mountain called classical music. I wanted to know what it was that scared everyone. I went into it and found out it wasn't anything but some more music. As far as both musics are concerned, I think – *I know* – it's harder to be a good jazz musician at an early age than a classical one. In jazz, to be good means to be an individual, which you don't necessarily have to be in classical music performance. But because I've played with orchestras and all that, some people think I'm a classical musician who plays jazz. They have it backwards: I'm a jazz musician who can play classical music. I *always* wanted to play jazz. Besides, if you love the trumpet, you have to love jazz because jazz musicians have done the most with the instrument. They have given it the most depth and the widest range of expression. I'm not saying that classical trumpet players aren't expressive artists. That would be dumb. What I'm saying is that jazz musicians have given the most to the trumpet's vocabulary in this century. What I'm trying to do is come up to the standards all of these trumpet giants have set – Armstrong, Gillespie, Navarro, Brown, Miles, Freddie Hubbard, and Don Cherry. And that's not an easy job.

Sleeve note from
Wynton Marsalis

Subversive

IMPROVISATIONS ON top of the elastic, swinging pulse of jazz cannot be censored because they exist only in the present. Jazz is hard to pin down, it appeals to both mind and body. It slips through the cracks, or at least did before it became a university major. There was a time when all establishments rejected it; it was subversive everywhere. Remember, now we are talking not about the tame dance bands, which were accepted by just about everyone, but savage exploration by a lone improviser. People who reveal themselves in public. Naked. These people stand for everything establishments are against. It can be argued that bebop lost its power and relevance when Jimmy Carter sang 'Salt Peanuts' with Dizzy Gillespie, and there would have been no 'Golden Age' had Joseph Goebbels sung 'St Louis Blues'.

La Tristesse de Saint Louis (1985)
Mike Zwerin

The Purist

'OF COURSE, to a purist like yourself . . . ' Me? To the purist all things are poor, making him worry whether the banjoist is standing or sitting, or denounce Louis Armstrong, and as I staggered into 1967, hearing that Ornette Coleman had been voted *down beat*'s Musician of the Year, I took stock of my position. True, I don't like fancy time signatures, or want any African or Latin-American or Indian or Caribbean tinges, or bass solos, nor New Wave nonsense, or free form fatuity; in fact, the whole thing has gone to pot since 1945, or even 1940, but this is no more than saying that I like jazz to be jazz. A. E. Housman said he could recognize poetry because it made his throat tighten and his eyes water: I can recognize jazz because it makes me tap my foot, grunt affirmative exhortations, or even get up and caper round the room. If it doesn't do this, then however musically interesting or spiritually adventurous or racially praiseworthy it is, it isn't jazz. If that's being a purist, I'm a purist. And the banjoist can stand on his head for all I care.

All What Jazz (1985)
Philip Larkin

Jazz-addiction and the Alan Plater Syndrome

WHEN I was about eighteen, and something of a veteran in the business of daring to bang out a small repertoire of ill-fingered tunes at jazz sessions around Birmingham, I started to form the idea of early retirement; and before I was twenty, I'd done it. For the first time, anyway. I couldn't imagine that I wasn't soon going to grow out of it, I didn't know I was hooked on this music, and was already part of a network which was spreading quietly and rapidly, particularly at the time, the late 1940s: a network made out of something strong, and so extensive that fresh bits of it are still coming into view, even now.

You can see evidences of it in what I think of as a benignly pathological jazz-addiction, or provocative, incantatory naming of jazz in places where it can't be guaranteed to produce goodwill, though it might. The playwright Alan Plater's a good example of somebody who uses his media-access to wave a jazz flag. The plot of the television series 'The Beiderbecke Affair', which could have started anywhere Plater chose, starts with an order placed by the amiable hero, Trevor Chaplin, for a set of tapes of recordings made by Bix Beiderbecke in the late 1920s. As a character, Trevor Chaplin is a sort of open space – an allotment, perhaps – rather untidily planted with a collection of Alan Plater virtues: innocence; suspicion; feeling; resistance to humbug; general Northerliness; a wary commitment to women; complete commitment to football; complete commitment to jazz. Now the football, for the purposes of run-of-the-mill television drama, would have done on its own; but it's played down in favour of the jazz, which gives the character a touch of irrationality the drama needs. I guess pathological addiction to football on its own wouldn't be thought irrational at all.

But Trevor Chaplin's jazz-addiction isn't the pin-headed, nit-picking specialism which could be offered as the jazz-collector's equivalent of blind loyalty to the home team. For him, the home team is practically the whole of jazz music, from King Oliver to Sonny Rollins, Miles Davis and Toshiko Akiyoshi and Lew Tabackin – all those names he rolls off his tongue as he rummages through the records in Big Al's warehouse. They're all emblazoned on the banner. It's not Swing against Bop, or Blues against Big Bands; it's Jazz in General against Creeping Evil. And it is, as I said, an incantation, a naming of names; not much actual jazz was played in 'The Beiderbecke Affair' for all the allusions to jazz in the jolly soundtrack. But the name Beiderbecke is, as anyone familiar with the history and hagiography of jazz knows, no ordinary word. It's a magical one, which works in much the way the name 'Gatsby' has come to do, suggesting far more than it denotes.

I picked on 'The Beiderbecke Affair' because it's a particularly meritorious example of the injection of a jazz loyalty which is, strictly speaking, somewhat surplus to the requirements of its surroundings. But you can spot others, once you know what you're looking for. There is in Bill Cosby a team loyalty to the work of black jazz musicians which goes a little beyond his general programme of systematically subverting all the old images of black people – whether as devils incarnate or Uncle Tom – by sanitizing them into the world of a Middle-American sitcom. He plugs the acknowledged heroes of black achievement like Count Basie, or Ray Charles, but there's a little extra warmth, a touch of the adolescent with a grown-up cheque book, about the way he makes sure it all gets in the script. And there's the curious matter of Cliff Huxtable's old father. This character is a tame and folksy old fellow, who looks as if he'd be an Uncle Tom if only there were any white folks for him to suck up to; but Cosby makes him a retired jazz trombonist, putting his feet up and dedicating himself to orgies of family piety after what seems to have been a career in a band of really hard men – something like one of the early editions of Art Blakey's Jazz Messengers. I can't really imagine Art Blakey himself getting like that; but never mind. The jazz fan in Cosby gets his foot in the door.

They're always doing it. John Wain wrote a jazz novel and some jazz poetry; and although they and their writings about it occupy separate compartments, away from their poetry and fiction for the most part, the way in which jazz fed Philip Larkin and Kingsley Amis from boyhood on is plain to see. The historian Eric Hobsbawm borrowed the name of the black trumpeter Frankie Newton for his critical writings on jazz. And I remember how the novelist Jack Trevor Story angled to get the American saxophonist and personage Bud Freeman lined up for a part in his fantasy-autobiography on television, only to be foiled by employment regulations.

Then there are the persistent players, the incurable second line; the people whose main career has been in another art, or a profession in which their eminence might not seem consistent with the need to slope off and play in the local jazz club, or drive to distant cities by night, unable to resist a gig. Even without crossing the Atlantic to recruit Woody Allen, you can make the point with better clarinet players. There was the acoustic architect Sandy Brown; there's the cartoonist Wally Fawkes; there's the film critic Ian Christie; there's the artist Alan Cooper. Other names: Alan Davie, painter and avant-garde jazz cellist; Barry Fantoni; Jeff Nuttall; Russell Davies.

Apart from sharing that habit of perpetual truancy into music, I've also gone out of my way to earn a modest place in the complete file of case histories of unwarranted jazz naming. A boyhood hero of mine was the Chicagoan pianist Joe Sullivan. By the mid-1960s he was an obscure and neglected figure and near the end of his life; his old records weren't getting reissued. While assembling poems for a collection I wrote one – I called it 'The Thing about Joe Sullivan' – which was really my version of what I'd have liked to read as the sleeve note of a new Joe Sullivan album, had there been one. It was about Joe Sullivan, and about my own abiding enthusiasm for his music. And I decided to make it the title poem of the book; not because it typified the whole collection, which it didn't, but because I thought it would be nice for me to see Joe Sullivan's name on the cover of a book. What with the ups and downs and ins and outs of publishing, the book when it finally appeared had a different form and had to have a different title; but I carefully kept that poem back, in case the chance came up again. And some ten years and three books later I remembered it and lifted it out of storage and on to a cover; so that the name of Joe Sullivan forced its way that year into the homes of some hundreds of members of the Poetry Book Society. And on the strength of that I somehow

managed to get Granada Television to have the idea of letting me play
in a group with Bud Freeman – who actually worked with Joe Sullivan
– on a programme where I read my Joe Sullivan poem. So I was one up
on Jack Trevor Story for a few minutes.

Five Radio Talks (1970)
Roy Fisher

Art or Entertainment?

WHAT HAPPENS is, you make 300 arrangements and you arrive at
one, say 'Begin the Beguine', and you like it; it's good enough, you
like the tune, you like the arrangement, it worked, and the audience
liked it, so everybody's happy. But all of a sudden, you try to go past
that. And you can't go past it. In a sense it's as though the audience is
insisting you put on a straitjacket: 'Don't grow anymore.' It would be
like putting a pregnant woman in something where she couldn't
grow. I happen to have a need to continue to grow. This is a curse I
have, an overwhelming compulsion to keep developing. Well, if
someone says to you, 'You can't develop; we want that, over and
over,' you can go crazy. I don't mind playing some of it – it's part of
my past, but it's one part of it, it's not the whole ball game – and in the
late 1930s and early 1940s, I was in a position where the audience
would not let me do what I wanted; they only wanted me to do what
they wanted. Over a long time of thinking about this, I formulated the
difference between an artist and an entertainer.

And unfortunately, I'm in the previous group. I don't mean that
people have to think I'm an artist, but I know what my temperament
is. The entertainer is out to please Helen and Sam and Joe and Mary.
And if he does, he's happy. He's succeeded. The artist is essentially out
to please himself. He hopes that Helen, Sam, Joe and Mary will like it,
because if they don't, he's gonna have a tough time paying the rent.
But if they don't like it, he's still gotta do it, anyway. As Joyce Cary
said in a book called *Art and Reality*, any original artist who counts on
reward or satisfaction is a fool. I guess I'm a kind of a fool, because if I

don't get reward and satisfaction I can't pay my men. If I can't pay my men, can't pay arrangers, can't pay musicians, I can't play anything. There isn't any band. It's a disbanded group of musicians all looking for a living.

Dialogues in Swing (1970)
Artie Shaw

A High-risk Music

BUD POWELL walked into his favourite café on Rue du Seine just in time to see this elderly Parisian wreck raise a glass to his lips, drain it, and immediately pass out cold. Bud pointed to the stiff on the floor and said to the bartender: 'I'll have one of *those*.' Now alcoholics are nothing to make fun of, certainly someone as talented and tortured as Bud Powell. But the story does illustrate the ambience and alienation involved in this *métier*. Somebody who decides to play jazz for a living knows he will struggle for the rest of his life, unless he opts for predictable and soothing compromise. Honest jazz involves public exploration. It takes guts to make mistakes in public, and mistakes are inherent. If there are no mistakes it's a mistake. In Keith Jarrett's solo improvisations you can hear him hesitate, turn in circles for a while, struggle to find the next idea. Bird used to start a phrase two or three times before figuring out how to continue it. The heart and soul of improvisation is turning mistakes into discovery. On the spot. Now. No second draft. It can take a toll night after night in front of an audience that just might be considering you shallow.

Close Enough for Jazz (1983)
Mike Zwerin

Is an Early Death Strictly Necessary?

I HAVE not yet defined precisely what I mean by the jazz myth. It is not simply animal vitality, or success, or misery and tragedy. It is something far more complex. In a sense, it is only a twentieth-century version of the myth of 'La Bohème' – the kind of thing that has been captured, on a rather cheap level, by Somerset Maugham in *The Moon and Sixpence* or by Irving Stone in *Lust for Life*. Art has the power to raise us above the exhausting complexity of everyday life. But much great art requires a long apprenticeship, as well as a certain detachment. A beggar on the Embankment is not likely to be led into forgetting his miseries by hearing Monteverdi's *Orphée*, or even Beethoven's Fifth Symphony. But an art that can stay 'popular', close to the complexities of everyday life, and yet make its audience feel detached from these complexities, has a power that is altogether more raw. It demands no down-payment of culture or study. This is the power of jazz. The lover of Beethoven feels that his music successfully transcends the sufferings of human existence, that such music was distilled out of torment by a man whose spirit could not be broken. Jazz does exactly the same thing on a lower level. Most lovers of jazz have never experienced anything like the long-drawn-out misery and degradation from which the American Negro created his music. And yet here it is, like the music of Beethoven, yet another proof that the human spirit cannot be broken, that it can create delight and love of life out of the most unpromising conditions.

This is the heart of the jazz myth. This is why the jazz enthusiast, trying to convert an unbeliever, emphasizes the violence and tragedy, the murder of Pine Top Smith and Chano Pozo, the frustration of Beiderbecke and Parker, the final agony of Bessie Smith. The 'unbeliever' might well point out that the jazz success stories far outweigh its tragedies. From Buddy Bolden to Clifford Brown and Stan Hasselgard, jazz can count about two dozen tragedies – and this by including minor figures like Robert Pete Johnson and Chano Pozo. But for every dead Bix there's a living Louis Armstrong and Duke Ellington; for every Charlie Parker, a living Dizzie Gillespie and Miles Davis. The successful and long-lived jazz men probably outweigh the tragedies by four to one. And in a profession that sprang up in the brothels, continued in prohibition speakeasies, and even today depends largely on short engagements and one-night stands, this is not unreasonable. But tragedy is part of the jazz legend, and must be taken into account in any attempt to understand the nature of jazz.

Colin Wilson on Music (1967)

Colin Wilson

No Such Thing

NOTE: I have used quotes around the word 'jazz' because 'jazz' never existed. There was then, as now, only musicians and their music. I didn't bother to use quotes around ragtime because I'm not so mad about there not having been ragtime as I am about there not having been 'jazz'. I thought there was, and I was had.

Sleeve note from *Dick Wellstood Alone*

Dick Wellstood

2

FIRST STEPS IN JAZZ

Being a jazz fan has overtones of activities as far apart as freemasonry and trainspotting – there is certainly a sense of belonging to a secret society with its own mysteries, passwords and signs; and for an outsider to be trapped in an uninhibited jazz conversation, with names, dates and prejudices flying around, can be as terrifyingly boring as being caught in a railway trivia conversation. As with most believers, even the life-long jazz listener or musician can often remember the exact moment of conversion, the first exposure after which nothing was ever quite the same again.

Choosing the Tenor Saxophone

I DIDN'T buy an instrument for the sake of the music. It's different if someone says he likes music and wants to get an instrument to try to be a musician. In my case I wanted the instrument for what it represented.

By watching musicians I saw that they drank, they smoked, they got all the broads and they didn't get up early in the morning. That attracted me. My next move was to see who got the most attention, so it was between the tenor saxophonist and the drummer. The drums looked like too much work, so I said I'll get one of those tenor saxophones. That's the truth.

from the IJS Archive
Eddie 'Lockjaw' Davis

Not Choosing Drums

DRUMS NOW? No eyes. I don't want to see them. Every time I'd be in a nice little place, and I'd meet a nice little chick, dig, her mother'd say, 'Mary, come on, let's go.' Damn, I'd be trying to pack these drums, because I wanted this little chick, dig? She'd called her once and twice, and I'm trying to get straight, so I just said, I'm through with drums. All those other boys got clarinet cases, trumpet cases, trombone cases, and I'm wigging around with all that stuff. And, Lady Francis, I could really play those drums. I'd been playing them a whole year.

from the IJS Archive
Lester Young

My First Alto

MY UNCLE died and left me my alto and I went for my lesson. I didn't want to, but they said, 'The man died. The least you can do is take a lesson.'

Jazz Anecdotes (1990)
Phil Woods

My Friend, the Piano

I THINK I must have first turned to the piano out of boredom and loneliness. We were a reserved and undemonstrative family. The only time my mother kept me close was when she was at the piano and I'd put my hands on hers while she played; that was a kick, her hands moved so beautifully and it was like I was playing.

After a few early years of church I was left to myself on Sundays, puzzled at why those people in my father's church had to go through so many changes to do things that are supposed to be natural. All that kneelin' 'n' shoutin'. Waving a cross to make a devil leave. Why not just beat him to death, tell him to get the fuck out of the way. If a kid gets up Sunday morning wanting to lay around, have peanut butter sandwich with jelly and a pop first thing 'cause he's feeling good, or an adult has eyes for some wine or a Scotch, get himself all tore up, I thought, Why not, if that's the way he wants to go? No need to be ashamed of your feelings, ain't hurtin' nobody. I felt pulled apart watching so many people acting one way in the church and a different way in the street or in their backyards. Too many Dr Jekylls in this show.

When I was six I was given a little gold Sunday school pin which was the reward you got for a year's good attendance. But three years later I had stopped going to church Sundays and was listening to Freddie Slack, Fats Waller (bad cats) and Earl Hines (very bad cat) playing his 'Boogie-Woogie on St Louis Blues', using the time the family was at church to pick out some of that stuff on our parlour piano.

The piano was the only sure friend I had because it was the only thing that was consistent, always made sense and responded directly to what I did. Pianos don't ever change. Sittin' there every day. You wanna play me, here I am. The D is still here, the A flat's still here, they're always going to be there and it don't matter whether it's Sunday, Ash Wednesday or the Fourth of July. Play it right and it comes out right; mess with it and it'll make you back up. A piano don't lie. Check the prancing players with the sparkles in their eyes and the pretty fingernails flashing up and down the keyboard – listen closely and that's all there is, just flash and icing, no more depth or meaning than a wood chip dancing down a waterfall. A keyboard is more consistent than life, it gives you back what you put into it, no more, no less. In the 1940s Bud Powell had grease in his veins and burned the motherfucker up; Thelonious Monk plays it strange and beautiful because he *feels* strange and beautiful. The piano was the first secure and honest thing in my life, I could approach it on my own and fail or be good. Straight to the point and quick.

Raise Up Off Me (1972)
Hampton Hawes

Colin Wilson, Trumpet Player

IN 1957 I bought myself a trumpet, resolved to learn to play it as Bix learned – by trying to play to records. Now six years later, I still play as badly as after my first week of practice. Also – and I hope this does not sound like intellectual snobbery – I think perhaps I am not inarticulate enough really to identify myself with the spirit of jazz. I have talked to many jazz men, including Coleman Hawkins, Roy Eldridge, Thad Jones, and Cannonball Adderley, and discovered most of them to be interesting and likeable human beings; but have found it impossible to connect these men, as human beings, with the excitement that I often derived from their playing. Now to some extent this is also true of writers; meeting an author one admires is usually a disappointment; but I have generally been able to recognize a link between an author's books and his personality. I suspect that jazz men are on a different wavelength. It is a disturbing thought that I would probably have found Bix Beiderbecke or Bunny Berigan as personally unsatisfying – in that sense of 'non-communicating' – as other jazz men; but I have no doubt it is true.

Colin Wilson on Music (1967)
Colin Wilson

Hero Worship

HIGH-SCHOOL hipsters slouched through my living-room, eyes red, leaning forward with horns in gig-bags cradled in their arms. They wore goatees and Dizzy Gillespie berets. Those who were not already junkies scratched themselves and spoke with the rasp to make believe they were. Charlie Parker was a junky and that was good enough for us.

'Groovy, man, what a gas!' they'd say as my father looked over his evening paper in disbelief. They'd climb the stairway to my little attic studio where there was a wire recorder, an upright piano and pictures of jazz giants on the walls. Earl Brew burned some piano keys but my mother did not say anything because Earl was black and she was liberal. She thought the burns were from cigarettes.

When we weren't playing music we were listening to or talking about it. 'What do you want to be when you grow up?' was not something that had to be asked.

We had cards printed with 'music for all occasions' on them. We took professional names. Bob Milner became Bob Mills, Frank Hamburger chose Duke Frank, I was Mike Wayne. Al Goldstein picked Al Young in honour of his hero Lester Young, but everybody called him Lester Goldstein.

My attic room overlooked the Forest Hills Tennis Club. The tennis players complained because our jamming jammed their concentration. We were the first Jewish family in Forest Hills Gardens, an exclusive semi-private enclave. My father suspected the tennis players were anti-Semitic. The tennis players accused him of operating a rehearsal studio in violation of zoning laws. Lester Goldstein loved to honk out the window during crucial rallies and Lester really knew how to honk.

I cut high school to catch noon shows at the Paramount, the Capital, the Strand – Broadway theatres in which my models rose hungover from pits for the first of five daily shows playing 'Blue Flame', 'Skyliner', 'Take the A Train' and 'Let's Dance', my 'Star-Spangled Banners'.

I was dazzled by the sparkle of spots off brass. I daydreamed of future hungover noons rising from pits. I knew name-band personnel like other kids know big-league line-ups.

My parents took me to a Catskill Mountain hotel for a summer holiday. After breakfast one morning, walking into the early mountain air, we passed the hotel band bass-player coming in with a dazzling woman on his arm. We had talked and he knew I wanted to be a musician. 'Boy, you're up early,' I said.

He hesitated. 'Yes . . . early.'

Later I realized he had not in fact been to sleep. How I envied grown-ups who could stay up all night playing music and be with such beautiful women. Now when I think back at what life must have really been like for that hack working the Jewish Alps for the summer, I wonder how children survive their fantasies. I was in love with music; she was my obsession; I could not see straight for the love of her.

But if music is, as Duke Ellington put it, my mistress, we have had a stormy relationship. I cheated on her, lied to, neglected and beat her. On the other hand, she was too demanding. When she nagged I left her and when I neglected her she left me. I was to spend my time under too many hats, between too many stools. It would be a stormy affair.

Close Enough for Jazz (1983)
Mike Zwerin

Sunday Afternoons in the 1930s

SITTING WITH a friend in his bedroom that overlooked the family tennis-court, I watched leaves drift down through long Sunday afternoons as we took it in turn to wind the portable HMV, and those white and coloured Americans, Bubber Miley, Frank Teschemacher, J. C. Higginbotham, spoke immediately to our understanding. Their rips, slurs and distortions were something we understood perfectly. This was something we had found for ourselves, that wasn't taught at school (what a prerequisite that is of nearly everything worthwhile!) and having found it, we made it bear all the enthusiasm usually directed at more established arts. There was nothing odd about this. It was happening to boys all over Europe and America. It just didn't get into the papers. It was years before I found any music as commanding as Jimmie Noone's 'The Blues Jumped a Rabbit', Armstrong's 'Knockin' a Jug' or 'Squeeze Me', Bessie Smith's 'Backwater Blues', or the Chicago Rhythm Kings' 'I Found a New Baby'.

All What Jazz (1985)

Philip Larkin

Jazz and Kingsley Amis

BORN IN 1922, I suppose I was one of the first British generation to whom jazz was a completely natural thing, not new, not a fad, not exotic, and certainly not in any way unrespectable, or suspect because 'negroid'. Older people were against it then, an added recommendation. As I grew up a little I found that a lot of what I had thought of as jazz was really dance music, or suspect because 'commercial'. I have already described how when I reached Oxford my enthusiasm soared and my knowledge expanded, chiefly under the influence of Philip Larkin. Jazz became a part of my life and still is. Every morning at home I play half a dozen tracks on my little tape recorder, mostly taken from radio broadcasts or off old 78s. Today for instance it was a couple of ferocious Dixieland numbers I taped so long ago that I have forgotten what the band was, 'Drop Down Mama' by Sleepy John Estes, a blues singer too obscure for an entry even in the monumental *New Grove Dictionary of Jazz*, a couple of Joe Turners with Pete Johnson at the piano and one of Muggsy Spanier's so-called Great Sixteen. Tomorrow perhaps Artie Shaw. Why not? How uncommercial he seems now that he belongs to a vanished world!

Because . . . In 1941, my first year at Oxford, I discovered that jazz could be not only entertaining and enlivening but emotionally moving too, if never quite as much so as parts of some classical works. I was particularly struck by what we called the Banks sides, twelve of them cut in 1932 by a small band that included the trumpeter Henry Allen, the clarinettist and tenor saxophonist Pee Wee Russell and, on four of the twelve, Fats Waller, whom most readers even today, nearly half a century after his death, will have heard of. Banks himself was the singer, a sort of counter-tenor, not very jazzy perhaps by

some standards but fascinating to me, especially in the words he sang.
I had not known then that such singers would have in their memory
several hundred blues verses which, in their allotted minute or so, they
would sing a few of more or less at random. I thought Banks was
performing connected songs or poems of a kind of awesome
surrealism. This certainly applied to 'Spider Crawl':

> Oh see that spider crawling up that wall . . .
> Let me be your little dog till the big dog comes . . .
> The graveyard sure is a mean old place . . .
> My gal is just like a weeping willow tree . . .

Trumpet and clarinet wove magic flourishes and arabesques between
the lines. Philip had a copy, I had none and could not get one: the
record was deleted, out of print. So much did this one piece come to
mean to me that when, in 1943 or so, it again became available, I at
once bought it, even though I was in the army and had nowhere to
play it. I kept it on the table by my camp bed just to look at, an icon not
even to be picked up unnecessarily for fear of scratching it. No
classical rarity can ever have been as rare as that in any sense.*

That tiny story will have to do duty for an account of the impact the
stuff made on me, serve instead of a list of the Armstrongs and Bixes
and works of the Chicago Rhythm Kings we played and replayed,
substitute for an analysis of its appeal, simple, strong, melodic, as
Bruce Montgomery always used to insist, rather than rhythmical. To
catch an earful was to enter a world of as yet uncharted, unwritten-
about romance, innocent, almost naive. I should have been horrified if
I could have known that in that very year of 1941 'modern' jazz, in the
shape of what Charlie Parker and Dizzy Gillespie were beginning to
play, was to begin the slow but sure destruction of the music I had just
begun to love.

'Spider Crawl', like three of the other Banks sides, is a blues, which
is to say it consists of short choruses of twelve bars each, using as

---

* In the early or middle 1950s Banks went on tour. This took him to among other places
Belfast, where Philip Larkin, still nursing the unconquerable hope, went to one of his
performances. Philip found he bore no audible resemblance whatever to the Banks of 1932. The
sole point of interest, and that social or anthropological rather than musical, came late, when
Banks announced he would end with a vocal impression by way of tribute to the man 'who has
done most to express the spirit of my race!' Not Louis Armstrong, not even Paul Robeson, but
Al Jolson singing 'Mama' or a comparable horror.

simple a chord-sequence as can be imagined, virtually confined to the chords of the tonic, the sub-dominant and the dominant seventh. Other standard jazz tunes used sequences not much more complicated. According to an account given a thousand times, Parker and his followers craved for something more demanding, more adventurous (oh dear), and wrote and played tunes in which the chord changed every *beat* – more fun to play. More fun, any fun, to listen to? Very much not to this pair of ears.

Memoirs (1991)

Kingsley Amis

Young Girl Meets Old Attitudes

IN 1961 I was 19 years old. Nineteen was young in those days and I was pretty naive despite my interest in jazz and blues. I'd started to write about Black music three years earlier and was already finding it remarkably easy, as well as rewarding, to track down those Americans who were beginning to play in Britain after a long period of musical starvation. Their appearance here was highly significant in the days predating the rise of British Beat and the period of affluence to come.

One of the blues artists so lionized during this period was Little Brother Montgomery, a versatile pianist from Louisiana via Chicago. I saw him play at the 100 Club in London and approached him for an interview. 'Just come by the hotel,' he said, 'and I did. He was in bed at the time but, excusing himself, struggled into a shirt and trousers and proceeded, with a characteristically sardonic air, to answer my tentative teenage questions.

A friend took a photograph of us: Brother sitting on the bed, his shirt hanging open to reveal a rather daunting paunch, me sitting on a chair beside him, pen and notebook in hand, legs crossed demurely. I'm wearing a Paisley dress made by my mother and an expression of truly painful seriousness. I rather like the picture, though, so I submitted it for publication along with the article.

'Very nice, dear,' said the Editor, 'but we can't really use that, can we? I mean, what would our readers say if we printed a picture of a white girl sitting next to a darky with his shirt undone?'

I've never forgotten those words and they have taken on increasing significance for me as the years have gone by. They say a lot about the patriarchal divide-and-rule system under which women and Black people are forced to live. Writing about the music was something that men did. There was a penalty to pay for being a woman in a man's world, and there were many who made sure to exact it. Often it took the form of sexual pressure, and surviving that required strength of a particular kind. But for a white woman to be concerned with something that Black people did meant to experience additional pressure. Ostracism was the penalty there and to survive that it was necessary to recognize why it occurred.

Why people cannot measure their worth in terms other than power over others is one of the questions posed by personal politics which have always disturbed me, though I doubt whether it would have been so immediately obvious to me without getting to know people from worlds outside my own. Through becoming immersed in Afro-American music I was made aware of certain realities that would surely have remained hidden had I stayed within the secure boundaries of my own culture. The experience was so startling, went so deep, that there is little I write that does not reflect this contact.

Mama Said There'd Be Days Like This (1989)

Val Wilmer

Jazz and Girls

ONE NIGHT when I was working with Charlie Miller at Waldorf Castle (I was still in short pants, I didn't put on long pants until I went to Boston), a woman came in there, she was about thirty, nearly twice as old as I was; a beautiful negro woman. She sat right there and looked at me all night. I looked down at her. I smiled and I let it go at that.

That woman knew Whithey, the drummer, who was like a father to me and told him: 'Tell that little guy there I want to see him.' So after work I went down and Whithey introduced me to her.

'I just love to hear you play,' she said. 'How old are you?'

I lied a little and said I was seventeen. I was a little younger than that. So she invited me around to her place. She was a widow and had her own beautiful place, a car and everything. She lived on the outskirts of Philadelphia, in West Philadelphia.

She kissed me and said – 'I'm going to keep you with me and I'm going to treat you like a baby.' That sounded good to me. The only problem was that I was supposed to go home to my aunt's. But that night I didn't go home. We got into bed. By now I knew what I was doing! We had a ball . . . In the morning she got up and made us some breakfast. She was a kinda heavy woman but well proportioned.

I had many girl friends when I was in my early twenties. In New York I had seven chicks each week. For months and months, for maybe a year, I had a different girl every day. I did it until I met my first wife.

I had them all trained. It wasn't a secret, each one knew that I had all the others. I had separate days for each one. On Monday was one, and so on.

One night at Smalls Paradise when I was working there, a chick came on a Tuesday night, who wasn't supposed to come until the Wednesday. I was drinking and she came in and sat right by me. I looked up all serious and said – 'What are you doing here, you know damn well this ain't your night!'

'I know, I know, Benny,' she answered. 'I just wanted to come and listen to your music.'

She stayed there for a while and then the 'Tuesday chick' came in, so she left and I was OK.

I was young then. It's a wonder I'm not dead a long time ago, but I paid for it. I had an operation for appendicitis that was due to drinking and fooling around. But I enjoyed it though I was raising hell then.

The Key to a Jazzy Life (1985)

Benny Waters

Learning from Records

As SANDY spent more time listening to blues singers – Sonny Boy Williamson (the *original* one), Kokomo Arnold, Blind Lemon Jefferson, Leroy Carr, Joe Turner, Big Bill Broonzy – and to the Gospel groups – The Sensational Nightingales, The Five Original Blind Boys – then to clarinet players or other instrumentalists, the copies came through, but somewhat unrecognizably. It all sounded convincingly original: only the tone was. This came from trying to play terribly loud. It seemed that Dodds must have been loud. No one could tell from records. Grand Funk Railroad *are* loud, although inaudible without 230 volts and 7000 watts. But Dodds must have been loud unaided. He had to be heard in the King Oliver band over two trumpets, one of whom was powerful young Louis Armstrong. So all the Dodds copyists tried to blow the insides out of their clarinets. Sandy had started with an Albert system, sometimes called simple system, as opposed to the adaptation of Boehm's flute fingering arrangement though it's anything but simple. The Albert is usually louder than the Boehm and has an unmistakably full tone. All the New Orleans players used various versions of Albert. When Sandy switched to the Boehm he missed the tone so much he huffed and puffed until he got an approximation. As for the notes he played, these were fragments cut from the archaic and modern blues and gospel singers, a kind of blues confetti stuck in the end of a kaleidoscope. You could switch it all round to get a new and brilliant picture every time, just from a few old blues remnants. Same old stuff really, but a lucky new way to put them together. 'Put your eye to this, sir.' 'Brilliant.' Shake, shake. 'Now this.' 'Brilliant again, like the stained glass in a cathedral.' Amazing what you can do with a few odds and ends: a permutable catechism rather than a liturgy. Perhaps there's no real difference.

The McJazz Manuscripts (1979)
Sandy Brown

My First Recording

THE FIRST number we did was an impromptu slow blues. I could handle that; the three chords I was getting by with were the chords of the twelve-bar blues anyway, and I think we did quite well. It was a thrill. The other tune was 'Honeysuckle Rose', which was one of the tunes I believed I knew. My job was to accompany a trumpet and a clarinet playing the tune in near-unison in the key of F. My ear had told me the first chord I needed to play wasn't F major; it must be one of the other two chords I believed existed. It isn't. But I chose one of my Flat-Earth Society chords, and banged it out for four solid bars every time it came round. It was B Flat Seventh. I also played it for the whole of the middle eight. Those who are not musicians need to be told only that these actions were very misguided indeed, and are still on my conscience, even though erased from the record, literally, by the scratching of needles, forty years since. It wasn't even an innocent ignorance: I'd got hold of the music, but had refused to believe it. G Minor Eleventh? C Thirteenth? Whose leg were they trying to pull?

My harmonies weren't the only blemish. After the opening ensemble, with its hints of Charles Ives, I had a solo piano chorus. Although continuing to use my wrong chords, I couldn't clash with anybody else, being on my own; I just seemed to be playing a different tune altogether. I also got excited, and speeded up dangerously. Then came a drum solo by the founder of the feast. It was loud, naturally. And it started at the speed I'd reached, and quickly accelerated even further. I forgot to mention that the drummer had a little red MG. The solo bore no relation to the shape of the tune; there was no way of knowing where to come in again. The closing ensemble was nasty, brutish and short. Another pound gone. And a very long three minutes.

We acknowledged the playback as pretty lifelike. It didn't occur to anybody to have whip-round to raise a pound for another attempt. That was how we sounded, and we didn't know how to do anything about it. I couldn't afford a copy of the record; and besides, the pickup on my 1920s acoustic gramophone was so heavy that it shredded even ordinary records. I heard it only once more, about a year later. In the interim, I'd accepted conversion to the correct changes to 'Honeysuckle Rose', and was glad the record was already wearing out. The copy was the drummer's own, and he'd been listening to his solo a good deal. The blues side wasn't much worn. I wish I still had that.

Five Radio Talks (1970)
Roy Fisher

Discovering Jazz in Dublin

I LEFT school and spent a lot of time on my own, brooding in a funk. Soon I'd be twenty and I hadn't led a teenage life according to the articles. One day I bought a record by pianist Jimmy Yancey. A flash conversion to his amazing quiet blues–boogie with its graceful jog and Spanish tinges! In his piano was the whole of beat! I wanted nothing else ever. Endless, satisfying music. I was determined to make some too. On sunny afternoons – Saturdays even – whilst others were out playing I sat at the piano trying to work myself into a blues frame of mind; learning to crush notes two or three at a time, flicking the wrist around for certain effects, wiping notes, and keeping a steady roll going. No teachers around – just Yancey on the gram. Yancey at half speed, at quarter speed. Yancey taken to bits. Who was Yancey?

A photo in a jazz book showed him standing melancholy and black on the front porch of his wooden shack. At one time he'd been a vaudevillian, was reputed to have tap–danced in front of the King and Queen at a Royal Command Variety Show in Edwardian times. 'For 30 years he was employed as a groundskeeper at a Chicago baseball park and only played piano at rent parties and private functions,' said the back of my record cover.

About the same time I discovered Scott Joplin and the real ragtime. Stately and exact, chaos elegantly caged, it went well with the more down–homey Yancey. Difficult music to read (I fumbled it but eventually approximated it) but reading *about* ragtime helped. I read Rudi Blesh's *They All Played Ragtime* several times. And I read all about early jazz: shining trumpets that could be heard for miles on a clear New Orleans night, blown by legendary bronzemen in gay bordellos with fancy iron-work railings. Good-time high-yaller girls, diamond teeth, grinding all night, sweet lotus blossom and keep a knockin' but you can't come in. Then they all sailed up the river to Chicago! Did I want to get to the USA! Sickening to close the book and face Putney Heath!

Next I went to Trinity College, Dublin, Eire. I took a course in modern history and political science. I'm not sure why. The head of our department gave us an introductory lecture which went: 'Freshmen! I ask you: what is history? History is the past,' and left it at that. Julian, the college postman, told me: 'History? Why study history? It's all happened and there's nothing you can do about it.' I was confused. We all scattered and I got going on other things. By now I was absolutely dying to be black. I was utterly hooked on black men, through reading and records. Luckily, there were a number of actual black men from Africa herself at Trinity. Quite a few sat together in our history class.

Mr Balloodadan, very friendly, wore a blazer with 'Mauritius' sewn on the breast pocket. I figured that it must be the name of the ocean liner he sailed over in, that he'd won the badged blazer in a deck quoits competition. My pal J. said no – Balloodadan was from a country called Mauritius where he owned a chain of brothels and he was over here on business, buying white slave girls. Also in our class was Mr Anangoola who had tribal scars on his face and applauded everything, especially lectures. I persuaded him to come out to my digs one evening to hear jazz records. He turned out to be a disappointment, enjoying the tea and iced cake but not really responding to the jazz. I thought it might trigger him off so that I could then quiz and study him but it didn't and that night I learned a truth: not all black men have innate beat. He returned to his degree course (eventually winning a first) and I dived headlong into college jazz life. That was the next best thing to being black.

After the Ball (1973)

Ian Whitcomb

~~~~~~~~~~~~~~~~~~~

3

PORTRAITS

Years ago a British record label issued an anthology of jazz pianists in LP form and asked a lot of other jazz pianists to write the sleeve notes, one pianist to comment on each performance. The idea, said the company, was to achieve honesty and objectivity. The company must have been mad, because almost all the pianists, of course, made nice insincere noises and retired to count the money. The single exception was Richard Rodney Bennett, who was extremely (and justifiably) rude about his subject, an Austrian classical pianist called Friedrich Gulda who fancied he could play jazz. Any ordinary musician, said Bennett, has times when he can't think of anything to play, so he falls back on a store of clichés he has minted to get him through such patches. Gulda, he said, hasn't even been able to dream up his own clichés; he only has an old sack full of other men's clichés to fall back on.

I wanted to get hold of that text for this book, but couldn't trace the record. Finally I tracked down Richard Rodney Bennett himself, who said apologetically that he had no memory of writing any such thing. Still, it was worth remembering, because I have now managed to get it in anyway, and because it is a good example of the way musicians in the jazz world acquire a knack for summing up their fellow musicians. Half anecdote, half portrait, there is a kind of sketch of musician by musician which is an art in itself. The story towards the end of this section about André Previn and Mel Powell is not even a jazz story, specifically, but I feel it couldn't have been told by a non-jazz musician.

Bunk Johnson, Drunk

BUNK PLAYED a beautiful horn and nobody else around New Orleans played the same style Bunk did. He played the most beautiful tones. After a while Bunk got to drinking so bad they fired him and then he went with Frankie Dusen's band.

Frankie Dusen was the only guy that Bunk was afraid of and who could make Bunk listen. Bunk would show up to play so drunk he'd be draggin' his coat across the floor and couldn't find the bandstand. He'd try to put his horn up to his mouth and hit his nose or chin, and couldn't even find his mouth. When he was like that or just passed out, the guys would say to him, 'Hey, Bunk, here comes Frankie.' Bunk would straighten right up. The reason was Frankie used to beat Bunk just like you beat a kid. He'd get a razor strap or his belt and whip him.

Bunk was a very nice guy when he was in the Superior Band, but when he went with the Eagle Band, he really got to drinking bad. In those days the saloons never closed and Bunk never left the Eagle Saloon. He'd drink till he passed out and then sleep it off on a pool table, get up, and start drinking again. If we came along and wanted to shoot pool, we'd just lift Bunk off and lay him on a bench. He got to drinking so bad that even the Eagle Band fired him about 1910 and no one else would hire him. He left town with a minstrel show and I didn't see him again until 1937 when I was playing with Louis Armstrong's band in New Iberia, Louisiana . . .

Bunk Johnson Vanishes

FROM 1910 to 1937, I didn't see Bunk Johnson. In 1910 he left New Orleans with a minstrel show. In 1937 Louis's band was playing a Catholic dance in New Iberia, Louisiana, and I saw Louis talking to this old guy. After we started playing, I said to Louis, 'Who's that old guy?'

Louis said, 'That's Bunk Johnson.'

I said, 'I didn't even recognize him.'

Louis said, 'I didn't either, man.'

The next intermission I went over and talked to Bunk for a while. He said he'd been driving sugarcane wagons. He sure had changed in those twenty-seven years. He didn't have no teeth at all. He said he'd been with the minstrel show for a long time. Those minstrel show cars were really funny. They'd hook them on the back of the train and then put them off at the siding at the town where they were going. The show people would mostly live in the car because people wouldn't rent them rooms. Show people would steal anything they could carry and then not pay the rent. They'd steal chickens, rabbits, sheets, clothes, or anything.

Both the above from *Pops Foster* (1971)
Pops Foster

The Return of Bunk Johnson

THERE MAY have been a variety of earth-shaking events going on in the world on that particular spring day in 1922, but only one thing mattered in the sun-drenched town of Perryton, Texas. It surely didn't look as though it were participating in Mr Coolidge's prosperity, with its dusty streets and its one-storey buildings with two-storey fronts. But nevertheless, all its flags were flying, flamboyant bunting was draped over a speakers' stand, and the mayor was about to open the festivities observing the town's first anniversary by dedicating the new wooden sidewalks. To help celebrate the gala occasion, a unit of the Greater Holcamp Carnival Shows had set up in the vacant square upon which the optimistic townsfolk proposed to erect a grand City Hall.

I suppose my memory could play tricks on me. I was only six years old, and the lingering images in my recollections could be confused with the sets of Jack Hoxie or Ken Maynard western movies – what with the real Indians on horseback, the cowboys in their big hats, their lariats hung over the pommels of their saddles. I remember very well that most of the cowboys were black and that they fraternized freely with the white ones. I hadn't yet seen that kind of social phenomenon in my native New Orleans.

My father had acquired ownership of this unit of the Greater Holcamp Carnival Shows, and I do recall a visit from Mr Greater Holcamp himself, a short, skinny, dyspeptic, youngish man in a golf cap (we call it a golf cap now) and a sweater with leather-reinforced elbows.

One of the feature attractions of his particular carnival was a real blackface minstrel show, complete with tambo and bones, the traditional interlocutor, and the pink top hats and gloves. Best of all though was the band, which consisted of five black New Orleans musicians. The leader's name was Willie, and he played the trumpet.

The music, of course, wasn't new to me, but it was a music that never failed to be exciting. I observed early that when this music was played, people listening couldn't keep still. They were impelled to dance, stomp their feet, and otherwise appear to have lost kinetic control of their appendages.

From time to time, when my parents were off tending to business, Willie would take temporary charge of me. It wasn't a difficult assignment for him, since I was a sober and sensible six-year-old, reasonable enough to understand that there were surely dozens of things Willie would have preferred to do. We carried on brief, desultory conversations, handicapped by the fact that I found it very difficult to penetrate his dialect. I probably asked him a question or two about the music he played, but I just don't remember. In any case, a season went by in which I frequently found myself in Willie's company. I would have to describe the relationship as sedate and uneventful. I still attended every performance of the minstrel show, mainly to listen to the band. I had, by this time, all of the routines and gags in my head, though I had made no effort to commit them to memory.

Back in New Orleans, I resumed my accustomed lifestyle, and I remained endlessly fascinated with the multifaceted French Quarter. I remember feeling considerable relief when I learned that my father had sold the carnival and that I wouldn't be required to repeat the tour. (Some kids have no sense of adventure.)

Now two dozen years go by. I have, by that time, learned a lot about this music and the people who played it. I had been producing my Journeys Into Jazz concerts for some time, and during 1946 and 1947 I had a regular Friday night series going in the Philadelphia Academy of Music. I did very little advertising, because I had a mailing list of devout followers of the music.

One day I got a call from Bob Maltz, who operated the Stuyvesant Casino in New York, asking me if I'd like to book Bunk Johnson for an appearance at one of my concerts. I had, of course, heard of the old man, since anything that happened in the jazz community of those years became common knowledge almost instantly. We all knew how several months earlier Bill Russell and Fred Ramsey, on a tip from Louis Armstrong, had discovered Bunk working in a canefield in New Iberia, Louisiana. It has become a jazz legend now, how they got Sidney Bechet's brother Leonard, a dentist, to make Bunk a set of false teeth, how they got him a horn and inaugurated his heralded comeback.

I thought my regular patrons would enjoy having a look at this ancient relic, so I hired him. Naturally, I assumed that very little could be expected of Bunk musically by now, and to be on the safe side, I also engaged Wild Bill Davison to take up any possible slack. The rest of the musicians I called were all New Orleans people, except trombonist Jimmy Archey, who really understood authentic jazz. The others were Albert Nicholas for clarinet, Sam Price for piano (come to think of it, *he's* not from New Orleans, either), and Pops Foster for bass. (I never hired anyone else if I could get Pops.) Baby Dodds, my choice for greatest jazz drummer of all time, was present, too.

Anyway, on the night of the concert, perhaps forty minutes before curtain time, this old, old black guy, wearing a brown homburg hat and a long, out-of-style overcoat and carrying a trumpet case, walks down the aisle to where I'm standing on the stage. When I saw him I'm sure I must have looked like I'd turned to stone. When I recovered my equanimity, I said, 'Willie! What are *you* doing here?'

'You got to know me a long time to be callin' me Willie,' he speculated. 'Most everybody calls me "Bunk".'

In a matter of seconds I realized that I had undergone dramatic changes in appearance since the time I was six, and I reasoned that it was perfectly logical that Willie – excuse me, Bunk – could fail to recognize me. After settling down to some coherent talk, we discussed who I really was and I saw a flicker of not-too-excited recognition on his face. We marvelled for a moment over the small world, and by this time other members of the ensemble had arrived.

Bunk said to Nick, 'Remember we played in that carnival in Texas and Oklahoma in the twenties? You remember the boss had a kid that hung around the jig show?' (Sorry – that's what they called minstrel shows in that era.)

Nicholas remembered vaguely. Bunk told him I was that kid. My discussion with Nicholas over this bit of history was more animated. I already knew him well, but had no idea he had been the clarinettist in that early venture. As I took another look at him, I found I could match his middle-aged face with that of the twenty-two-year-old from that Texas spring. He then told me, 'You know, Dodds, here, was with us in that band.' I was amazed. The whole story was carefully repeated to Baby, who didn't remember the boss's kid. He also didn't remember the boss, the Greater Holcamp Carnival Shows, and was somewhat surprised to learn that he had ever been in Texas. He wasn't sceptical about it. He just expected other people to remember things for him. (Most of Baby's life was spent in an unfamiliar galaxy.) Bunk, however, corroborated Baby's presence on that tour. I was, of course, overwhelmed to learn that these great jazzmen had been part of my childhood.

I Remember Jazz (1987)
Al Rose

Louis Armstrong

DURING THE time that he was playing with me – well, word was getting around that Louis was a good trumpet player. So, one night Freddie Keppard came in to hear us and the bandstand was down low and Freddie stood there by the bandstand and he listened awhile, and then he said to Louis, 'Boy, let me have your trumpet.' So, Louis looked at me and I bowed my head, so Louis gave him the trumpet. So, Freddie he blew – oh, he blew and he blew and he blew and then the people gave him a nice hand. Then he handed the trumpet back to Louis. And I said, 'Now get him, get him!' Oooh, never in my life have I heard such trumpet playing! If you want to hear Louis play, just hear him play when he's *angry*. Boy, he blew and people started standing up on top of tables and chairs screaming, and Freddie eased out real slowly. Nobody ever asked Louis for his trumpet again!

The Jazz Word (1960)
Lil Hardin

Louis Armstrong and Jabbo Smith

JABBO SMITH tried on several occasions to prove he was better on trumpet than King Louis. He was never able to convince any of the other musicians, but he certainly tried hard.

One such occasion comes to mind. It was an Easter Monday morning breakfast dance at Rockland Palace, Harlem's biggest dance hall. Jabbo was starring in Charlie Johnson's band from Smalls Paradise, but Don Redman's band, featuring Satch, from Connie's Inn was the top attraction. For weeks before the dance arguments raged, bets were made, and finally the great moment came.

When I entered the hall I found that more than a hundred musicians had beaten me to any choice spot, so I pulled out my horn and got on the stand with Charlie's band. Nobody said anything, which figured, because I always sat in with anybody around town in those days.

Jabbo was standing out in front, and I'll say this, he was *blowing* – really coming on like the Angel Gabriel himself. Every time he'd fan that brass derby on a high F or G, Altis, his buddy from Smalls, would yell, 'Play it, Jabbo! Go ahead, Rice!' (Everybody from Charleston called each other Rice. It was the hometown nickname.) 'Who needs Louis?' he yelled. 'You can blow him down anytime.' When Johnson's set ended with Jabbo soaring above the rhythm and the crowd noise, everybody gave them a big hand. I could tell from the broad grin on Jabbo's face that he felt that once and for all he'd shown Satch who was king.

Then all of a sudden, the shouts and applause died down as Louis bounced on to the opposite stage, immaculate in a white suit. Somehow, the way the lights reflected off his trumpet made the instrument look like anything but a horn. It looked as if he were holding a wand of rainbows or a cluster of sunlight, something from out of this world. I found out later that I was not the only one who had the strong impression of something verging on the mystical in Louis's entrance. I can still see the scene in my mind's eye. I've forgotten the tune, but I'll never forget his first note. He blew a searing, soaring, altissimo, fantastic high note and held it long enough for every one of us musicians to gasp. Benny Carter, who has perfect pitch, said 'Damn! That's high F!' Just about that time, Louis went into a series of cadenzas and continued into his first number.

Since everyone is not a trumpet player and cannot know how the range of the instrument has grown over the years, I should explain how significant a high F was. Back in the 1920s, the acceptable high-note range for the trumpet was high C, and to hit or play over C made the player exceptional. That is until Louis came along with his strong chops, ending choruses on F. Lots of guys ruined their lips and their career trying to play like Satchmo.

Louis never let up that night, and it seemed that each climax topped its predecessor. Every time he'd take a break, the applause was thunderous, and swarms of women kept rushing the stand for his autograph. They handed him everything from programmes to whisky bottles to put his signature on. One woman even took off her pants and pleaded with him to sign them!

Jazz Anecdotes (1990)
Rex Stewart

Kid Ory

LIKE I said before, Ory and I would go catching crawfish together a whole load of times, then we would go back to his house and clean them and cook 'em. One day we were sitting in his house preparing these crawdads when out of a clear blue sky I asked him, 'How much royalties do you get out of "Muskrat Ramble"?' I don't even know why I asked. I guess more out of conversation than curiosity. 'I don't get nothing,' came his reply and I almost fell off the chair. He said he never sold it to anyone since he had composed it that day for the Louis Armstrong Hot Five recording. That was some twenty years before and it had become one of the all-time dixieland hits in the meantime.

His publisher years ago had been Melrose Publishing Company and they had sold the song to another publishing company and Ory had never gotten 'nickel one' from the song. I had some friends in the music publishing business on Vine Street in Hollywood so I called and asked them who published 'Muskrat Ramble'. These friends looked it up and said that the Levy company had it. I took Ory down to this Levy Publishing next day. They were on the second floor of a big office block. We got there and the secretary said that Mr Levy was in and for us to wait a moment. 'Who shall I say wants him,' she asked. 'Just tell him Barney Bigard,' I said. I didn't want to mention Ory just yet. We waited a few minutes and in we went. 'Hello, Mr Levy,' I said, 'I'd like to introduce you to a man who composed a tune that you publish and it gets played all the time. This is Edward "Kid" Ory, and he has never gotten a dime in royalties.'

'Kid! We've been looking all over for you for years. We have some money right here for you that we wanted to turn over,' said Mr Levy.

They must have looked high and low for him all right. All they had to do was look in the union book. Anyhow, this Mr Levy turned over a cheque to Ory for around $8000 right there and then, and furthermore he got royalty cheques of $600 or so every quarter from then on. That started him buying his new home.

It seemed from then on I noticed a change in Ory. At first it was nothing big, but do you know that he never thanked me for getting straight with his royalties. He never said a word. Maybe success was having something to do with it. He split from his first wife and married another woman who kind of made suggestions to him about running his band. The way they had it, after a few years you wouldn't believe it was the same guy running that band. He left his first wife in a pretty underhand fashion, but that wasn't nothing to do with me. But as far as the musicians in his band went, those guys were my friends and I didn't appreciate the way Ory treated them as time went by. I mean Minor Hall got sick when they toured Europe and they just left him without a round-trip ticket and the poor guy had to get home best as he could. Wellman Braud, my old bass-playing friend from Ellington's days, was on that trip and he told me they didn't get paid. Ory owed him around $200 and he had to go to the union, in other words to take Ory to the union, to get his cash. Another time I heard Ory and Ed Garland had a fist fight on the bandstand at the Hangover Club in San Francisco and Ory got knocked from the raised-up bandstand on his ass. I didn't stay around till the end, but he was making a lot of enemies. He just was a different guy than I had known and helped – been glad to help in fact. And do you know he never said a word about me in all of his interviews, not one good word. Not nothing at all.

I went to his funeral in 1973. They put him away New Orleans style with a band of music and some of his old buddies played for his last ride: Andrew Blakeney, Teddy Buckner, Norm Bowden, Sam Lee, Alton Purnell. I know they played 'Just a Closer Walk with Thee' over him and cut out down the hill with 'Muskrat Ramble' and 'Ory's Creole Trombone' and that was the end of an era.

With Louis and the Duke (1985)

Barney Bigard

Jelly Roll Morton

IN 1939 I was a delegate to the KEEP AMERICA OUT OF WAR convention in Washington, DC. My hotel room had in it a flyer announcing:

THE JUNGLE CLUB
JELLY ROLL MORTON (IN PERSON)
AT THE PIANO

The flyer gave an address on U Street. I think it was a Tuesday night when I paid a cab driver and found myself standing on this unattractive street making a decision about whether it was worth going up the narrow staircase of the dingy building to the Jungle Club on the second floor. Even though it was about ten o'clock, I heard no sounds of music. I was about to turn and leave just as Jelly Roll joined me in the doorway.

'I remember you,' he said. 'You're Eubie Blake's friend. It's pretty early for things to start around here. Come on up and I'll show you the place.'

He had his keys out as we went up the stairs. He opened the door to display the poorly executed African jungle decor. With an all-encompassing sweep of his hand to indicate the grandeur of what I was seeing, he announced, 'All genuine bamboo.'

In 1939, the cheapest furniture you could find was 'genuine bamboo'. It was the hallmark of poverty – certainly nothing to boast about. But Jelly seemed oblivious to all that.

'A dollar cover charge,' he informed me. 'The first drink is free. After that, it's sixty cents a shot.'

'Cover charge?' I inquired. 'You've got a show?'

'I'm the show,' he assured me. 'Jelly Roll Morton in Person.'

I gave him a dollar, and he asked what I was drinking. I asked for Laird's Applejack, which he didn't have, then settled for Canadian Club and soda. He settled himself down on his piano stool. The piano was an antique upright that had obviously had a lot of work done on it. We were still alone. I was the only customer. That scene would be duplicated on many succeeding nights.

Mezz Mezzrow and Eubie Blake

EUBIE AND I were having dinner in the Theresa Hotel, Harlem's showplace, when Mezz walked in scanning the place. I realized he might be looking for me. As the only other paleface in the crowd, I wasn't hard to find. He came over to our table and paid his respects politely to Eubie. Then he handed me a square package, about the size of a deck of cards.

'This is just to show my appreciation, pal,' he said. 'I just want you to know I'm stayin' straight and I'm going to do the best I can to stay out of trouble and play jazz.'

Eubie said, 'Anybody who's playin' jazz is *already* in trouble.'

I thanked Mezzrow and wished him well. He said, 'Don't open the package until you get home.' Then he told us goodbye and left.

'Put that *away*, Shazzam.' (That's what Eubie and some other people called me in those days.) 'It's probably some kind of dope.' I laughed and so did Eubie.

When I got home, though, which was in Philadelphia at that time, I opened the package and found a beautiful sterling silver cigarette case full of – you guessed it – marijuana joints. Or, as they called them in those days, 'muggles'. I called Eubie on the phone. 'I opened Mezz's package and what do you suppose it is?'

'I already told you, Shaz. Dope.'

'Yeah,' I admitted. 'But how did *you* know?'

He said, 'What else would Mezzrow give to somebody he really liked? Don't smoke any of it. It ain't good for you.'

I confess that I *did* smoke one – first time in my life. It scared the hell out of me and I flushed the rest. I had seen enough muggles smoked and knew how to do it. I did get high and it did feel good. After all, it was Mezzrow's celebrated 'golden leaf'. But I knew I didn't want to do that any more.

Eubie Blake

EUBIE HAD an extended string of affairs from his extreme youth, through both his marriages and the last of them when he was in his nineties. I asked him when he was ninety-seven, 'How old do you have to be before the sex drive goes?'

He answered, 'You'll have to ask somebody older than me.'

Eubie wasn't a man to pursue the ladies, but he was certainly quick to yield to temptation. After all, when *Shuffle Along* became a smash on Broadway, he was rich, talented, and personable. He was an international celebrity; his songs like 'Memories of You', 'I'm Just Wild About Harry', and 'You're Lucky to Me' were part of the main body of American music. The ladies, especially the show business ladies, were all over him. He was lionized.

Certainly everybody knew he was in love with Lottie Gee, his *Shuffle Along* ingenue. The cast knew it, his partner Sissle knew, his wife Avis knew, and all of Broadway knew. Both Avis and Lottie were jealous as they could be, and Eubie's attitude was one of complete helplessness. He never felt he was cheating on anybody. It was just that all women were always taking advantage of the unfortunate fact that he couldn't resist them. He once confessed to me, 'I been gettin' away with that act for sixty years.'

He told me that every time he left his house, Avis would insist on making love to him until he climaxed and then when he left Lottie in the apartment he kept for her, she'd do the same thing; then, he added, ruefully, 'there were the *other* girls'. The roster of Eubie's lady friends read like a directory of black soubrettes, ingenues, chorus girls, and showgirls. That, he said, was the *big* thing about being a success in the music business. He was saddened by the girls – and there were several – who committed suicide over him, two who were killed by their husbands – yet he discussed all these events as an outsider, as one who had exercised no initiative in these matters. He viewed it all as an innocent bystander.

All the above from *I Remember Jazz* (1990)

Al Rose

Duke

WHEN AN earnest interviewer asked Joe Nanton if he considered Ellington a genius, Nanton replied, 'I don't know about that, but, Jesus, he can eat!'

Jazz Anecdotes (1990)

Bill Crow

John Lewis and Miles

ON TENTH Avenue one evening I went upstairs to ask John Lewis if he couldn't stop playing his harpsichord at 3 a.m. because it was directly over my pillow. He apologized, explaining he was preparing a piece to a tight deadline and it would all be over tomorrow. We were in his doorway. To be polite, I asked him if my trombone practising was too loud. He shook his head in that kind, diffident manner of his.

Oh yes, I seem to have forgotten to mention that Miles Davis lived on the same floor as John. Just then a grumpy voice behind me rasped: 'Yeah, it's too loud,' and Miles dumped a bag of garbage down the incinerator.

Close Enough for Jazz (1983)
Mike Zwerin

Duke

DUKE ELLINGTON was one of the two geniuses I have ever worked with. That word is used so much nowadays; they call guys geniuses that I would have just called damned hard workers. But as to the real McCoy, I have only ever worked with two. The other was Louis Armstrong. They were both geniuses in different ways though. Duke is a composer and writer of ideas whereas Louis was a player of ideas. Louis could take any tune and make it interesting and beautiful and yet still you know that it's the tune. That's where his creative ability came from. Duke would actually write most of his own stuff. He would take an ordinary situation and put it into some music – orchestrate it – and before you could turn around there was a whole band orchestration based on some ordinary everyday occurrence. Like for instance 'Harlem Air Shaft' or later his Sacred Mass stuff.

When I first met him I knew there was something different about him. Something that put him outside of other men. I couldn't figure out what he was doing with his music but I played it every night. I gradually got used to it and came to realize that he always knew exactly what he was doing. He never hit on things by luck; it was always in his plan musically. He came up with a different sound from all the other bands. Every time you would hear him on the radio you would know that it was his band. He had a distinctive touch to everything. He would take my clarinet part and make the trombone play it. He had the whole front section in different keys for some measures. Anything you like to name. But it was his music. The man and his music were one and the same after a while.

We were playing a concert for the New York School of Music and this professor of music had his class there. We were playing 'Crescendo in Blue' and the professor had the class to figure out what Duke had done as a lesson. They couldn't grasp what Duke was up to and neither did their professor. Duke had to stand out in front of the class and go over what he had just played step by step. He had to explain it to the professor too. I remember that Gershwin wanted to collaborate with Duke once on an extended piece, but Duke turned him down. He thought it was 'old hat'.

Of course he was an open-minded man too. I mean if we would come up with a good suggestion, anyone in the band that is, he would generally take it. He would at least try it out. If you took a chorus and played a little piece of improvisation that he liked he would take it out and score it to make up a whole new tune. Then he would call a rehearsal. He would come there with maybe about sixteen bars. He would tell the guys, 'Play this that's here, then Barney, or Tricky or whoever, you just ad lib from there.' Open space completely. He'd figure out a chord structure to put behind it, then come up next day with a last chorus written out, and that would be how we'd record it later that same week. He could write around you. He knew your limits up and down and he would build the things around a given soloist's voice.

He would hear things and start to write even without a piano. That's where that number 'Daybreak Express' came from. These southern engineers on the railroad, they used to have a fireman that would blow the whistle on the train. We'd all be up at night gambling and we'd hear the whistle blow as we went over a crossing. Duke would hear all the same things. The only difference was, we were playing poker and he was writing music about that whistling. He somehow got the effect of the train all into the music. He'd write all the ideas down and next day he would bring them to rehearsal all wrote out. You see Tizol was the extractor of Duke's ideas. Tizol had such beautiful handwriting. He would write all the individual parts out and give them back to Duke, who would in turn check them over then pass them out to the band.

Duke was a very patient man at rehearsals. Not like some bandleaders. Like if we were going to phrase a section part he would just sit quietly until whoever had the lead phrasing would get it down. Then the other men in that section would add their harmony parts or whatever. Duke would never get excited. He knew that it would all work out in the end.

The other thing writers all forget to mention is that Duke Ellington was a terrific band pianist too. He wasn't much on solos. In fact people would always be wanting him to come places to play and he told them directly, 'Oh! I'm no good without the band.' He genuinely meant it too. But like I said, as a band pianist he was just great. That is, once you got used to his chords. He would make the weirdest chords on practically any number. For instance if we played an old hat number like 'Who's Sorry Now', out would come those 'funny' chords even for a number like that. I understand that he got a lot of his chord ideas from an old guy named Will Vodery that used to arrange for shows. He was the first Negro that went to Hollywood to arrange for a motion picture. He taught Duke a lot and Duke just kept on adding to it.

Another nice thing about Duke Ellington. He wasn't a surly kind of fellow in any way. He spent plenty of time with his fans, talking to them and giving them autographs. Most people don't know that side of him at all. All they know is the composer side. Of course that is what he spent the majority of his time doing. He wrote so much stuff you wouldn't believe it. Of course some of the guys in the band did contribute even without getting any credit. They didn't care about the credit; they were just musicians. Like Lawrence Brown had something to do with 'Sophisticated Lady', and Johnny Hodges had some part of 'Don't Get Around Much Anymore'.

Duke and I had gotten together on 'Mood Indigo'. I'll tell you what happened, just to set the record straight. My old teacher Lorenzo Tio had come to New York and he had a little slip of paper with some tunes and parts of tunes that he had written. There was one I liked and I asked him if I could borrow it. He was trying to interest me in recording one or two maybe. Anyway, I took it home and kept fooling around with it. It was just the second strain. There was no front part on what Tio gave me. I changed some of it around, for instance the bridge on the second strain, and got something together that mostly was my own but partly Tio's.

Duke had a date for a small group recording which in fact was supposed to be my group. We would record for all kinds of companies in those days and put the band under any kind of name with one of the sidemen signing in as leader. That was to avoid contractual complications. All the bands did it. Anyway, I brought what I had of the number to the date and we tried to work it out. We just used Tricky, Artie Whetsol and myself, along with the rhythm section. Duke figured out a first strain and I gave him some ideas for it too. He wrote out a three-part harmony for the horns, we added my second strain and recorded it. Whetsol had the lead, I had the second and Tricky Sam had the third. We didn't think anything of it and all of a sudden it began to get popular and that was it.

I missed the boat for twenty-eight years on royalties. I didn't get a dime. It was all under Ellington and Mills's name. You see in those days – just to show you how stupid we were – we would write a number and sell it to Mills for twenty-five or fifty dollars. If we had kept the numbers with our names on we would have had royalties for years and years. Now it has finally been legally cleared up for 'Mood Indigo' and I do get my royalties from it. In fact I had an offer from a guy to sell the rights to it for $5000 plus 50 per cent of any forthcoming royalty. I told him no. With any song you can register it every twenty-five years I think it is, then re-register it until seventy-five years are up then it's public domain. As you go along you get smarter and smarter but after you get taken a few times you know what is going on. Somebody that was doing a discography asked me why the number came out first as 'Dreamy Blues'. That was never the title. I always called it 'Mood Indigo' but maybe the record company put the wrong label on the record. I never heard of 'Dreamy Blues'; it was always 'Mood Indigo' to me and I ought to know.

In the Duke Ellington Orchestra a lot of the music would be unrehearsed. Especially the soloing order. Duke would never have a set pattern, like clarinet then trumpet then bass or that sort of thing. After we played down his intro and main theme parts he had written for us then we would just take extended solos as we wanted. Duke himself would give us such great rhythmical backing at the piano. He knew how to 'feed' somebody that's blowing a solo.

Duke only ever missed a job once to my knowledge. His mother had died and he had to bury her so he took off for a couple of days. They got Don Kirkpatrick, who was Johnny Hodges's brother-in-law, to take Duke's place. He did a fine job but the band wasn't the same. Everyone in that band knew they were working with a genius.

Do you know till this day he has never had all the credit that he deserves. Like all other great artists. They have to be dead a hundred years before the world will really know their worth.

With Louis and the Duke (1985)
Barney Bigard

My Father, the Duke

ALL OF a sudden, I was someone who had to be spoken to. There was always just this little distance between us. He was never able to adapt himself as a father, and it got to a place where conversation was difficult. When I was first on the road with him, we didn't know each other well enough to really have anything to talk about. Gradually, however, he began to teach me music, which was one of the best things that could have happened. As time went by, it became more and more obvious that I could write with satisfaction only for his band. Well, I did do two or three things for Charlie Barnet, and tried a few for Basie, out of friendship. But right away Basie said, 'Sorry, I can't use these. They're too close to Ellington.' So all of a sudden I realized that I was enmeshed in a way of musical thought from which I wasn't really able to tear myself away. Therefore, if I couldn't write for the band, I either had to write for myself or nobody. This sort of like a shell I got into I guess over the last ten years.

Everybody's always asking, 'Is this the *real* Ellington? What is the real Ellington? Who is the real Ellington?'

Well, Ellington is a chameleon-type person. *This* is the real Ellington. He changes. For instance, I've seen him leave a big dinner of some sort and wind up in a dive. And he is equally at home in either place. I've seen him talk to people of intelligence and people of ignorance, and keep the conversation going without embarrassing anyone, or making anyone self-conscious of his status.

Ellington was never one to get into the middle of a battle. He's never going to take up one side or the other. If two people differ, he'll sit there until the discussion has been settled and then he'll probably say something that changes everything anyhow.

And he can get away with it because *this is Ellington* . . .

The Jazz Word (1960)

Mercer Ellington

Django Reinhardt

ANOTHER THOUGHT that occurred to me. You read all kinds of stuff about the jazz in Europe being so great. I think the only great jazz musician to come out of Europe was Django Reinhardt, the guitarist. He was the only completely original one that played jazz in the American way, with that same swing. Most all of the other musicians seem to take practically all their stuff from records. It's that lack of originality that worries me. They don't have the same feeling as Americans have. Maybe in time they will get it. Only time will tell. But this Reinhardt guy was unbelievable. I recorded with him in Europe on one of my trips and, as I said, he was a complete original. Even today his talent has never been matched but in those days he stood out alone.

With Louis and the Duke (1985)

Barney Bigard

Jack Teagarden

BIG T was on first-name terms with the great and famous – not just musicians, but movie stars, a king or two, big industrialists. But he considered that the most important person he knew was Mr Van Sweringen of Cleveland who built and owned the Nickel Plate Railroad. If there was ever anybody in the world he envied it was this man who had been able to build and operate his own railroad. Jack did a brief tour with me one time. St Louis, Minneapolis, and Cleveland. He couldn't wait to get to Cleveland. Maybe he only came with me because he was sure Mr Van Sweringen would let him ride in the cab of a locomotive.

Working with jazzmen you get inured to all kinds of idiosyncrasies and after a while nothing surprises you. That Jack knew the owner of a railroad well enough to call him on the phone and ask to be permitted to ride in the locomotive was credible to me by that time. What wasn't credible was that when T got ready to go for his ride he was able to pull a motorman's hat out of his suitcase. I discovered he wore that to drive his car, too. Even more astonishing was the fact that Mr Van Sweringen joined him for the ride in the cab of the locomotive.

I Remember Jazz (1987)

Al Rose

Charlie Parker

I NEVER crowded or bothered him. I was busy trying to figure out my own life and I sensed that aside from his music it wasn't going to do me any good to be spending a lot of time around Bird. But he was the best player in the game, and on the stand when he'd sometimes look around at me and smile I knew I had played something good.

He was a sad driver – when his two-year-old car fell apart he left it in the street; borrowed mine once and tried to shift without using the clutch – so I'd pick him up every night at the madame's house in my '37 Ford, take him to work and bring him back. When I came early one night he motioned me to follow him to his room. I waded through piles of sandwich wrappers, beer cans and liquor bottles. Watched him line up and take down eleven shots of whisky, pop a handful of bennies, then tie up, smoking a joint at the same time. He sweated like a horse for five minutes, got up, put on his suit and a half hour later was on the stand playing strong and beautiful.

For two weeks he never said a word to me – going to the club, on the stand, or driving home. But it wasn't an uncomfortable silence; he was either stoned, froze, or just off somewhere else, and I respected whatever trip he was on and whatever distant place it carried him to. It was never an ego trip. If someone were to ask him who he liked better on alto, Henry Prior or Sonny Criss – it was the sort of thing a young player starting to come up would ask – he'd shrug and say, Both. They're both cool. Shooting down other players was as foreign to his nature as a longing for sharp clothes and a Cadillac or whether or not he had a white woman, which were the black badges of success in those days. He had plenty of white women but it never interfered with his music.

Sometimes I'd pull up in front of the club and he'd be too high to get out of the car. Howard McGhee would ask me where Bird was. I'd say, Sittin' in the car. No point in trying to pull him out, he wouldn't have been able to play anyway. After a while he'd get himself together, walk in and start blowing – even before he reached the stand, weaving his way through the tables playing in that beautiful, fiery way.

At the end of the second week of the gig he spoke his first words to me. It was close to three in the morning when I left him off at the madame's house. He got out, started walking toward the house, then stuck his head back in the window and said, 'I heard you tonight.'

The next day I told the guys in the band I was going to drop by Bird's place and see if he wanted to go to a movie. Everybody said, That's a dumb idea, he isn't going to want to go to any show. That's too square for him, too bourgeois. I dropped by anyway. He came to the door in a T-shirt and the same pin-stripe suit he wore on the stand. Said it was a nice day and a show sounded like a good idea. We went to a newsreel playing nearby. As I was buying my ticket I realized Bird was no longer with me. Looked up and down the street and saw him coming out of an alley halfway down the block. He wandered up to the box office and laid out his money, not saying anything about the little side trip. Afterwards we ate a hot dog and drove around downtown in my Ford, enjoying the spring day. When I dropped him off back at the house he said, 'I had a nice time.'

That weekend I smoked my first joint, some light green from Chicago Bird pulled out as we were driving down Avalon Boulevard to get a hamburger and Coke. Didn't feel anything till after we ate and I started driving home. I said, Man, why are all these horns honking at me? Bird said, You're driving backwards. I stopped and let him take over the wheel. He made it back to his place, stripping gears all the way. I walked the ten blocks to my house and was weaving up to the door when I saw a tiny old lady from my father's church staring at me. Watched me trying to make it to the door and said, 'Young man, are you behaving yourself?' I made it up the stairs, lay down under the bed, and getting a flash from the old church days asked God aloud to deliver me from the devil.

Next day Bird phoned me and said, 'That was some powerful light green.'

His uncle was Bishop Peter E. Parker and maybe he was close to God. I know he was damn near like a prophet in his music. He scared a lot of people over the years and died of pneumonia, so they say, in Baroness Nica Rothschild's Fifth Avenue living room when he was thirty-four. But as long as I knew Bird, I was never awed or afraid of him. I loved him. And how can you be afraid of somebody you love?

Raise Up Off Me (1972)

Hampton Hawes

Allen Eager, Miles Davis et al

TOWARDS THE end of John Coltrane's period with Miles, Trane was searching desperately to find his own personality. His solos were getting longer and longer, sometimes lasting for forty-five minutes in the middle of a forty-five-minute set. Miles said to him: 'Man, why don't you try playing twenty-seven choruses instead of twenty-eight?' Trane answered: 'I get involved in these things and I don't know how to stop.' Miles said: 'Try taking the saxophone out of your mouth.'

It was once said of a playboy: 'He would rather not make love to a beautiful woman and have everybody think he had than make love to her and have nobody know it.' There must be a little bit of that in every man. Even though wooing Eugenia and Ursula had produced no physical contact with either, I revelled in my big splash descending into the basement Club St Germain, one on each arm. Everyone would think I was making it with both of them at once; an entrance worthy of Allen Eager.

'Allen Reluctant' we used to call him, the granite-faced tenorman who played more like Lester Young than Lester Young. The first time someone told me about Stan Getz, he was described as 'playing even better than Allen Eager'. There were many other white Presidents – Stanley Kosow, Brew Moore, Johnny Andrews – and I had played with all of them in Brooklyn strip clubs. They had taught me tricks like running augmented arpeggios on dominant seventh chords; listening to them had been my school, but none of them had taught me more than Allen Eager. Allen was my Joe DiMaggio; I modelled my swing after his. He listened to Prokofiev, drove racing cars (once won Sebring), frequented Swiss ski resorts, lived with high fashion models (boy were they high), patronized the best English custom tailors. He could also be a nasty bastard when strung out, which was not infrequent. Miles kept trying to find out the name of Allen's tailor but Allen wasn't talking. This was no nodding-out, nose-scratching junky fixing in dirty toilets. He was always sharp, bright, on top of it. He could hold his own with poets, writers and classical musicians. He was a model to me of what hip should be. How have I survived my heroes? How I envied Allen Eager. Much later, not too many years ago, I ran into him living in a broken-down house in the black slums of Coconut Grove. He had lost his teeth, was a born-again Christian, on welfare and the food-stamp programme.

In Paris in 1957 Allen Eager was rooming with Beat poet Gregory Corso in the 'Beat Hotel' and I was pleased to imagine myself in his image walking into the Club St Germain with Eugenia on one arm, Ursula on the other. Miles was between sets in a dark corner. I always seem to see Miles in dark corners. He put his arm around my shoulder, asked about my health and generally made it clear that he was concerned with my welfare. His smile went a long way with the ladies. A clubowner once said to him: 'The trouble with you is that everybody *likes* you, you little son of a bitch.'

He joined us after the first set. I had to take Eugenia back to her university dormitory, where there was a curfew. When I returned I found Miles and Ursula in deep eye-contact. With his best evil ray, he looked at me and asked her: 'What do you see in a dumb cat like this? He's too fat anyway.'

I could never take his salty act seriously. He was so up-front about it for one thing. They were more jabs than anything. It was not really a knock-down round, he was just sparring. He went back for another set.

'Well, I guess I have a decision to make,' Ursula said. Was it possible? She was deciding between me and Miles. You can understand the nature of groupiedom from the beginning of time when I tell you I almost recommended Miles, pleased to be able to furnish him a beautiful woman. As we walked up the stairs together, Miles squinted at us from the bandstand. He looked so tragic, so Byronic, like a little lost poet as he opened up the melody of 'When I Fall in Love' like a flower.

Close Enough for Jazz (1983)
Mike Zwerin

Charles Mingus Tackles the Audience

ONE SUNDAY afternoon when Mingus was leading a group at the Village Vanguard, the audience was particularly noisy and inattentive. A couple of tables of patrons right in front of the bandstand seemed completely oblivious to the music. Their animated conversation was distracting to the musicians and made it difficult for the patrons sitting farther back to hear. Indignantly, Mingus hauled his bass up to the microphone and made a few scathing remarks about the noise, but the offending patrons were so wrapped up in their conversation that they heard none of Mingus's diatribe.

'Okay,' said Mingus, 'we're not going to fight you any more. On this next number, we'll take turns. We'll play four bars, and then you-all talk four bars. Okay?'

He stomped off a tune, and after the opening chorus Mingus played a four-bar break and waved the band out. The loud conversation at the front tables continued. The musicians carefully counted out four measures during the hubbub and then the band took the next four, with the solo tenor playing as loudly as possible. Another four for the oblivious talkers, another for the band. As the rest of the audience laughed, Mingus continued grimly with his announced format until the end of the number. The talkers never knew they had been featured, but they joined the applause at the end.

Jazz Anecdotes (1990)
Bill Crow

Oscar Peterson and Charles Laughton

OSCAR PETERSON tells the delightful story about meeting Charles Laughton in Edinburgh, Scotland. Oscar was there playing a concert and the great actor was there on a lecture tour (shortly before his death).

As Oscar was waiting for his train at the station, he saw a man who looked very familiar. He walked over to the man and asked:

'Are you Charles Laughton?'

'I am indeed,' said the man.

'I've admired you all my life,' said Oscar.

'Really? And what is your name?' asked Laughton.

'My name is Oscar Peterson.'

'And are you an actor?'

'No,' said Peterson, 'I'm a musician.'

Laughton asked: 'Jazz or classical?'

'Jazz,' said Oscar.

Laughton looked Peterson up and down for a moment and then asked: 'You got any pot?'

'No, I haven't,' said Oscar, whereupon Laughton walked away without saying a word.

If You Know of a Better Life (1982)
Bud Freeman

The Meanness of Nat King Cole

IN THE early days of my association with Nat Cole as his manager, when the King Cole Trio was just beginning to make some noise, we went out and did a series of one-nighters with Benny Carter's band, Savannah Churchill and Timmie Rogers. We got to Chicago, the city where Nat was raised. We played a new theatre between the loop and the South Side.

Opening day the place was jam-packed. The trio closed the show, and after that opener that he always used to use, 'The Man with the Little White Keys', Nat went into 'Gee, Baby, Ain't I Good to You'. You know how the song goes. A very romantic lyric, and the house was just so quiet you could hear a pin drop. Nat got to the part where he sings, 'I bought you a fur coat for Christmas and a diamond ring . . .'

And some guy stood up in the balcony and shouted, 'You ain't bought —— , man!'

Another guy stood up and said, 'Yeah, I know you're right – I went to school with this cat!' And in a matter of moments the whole place was in a complete uproar.

What the hell are you going to say? There was only one thing to do. We closed the curtain.

I doubt very much that Nat would get that kind of interruption today.

Carlos Gastel
Nat's manager

George Shearing,
and How to Smell Money

MY WIFE and I have had a gimmick going for years: I tell people I can smell money.

If it's a one-dollar bill, she does nothing. If it's a five she taps me once, with the knee or the hand. If it's a ten, she taps twice, twenty three times, fifty four times.

Once we were sitting around in the Papagayo room in San Francisco, Jimmy Lyons, Nat Cole, June Christy, Billy Eckstine, Stan Kenton, Trixie and myself, and the subject of money came up.

Trixie said, 'You know, of course, George can tell the denomination of money by smelling it.'

So they were handing out bills and she was tapping; they said, 'Well, you're giving him some kind of signal.'

Trixie could see there was a one-dollar bill coming so she said, 'All right, if you think I'm giving him any signals, I'll move over here,' and went clean over to the other side of the table.

The money came out and I knew that because she was moving away, it was a one-dollar bill, so I smelled it and said, 'It's a one.'

Nat Cole said, 'How do you do it?' and I said, 'Nat, it's very simple; for different monetary denominations, they use different grades of ink. Each grade has its own peculiar smell.' He shrugged his shoulders and said, 'All right. If you don't want to tell me, that's all right.' And he walked away.

Five years later I told him.

Both the above from *Laughter from the Hip* (1963)

George Shearing

Billie Holiday

RED NORVO offered me a job at Café Society in San Francisco. I couldn't read chords too well at the time and had to rely on my ear. Whenever I played a wrong chord, Red – he had a big pot belly then – would turn round, bug his eyes, wave his mallets at me and go '*Accchh!*' I hated that bogey-man stuff, but it's partly the reason I hear so good today.

Billie Holiday was working opposite us, sounding so good, like her heart was breaking on every tune. She was a rowdy, soulful, bighearted woman; carried around a pair of those little dogs you put sweaters on. At that time she was already famous and narcotics agents were harassing her. She got so she could spot them at fifty feet through a haze of smoke. 'See the little cat drinking Manhattans in the brown suit? Po- lice,' she'd say.

She could be tender and show a temper that would scorch you. 'I'm gonna come down off this stand and kick your ass,' she said to a chick who had been talking non-stop through her opening-night show; and afterwards told the bass player, who liked to stretch out behind singers, 'Why you have to play so wild? Cut out that devil music.' That cat took it so to heart he just looked at her quietly and his eyes filled with tears.

Later that night some of the musicians were arguing in the band room when she hollered from her dressing room – banging on the wall separating the two – 'Shut up all that noise in there.' They yelled back, 'Shut up yourself, broad' . . . 'Come in and make us.' We heard her door slam and a second later she came barging into our room in her drawers. She was big and strong, had some righteous meat on her, and those cats flattened against the wall, grinning, their arms raised. I watched it all from my chair in the corner. She glared a minute, then walked back out, talkin' about crazy motherfuckers, and said to me, 'You don't need to flinch, baby, I know it wasn't you.'

From that night on she began coming by the piano after her show when I would play intermission music. Would lean over me and say stuff like, 'You're about the sweetest quietest cat I ever seen, you play so pretty. Takin' care of business and not chasin' the scroungy ass bitches that come in here . . . ' She was always having trouble with men – when she went for someone it was wholehearted, she'd really mix it up with him and he usually had the bag* – but I was barely twenty, never jived or bothered her, and maybe that was why she liked to come over and talk. She made it her business to see that the chicks who hung out in the club didn't hit on me. 'You leave him alone, he's nice, keep your funky hands off him.' I had the feeling she hoped I wouldn't have to go through any bad changes, almost like a mother anxious for her son to steer clear of booze and drugs and sin; didn't want anyone polluting me. I didn't realize at the time that there was no way of escaping all that, I'd eventually have to go through it; you got to wade through a certain amount of mud to get to the pearls. We were leaving the club together one night when some photographers started taking pictures of her. 'If you're gonna snap me,' she said, 'you gotta include my son,' and she pulled me over, hugging and

* Narcotics and works

squeezing me. It was a hoked-up but nice picture and I still have it hanging over my mantel in East LA.

One afternoon toward the end of the gig some agents broke down the door of her hotel room looking for dope. If they'd come an hour earlier or an hour or so later she could've handled it, but at the time they broke in she and her man had their clothes off. They searched the room and busted her, but a good criminal lawyer up there, Jake Erlich, got her off. It was only temporary relief though. They kept hounding her till the end of her days, and despite what the obituaries and the movie said, I know she died because she was too emotional and bighearted, always racing. She lived her life so full it was inevitable she would go down fast.

In the shadows of the Cleveland airport cocktail lounge I spotted the lady, familiar heft to her, sitting at the end of the bar. I hadn't seen Billie Holiday in almost five years – those early days when she was watching over me, trying to keep me pure and free of sin.

'Hey, Billie.'

She looked at me a long time before she said, 'You too, baby? I didn't think it would ever happen to you.' Probably had heard I was strung but didn't believe it, remembering me as a nice, together twenty-year-old kid playing pretty tunes at Café Society.

I said something, asked her where she was headed.

'I thought you were going to get by,' she said and the tears came into her eyes.

Still wanting me to escape all that. *But you ought to know, you went through the same garden, went out in the rain and got wet, how was I supposed to stay dry?*

There was nothing I could tell her. A few minutes later she got on a plane to Detroit. It was the last time I ever saw her.

Raise Up Off Me (1972)
Hampton Hawes

Erroll Garner

NAT PIERCE attended one of Garner's record dates in 1969:

'The red light went on and he started to play. The red light went off and he kept on playing. Everybody waved to him from the booth, and when he eventually finished they said,

' "Erroll, we turned off the light. You were supposed to stop." He looked at them and said,

' "I couldn't stop. I wanted to find out how it would come out." '

Jazz Anecdotes (1990)

Bill Crow

Bruce Turner

BRUCE'S APPARENT distance from the realities of life was revealed at Gloucester Place when he bought a second-hand motor car. It soon broke down and he was asked why he didn't take along someone who knew about motor cars when he made the purchase. Bruce replied, 'But, Dad, the guy who sold it to me knew all about motor cars.'

All This and Many a Dog (1986)

Jim Godbolt

Roland Kirk

I DON'T know how he did what he did. He knew who you were *immediately*, one word. I went to his house in New York, hadn't seen him for two years, I just said hello. We got raided one time he was here. We didn't have a proper club licence. Members-only club, but it didn't work that way, it was impossible to function. So we just ignored it. And we got raided.

Roland was doing that pennywhistle thing. He distributed about a hundred pennywhistles to the audience, and everyone was blowing like mad. It was like a madhouse. About twenty plain-clothes men and women came in. And no one took a bit of notice. Just went on blowing, like an aviary. Roland couldn't see what was happening, of course, just thundered on.

All this law trying to get names and addresses. Policeman says to me, 'Go up and tell him to stop.' I said, '*You* go up and tell him to stop.'

Jazz at Ronnie Scott's (1981)

Ronnie Scott

Roland Kirk

SHUFFLING ON to the stage to begin his night's work, Rahsaan Roland Kirk looked for all the world like a mobile musical junk shop. Hung around his neck, on a cat's cradle of cords and straps, were a tenor saxophone and two curious hybrid instruments called a stritch and a manzello. In one hand he carried a clarinet and in the other a bag containing a variety of noise-making devices. Also attached to his person were a whistle, a nose-flute, a stylophone and a mini-cassette recorder. A flute was planted in the bell of the saxophone.

He was blind, and with a blind man's ponderous care he placed his equipment within reach. What happened after that was always an overpowering and quite unforgettable experience.

He would play two, and even three, instruments at once, range with complete authority over the whole stylistic history of jazz, fix noisy punters with his sightless stare and scold them into silence, and generally frighten the life out of every musician in the place.

God knows what compulsion drove him to do these impossible things. Perhaps being blind, he didn't know how impossible they looked. In any case, there was no denying the musicality of it all. When he played a three-instrument passage the harmonies were exact, his tone full and rich. When he sang while playing the flute the unison was impeccable. He set himself the kind of problems which only a lunatic could devise, like taking the reed off the saxophone and blowing the thing like a trumpet – not just the odd note, you understand, but a complete version of 'Body and Soul'.

His records never really did him justice; you had to *be* there. Recording studios can do anything, and it would be easy to believe that some subtle engineering had gone into creating the effects. Despite declarations on record sleeves that the whole thing had been done without the aid of mirrors, no sensible person could be expected to fall for such an outlandish claim.

And then, early in 1976, Kirk suffered a stroke which paralysed his right hand. According to all the rules it takes two hands to play any woodwind instrument so everyone decided that this was the end of his career. But we had reckoned without his superhuman willpower and the extraordinary pragmatism with which he had always approached his art. The music was in his head; getting it out was a technical problem, and technical problems can be overcome.

When he came to Ronnie Scott's in 1977 – for the last time as it turned out – he opened each set with a twelve-bar blues which changed key every chorus: twelve choruses, twelve keys, requiring the use of every note on the instrument. Night after night he raised two defiant fingers at fate and roared through that blues at full throttle.

At the end of his first set one night I went backstage to pay my respects and, mindful of his somewhat prickly temperament, gingerly advanced the question of how he had felt immediately after his stroke.

'Doctors,' he snorted contemptuously, 'what do they know? They said I could still write music. *Write!* But here I am and I'm still playing. You heard it, man, right down to the low D. When I get some movement back in this hand I'll be able to get the bell-notes too.'

His extraordinary ability to blow an instrument and breathe in at the same time was still intact. Other musicians can do it, but not as seamlessly, and not always while playing over the whole range of the instrument. This, he thought, would be his lasting contribution to instrumental technique.

Meanwhile the stroke was 'a blessing in disguise', forcing him to concentrate on the tenor saxophone, which had always been his favourite instrument.

We had quite a long talk about the technical problems of playing the saxophone with one hand and he showed me the modifications he had devised to make it possible. Looking at them, the thing I couldn't get over was the physical *weight* of it all. A tenor saxophone weighs about seven pounds. When it's being played half of that weight is carried by the player's right thumb. But Kirk didn't *have* a useable right hand, so the whole lot was hanging unsupported from his neck by a strap. The additional keywork must have added an extra couple of pounds at least.

The mechanism itself looked like something by Heath Robinson from an idea by Rowland Emett. Each joint of each finger had at least one job to do. Some of the longer rods went through three or four stages of articulation, and it took quite a lot of force to shift them.

To play one of these altered instruments meant mastering an entire new technique, and this is what Kirk had done. But bear in mind that it was then barely a year since he had suffered a severe stroke. For some of that time even he would have been out of action; devising the modifications and having the work done must have taken a few weeks. So in not much more than six months he had practised the one-handed saxophone until it sounded better than most people playing with two, and resumed a full touring schedule.

It is impossible to imagine Rahsaan Roland Kirk accepting the status of invalid, although he might have lived a little longer if he had. Now that he has been dead for ten years, I wonder what happened to those instruments with their fantastic assemblage of keys and rods. I hope they're safe, and that one day some museum will acquire them. Apart from perpetuating his name, the Rahsaan Roland Kirk Collection would be an inspiration to generations of musical technicians.

There was never anything but optimism in what he said that night. He spoke about his new album and his plans for the future as though the recent disaster had never happened. I left him assembling his armoury for the last set of the evening, his good hand checking methodically over every key and spring.

Roland Kirk died on 5 December 1977.

Wire, December/January 1987/8
Dave Gelly

Eric Dolphy

THE LARGE bump on his forehead exaggerated Eric's eager tilt forward. His instruments were like an extension of his body; he was never without one. I once saw him walking down 48th Street playing his flute.

He was a reedman, not in the sense that he played reed instruments. He was *made* of reed instruments. He did not speak, he blew. He played what might be called the Dolphyphone; whatever instrument was in his hands sounded as though he had invented it. In the *New York Herald Tribune* of 30 October 1963, Eric Salzman reviewed an Orchestra USA concert: 'Mr Dolphy, for those who don't know, is a brilliant wildman, an undisciplined musical genius who produced frantic, incredible cries from the bottom to the tip-top of a whole range of woodwind instruments . . . Mr Dolphy can no doubt produce his fantastic sound on anything you can blow a noise out of; he could, I'm sure, play with the same extreme expressive intensity on a pop bottle . . . you never know if he'll make it, but when he does – WOW!'

I met Dolphy when we were both part of a package tour called 'Jazz for Moderns'. I was with Maynard Ferguson, he was with Chico Hamilton. We travelled by bus or chartered DC3 for three weeks. Eric practised his piccolo travelling, while his buddy Ron Carter, bassist with Chico, had long and bony knees. By our coincident preference for the back of vehicles, we often found ourselves a row apart – Ron's knees in my back. Eric's piccolo was in my ears for three weeks. It still is. I can still hear its tension and polytonality. Like Lee Konitz, Eric Dolphy was one of those few musicians who could be polytonal a cappella. I'm not talking about multiphonics, playing one note and singing another at the same time. Tonality is a natural force, like gravity, and Dolphy had more than one centre.

Genius is intangible, by definition it does not fit in. Eric did not fit into the prejudgements of the Orchestra USA power structure. He tried, it's sad how hard and futilely he tried to please the bosses. But his own orbit was already inevitably fixed. The orchestra's instrumentalists were more necessary tools than vital cogs, and Eric was a hand-made product in any case.

Nothing sadistic about it, Eric was feared. How could you be sure what he'd come up with next? Let's hear one for reliability. Eric *was* a 'wildman' who could never adapt to the calm currents of the Third Stream. John asked Phil Woods to play one solo after another. This is not to denigrate Phil, a thrilling player, but Phil was not, like Eric, in the process of changing our ears.

On one of Eric's rare solos, Gunther asked him to 'play closer to the melody'. The mind boggles recalling it. Here was a musician who could invent melodies never before conceived. We should have played closer to *his* melody. Imagine what Eric might have done with Darius Milhaud's saxophone melody at the beginning of 'Creation of the World' had he been permitted to stretch out on it. Jerome Richardson, who did play it, was told to use his 'classical sound'. This in an ensemble formed to explore new musical forms and bring older ones closer together.

Eric loved to play the classics. He became totally immersed in his flute part on a Mozart work we prepared for several weeks, practising it during breaks and while everyone else was packing up. Although he was no Jean-Pierre Rampal, his classical flute playing lacked experience more than ability. He played Mozart appoggiaturas inside out, but then for a long time many experts thought Glenn Gould played Mozart wrong too. If Eric's intonation was questionable at times, he did get a fat sound and was in any case a charter member, and some of us back in the brass section thought it was shameful when, after Eric had rehearsed the part for weeks, a classical flautist was brought in to play the concert.

Besides hurt sensitivity, this was directly contrary to the announced purpose of the orchestra, which was to be 'an exercise of mutual respect and compatibility between classic and jazz forms'.

Orchestra USA was very important to Eric. He was involved on some deep level with it. It failed him like it failed most of us. When the classical flautist took Eric's chair, he walked up to me, looked over his shoulder, pulled up his collar and asked: 'You feel a draught?'

Before leaving for Berlin on what turned out to be his last trip, Eric asked a friend in the reed section: 'Make sure my chair's still here when I get back.'

Close Enough for Jazz (1983)

Mike Zwerin

Wally Fawkes

WHEN HUMPH joined George Webb's band in 1947 he and Wally became close friends. On the journey to Hawick, Humph got into a carriage, saw that Wally wasn't present and hastily retreated to seek him out. It hadn't taken him long to assess the rest of us. We were not on his wavelength. Fawkes was, and in his quiet, steely way, he was a match for Lyttelton. Humph's respect for Wally was revealed, albeit unintentionally, one night at the Blue Posts. The Lyttelton band were taking a rather lengthy interval and after manager Lyn Dutton's almost tearful pleading that they return to the club, Humph addressed his men. 'Right! Off we go! *Bray! Parker! Hopkinson! Picard! Turner!* Ready, Wal?'

Wally based many of his characters in his cartoon strip 'Flook' on people in the jazz world. One of them was Len Bloggs, a snarling anti-social inverted snob with a chip on his shoulder. For some reason I was the inspiration for this disagreeable misanthrope. So accurate was Wally's draughtsmanship that I was recognized by total strangers as the model for Bloggs who, in one story, was a schoolmaster. A man I had never seen before in my life approached me in a pub in Earl's Court and asked me if that was my profession. The question came as no surprise. I explained the connection and the man returned to his friend highly delighted with himself for recognizing me. On another occasion, at a jazz concert in the Festival Hall, I was again hailed by a total stranger, this time by name. The stranger was Steve Voce, a jazz critic, who informed me that he knew who I was from reading 'Flook'. He was inordinately proud of his smart deduction. I was a little icy in acknowledging the recognition.

All This and Many a Dog (1986)
Jim Godbolt

André Previn and Mel Powell in the Snow

WHEN MEL Powell was working at MGM, he and I were very good friends. Once we had some time off. We hadn't seen snow in a long time; so Mel said, 'I'll tell you what. I have some studying to do, and you have some work to do on some scores; now somebody has told me about a place up above Idyllwild, very high up in the mountains, with a cabin. Let's go up there and tramp through the snow and relax.'

So after Mel said to his wife, Martha Scott, 'Why don't you pick us up in three days,' we drove up there.

It was so deep in snow up there that I can't describe it; and the logs were all wet. I found a bottle of coal oil, and I said, 'I think if we sprinkled this on the logs they would catch fire.' And Mel said, 'That's a marvellous idea; but they look pretty wet. Empty the whole bottle out in the fireplace.'

We did, and lit a match.

Well, the whole thing just went up like the bridge on the River

Kwai. We literally charred down one whole wall of the cabin – for which we had to pay – didn't burn ourselves, because we had thrown the match in; we were cowards. And we moved to another cabin.

Finally, by the third day, we were both so nervous from not having played the piano that we went to the man that owned the cabins and asked him whether he had a piano. And he said, 'Well, there's an old upright piano over in the tool shed, which we bring out only for our summer guests. You can't play on it in there – it's dark and damp in there.' So we said, well, suppose we move it over into the cabin? And he said that was just about impossible – it was something like five hundred yards, and the snow was up to our ears, practically, but still we said we'd try it.

So we got hold of this piano somehow between us and we got going. We eventually managed to drag it maybe a hundred or two hundred yards, and by that time both of us were utterly pooped. It was impossible; we were just about dead.

Mel said, 'Listen, it's a lovely night. Why don't we just play out here?'

I said, 'Fine.' We had brought with us a Haydn Symphony for four hands, so I ran back to the cabin, got two flashlights, propped them up on the piano and we started playing.

It was so cold that we had to keep our gloves on, and we wore those wool hats that you pull down over the ears.

We were right in the middle of the third movement – I even remember which symphony it was, 104 in D Major – when Martha Scott drove up.

The tableau of the two of us, both sitting out there in the snow in a moonlit forest, at an old upright playing Haydn with our gloves on, was something she never got over, and especially the fact that we couldn't quite understand why she was so amazed. Because we were having a very good time.

I'm afraid the story has an anti-climax. We hired some people to schlepp the piano back.

Laughter from the Hip (1963)
André Previn

Owen Bryce

APART FROM the ebullient George there were other rare characters in the [Webb] band. Owen Bryce, second trumpet and founder member, was a strict vegetarian who walked sockless out-of-doors in the coldest of weather. He wore a pair of brown corduroy trousers that came almost up to his nipples. He had a large upturned nose and was dubbed, among other things, Cyrano. He came in for a lot of ribbing. It bounced off him. His ego, largely deprived of praise, fed on antipathy. He had a fine conceit of himself and was severely astringent in his criticism of others. He made few exceptions in his blanket criticism of the human race. It was he who stood alone.

He worked extremely hard to make his record and radio shop a deserved success and although an avowed socialist, he sanctimoniously preached honest endeavour and self-reliance with the fervour of a Samuel Smiles. Owen was a very Smilesian man. He had a withering contempt for our 'incorrect' diet and a missionary zeal to convert us all to vegetarianism. Every morning, winter and summer, he would go for a swim in the local baths, emerge, have a hot shower and plunge straight back into the pool. The band vehemently refused his insistent invitations to join him in this health-giving exercise, nor were they enthusiastic about the nut cutlets, raw vegetables and dandelion coffee so much a part of his diet. They were in stupefied awe when he fasted for up to three days. Like most fervent missionaries, his terminology rationalized his beliefs. If I had a boil on my neck, I was eating the wrong foods. If he had a boil on his neck, it was the poisons coming out thanks to a correct diet. Against such sophistry it was hard to win.

I admired and liked Owen and was considerably influenced by him. Despite his massive egotism he was a staunch, honest individual, although my faith in his vegetarianism was considerably strained when he became a pig breeder.

All This and Many a Dog (1986)

Jim Godbolt

Jimmy Knepper

PLAYING DUETS with Knepper is one intense learning experience. Out of the corner of my eye, I watched him articulate out in the fourth, fifth and sixth positions, false positions, difficult to ring and play in tune, but you can play faster out there because the notes are higher up in the overtone series and thus closer together. You can play fast like a fast trombone rather than machine-gun triple-tonguing imitation trumpet. He showed me the scales out where the slide must only move fractions of inches between notes. Most trombone-players are aware of those positions and can read in that fashion but Knepper uses them improvising. You wouldn't hear that just listening and it's not really essential knowledge, it is however the hidden truth behind the virtuoso, his musical silent 'K'.

Knepper is a mine of Mingus folklore: 'We were driving from New York to LA for a gig. When I got to his house I found out that he and I were going alone in his Cadillac limousine. "You're driving," he told me. "But Mingus," I said, "I don't have a driver's licence." He didn't mind at all: "That's cool. Nobody ever stops a Cadillac limousine." He was right.

'Mingus was unavoidable for me, I used to get very depressed. Good God, I'd say to myself, I'm stuck with this guy for the rest of my life. His music was so difficult, with all those time-changes and different sequences. You had to concentrate real hard just to get through the lines. They seemed to be purposely written to trip you up. I wanted to relax and play "All the Things You are". But Mingus had an innate musical instinct that could come up with something coherent by putting little bits and fragments together. He took snatches of different little melodies he sketched out here and there and hooked them together. Some of them he might have written years ago and not known what to do with at the time. He didn't call it "free" but he used to talk to us about "peaks of intensity". And he could make a whole tune out of a vamp-till-ready. A lot of rock is based on that – the introduction becomes the entire piece. Outwardly he came on like "this is my music and don't you dare mess with it", but privately I don't think he had that much respect for the stuff. He once told me: "I realize I'm only writing ditties."'

One night off when we were on tour in Germany with Gruntz, I said to Knepper: 'Hey, let's hang out and get drunk.' He moped and said: 'Naah. I think I'll go to my room and mope.' He knows how to mope all right. We were playing with one of the best drummers in the world (this guy would be on anybody's five-best drummers list), but Knepper abhorred his abstract time. The drummer likes to come off a long roll crescendoing right to the second beat, for example. Hearing this one night, Knepper got up and looked under his chair: 'Seem to have lost one.' This was during a gig, we were on the bandstand. He looked under my chair, then behind the saxophones: 'Hey, I'm looking for one. Anybody know where one is?'

Knepper leaves as little as possible to chance. One silent 'K' is enough. He knows where he's going and how to get there. The slide never moves more than the minimum distance necessary to get from one note to the next. If that means G in the sixth position, so be it. He improvises like he dresses, rather rumpled. There's a certain amount of disorder which, given his flawless technique, serves to humanize what otherwise might come out cold. You keep wondering . . . is he going to make it? Suspenseful, dramatic, he straddles the beat like a loping halfback in the clear, running only as fast as he has to. You shouldn't really hand the ball to Knepper for short yardage. This is no bone-shattering fullback, it takes time to get in the clear and finesse to stay there. He's brittle, avoid power-plays to avoid injury. Enough of this stupid football analogy. The season is over anyway.

Close Enough for Jazz (1983)
Mike Zwerin

George Melly

FOR THIRTEEN years George wrote the script for Wally Fawkes's strip cartoon, 'Flook', in the *Daily Mail* and there were occasions when he tended, perhaps unconsciously, to overlook Wally's contribution. Wally was in a Chelsea pub when he was asked what he did for a living. Wally's reply naturally mentioned Flook. The questioner's eyes narrowed. He looked hard and long at Wally and said, menacingly, 'Now look here, chum, whoever you are, I'd be more careful if I were you. I happen to be rather a close friend of George Melly's.' Mick and the band quickly spotted this quirk of George's and would pointedly ask how *his* illustrator was behaving, inquire if the fellow was toeing the line, etc, etc, and affect not to remember his name.

And he could be most patronizing. We met in the King's Road, Chelsea, one Saturday, the day the 'Beautiful People' make a ritual of parading this fashionable highway, heads constantly jerking from side to side to see and be seen. George was with a little clique of preening Chelseaites. He wore a wide-brimmed hat, a black cape and carried a silver-topped walking stick. He stared at me. 'What on earth are *you* doing here?' he exclaimed, as though I hadn't the right sort of credentials to use what, after all, is a public pavement.

Indeed he loved being among these 'Beautiful People'. He frequently joined them for what I mockingly described as 'George's Little Dinners' – really quite prolonged and expensive affairs in chic Soho and Kensington restaurants with obsequious waiters encircling candle-lit tables and the rest of the flim-flams of 'good eating', a striking contrast to the roadside greasehouses he was forced to patronize on tour.

Although passionate about the blues which he sang with the utmost sincerity, I don't think George managed to assimilate the blues feeling. Other British singers, notably Sandy Brown and Long John Baldry, have been infinitely more successful in projecting a blues sound. It was as a showman that George excelled. His act, exhibitionistic and flamboyant, included exaggerated hand and body movements with much facial distortion and rolling of the eyes. In essaying the female role he stuck beer mugs up his sweater to simulate breasts and sang in a squeaky falsetto.

In his *tour de force*, 'Frankie and Johnny', he fell about and off the stage with quite alarming realism to lend emphasis to the line when Frankie shot her faithless lover down. It was a unique act; there was nothing like it anywhere. The voice and the movements were the camp Melly imbued with *bravura*, the theatricalism of the congenital show-off, but his pronouncements revealed a razor-sharp wit, his conversation and writing showing considerable erudition. He was an intriguing combination of ham and intellectual. Understandably, he revelled in the surprise at the apparent contradiction.

George has long professed a hedonist's philosophy. In the austerity of the late 1940s and early 1950s, coming after the relative puritanism of the 1930s, his bisexual promiscuity, heavy drinking and bad language were seemingly quite outrageous and much of it was deliberately intended to shock. He can look back on himself as a pioneer of permissive behaviour, or 'raving' as it was called in the jazz world. It was an infectious philosophy. A lot of people happily embraced it, although few were able to extend themselves with the panache of Melly.

While I have derived much pleasure from watching George's act over the years, I still feel a twinge of embarrassment at the spectacle of an English, white, affluent, middle-class man singing the songs of the oppressed and poverty-stricken Negro. I admit it's an illogical objection. I have no complaint about English, white, affluent middle-(or upper-) class men playing the blues through factory-manufactured instruments.

All This and Many a Dog (1986)

Jim Godbolt

Pee Wee Marquette

I NEITHER can nor want to stay serious writing about jazz, which should be above all fun. Breezy swing interests me more than accuracy. Not that I don't try to be accurate, but who cares about accurate unreadable prose. 'You can't beat fun,' someone said.

My memorial piece about Birdland when the jazz landmark closed included amusing Pee Wee Marquette anecdotes. This black midget master of ceremonies had processed hair, wore a cummerbund, walked with a fancy cane and his tiny fingers were covered by diamond rings, one of which was a present from Dinah Washington. Pee Wee would be sure to announce a musician's name at the end of a set for a fiver a week. For ten he'd pronounce it correctly. Doug Watkins was 'Grub Hawkins' until he wised up. When Irving Levy, the best-liked Birdland partner, was stabbed to death, Pee Wee wept in a corner. Irving had treated him like a big man, a normal human being, dinner with the family, for example. On crowded weekends,

Pee Wee would grope through the forest of standees' legs with a lit flashlight looking for loose change on the floor. Just before dawn after the customers were gone and the naked cleaning lights had been turned on, he sat on the bandstand with a microphone in one sparkling mini-hand singing 'South of the Border (Down Mexico Way)' all by himself. Lester Young once responded negatively to Pee Wee's request for a tip: 'Leave me alone, you half a motherfucker.'

Pee Wee sued the *Voice*. Our lawyer, Ed Koch, later mayor of New York, asked for testimonials from musicians verifying my Pee Wee stories. Everybody said of course everybody knew they were true, but nobody but Pepper Adams and Patti Bown would sign their name to anything because they were afraid of being blackballed. Koch thought it was very funny being sued by a black midget. The case was settled out of court.

This taught me a lesson. You *can* beat fun.

Close Enough for Jazz (1983)
Mike Zwerin

Me and My Club

DEAR FRIEND

Little did I think, when I opened the Club in a Gerrard Street cellar thirty years ago. But that's the story of my life.

However, it's been a great thirty years and I feel very privileged to have had the opportunity to make some contribution towards gaining wider appreciation of the marvellous music around which my life has revolved for the last forty-five years.

I would like to express my thanks for the wonderful press coverage the Club has enjoyed over the last thirty years – it certainly has been a major factor in helping to put the Club so firmly on the jazz map. Without the encouragement from the writers, reviewers, interviewers, broadcasters and critics, I don't think we'd have had quite the same degree of determination to continue.

I want especially to acknowledge the debt of gratitude I owe to my friend and partner, Pete King, who must take the major share of the credit for keeping us in business despite the many problems and difficulties we have encountered over the years. Pete's been a real stalwart and I don't think I've ever said a word in anger to him. He's bigger than I am.

It's gratifying to look back over the last thirty years and recall the many fine articles, the hundreds of reviews and features which have been published about the Club. It's a tribute to Britain's jazz writers that they are so perceptive, so musically aware and so easily bribed. We've always been glad to welcome the press to the Club – along with the dead Greeks, the cement drinkers, the smoking dead, the people drinking on an empty head, the credits to Poland and those iron-willed members of the audience who control themselves so impressively. We hope we can count on your support for the next thirty years; we'd like to reaffirm our gratitude for your past endeavours. And we'd like all our ashtrays back.

Finally I want to pay tribute to all the musicians, the famous and not so famous, who have brought lustre to all the Club's reputation; and I want to express my gratitude to all the people who worked for us over the last thirty years. Their loyalty has really been outstanding – and I still remember with a glow of pride that one moment one evening in 1973 when all the waiters and waitresses were actually moving at one and the same time.

Thanks again to all of you – you've made a happy man very old.
Sincerely

RONNIE SCOTT   From Thirtieth Anniversary
                                                brochure of Ronnie Scott's

Humphrey Lyttelton's Obituary by Humphry Littelton

HUMPHREY LYTTELTON, the well-known Old Etonian ex-Guards Officer jazz trumpeter, was born on 23 May 1921 at Eton, the only son (among four daughters) of an Eton schoolmaster. It was, many observers agree, the turning-point in his career. Up till then he had led what can only be described as a sheltered life, taking little active part in public life and relying heavily in most matters affecting his livelihood upon his mother. It is not known exactly when he came to a decision about a career, but it is safe to say that, at an age when the average, healthy boy is grappling with the choice between growing up to be an engine-driver or a sex maniac, Lyttleton had already decided that for him it was to be a well-known Old Etonian ex-Guards Officer jazz trumpeter.

To be born on 23 May 1921 at Eton, the only son of an Eton schoolmaster, was a brilliant first step in a career marked by many examples of such forethought and inspiration. The location and circumstances speak for themselves. It was one of the dispensations of Henry VI Our Founder, his heirs and successors, that the son of an Eton master should be educated at the College free, gratis and for no more than it takes to equip him with a top hat, a suit of tails, two sets of underwear and an allowance of seven and sixpence a week at the school tuck shop. It follows that, short of accident or miscalculation, such as being born the fifteenth son of a ferret-handler in Thursoe, Littleton could scarcely fail to become an Etonian and, in the fullness of time, an Old Etonian.

The date of his birth also displayed that degree of ruthless calculation which was to mark his subsequent career. It ensured that, by the fateful year of 1939, Humphery would be eighteen years old and of military age. In the carrying out of this phase of his plans, Littelton received – and was ever quick to acknowledge in later life – invaluable assistance from the late Adolf Hitler, of whom it has been said Herr Hitler used his not-inconsiderable influence to make it possible for the young Old Etonian to become a Guards Officer and an ex-Guards Officer within the short space of six years.

At least one authoritative history of World War Two claims that by landing at the Salerno beach-head clutching a trumpet in his hand, Humphrey almost single-handed brought the Italian campaign to a successful conclusion. It is now thought that his role in the affair has perhaps been exaggerated and that his gallant and persistent trumpeting in the face of the enemy was responsible for fewer German casualties than at first claimed. Nevertheless, he was mentioned frequently in dispatches, leading eventually to his withdrawal from the Front and return to England. The scenes on VE Day, when the ex-Guards Officer designate was hoisted on to a handcart and towed, still trumpeting, through Piccadilly to the cheers of grateful Londoners, have been described in vivid detail by an eye-witness.

Within months, Middleton, now a successful Old Etonian ex-Guards Officer, was poised for the most crucial phase in his career. It has been suggested by at least one base calumniator that the road to becoming an Old Etonian ex-Guards Officer jazz trumpeter was a smooth one. It must be borne in mind that the Luttleton family, as it was originally spelt and often still is, goes back a long way into English history. The Luttletons were sturdy cricketing folk much given to original and fascinating hobbies, and the pages of their family history teem with Archbishop-cricketers, Cabinet Minister-cricketers, Public School Headmaster-cricketers and at least one Old Etonian Chief of the Imperial General Staff-cricketer.

With such a background, there was naturally enough considerable pressure upon young Humphrey to go into the family business. It should not be thought that he was ind altitude, a distinction which for many years was marked by a commemorative metal plaque in the knee-joint of a Mr Joby who recklessly sold sweets and soft drinks on the boundary immediately behind the bowler's arm.

It was in 1936 that Lyttelston made perhaps the most coolly-calculated move in the furtherance of his career, going with his mother during the Eton and Harrow cricket match at Lord's to buy his first trumpet, dressed in the full top-hat-silver-waistcoat-tailcoat regalia of the Eton First XI Supporters' Club. One half-hour lesson, a quick flip through the pages of the Nat Gonella Trumpet Tutor, a few hours' practice in the lavatory (now preserved for the nation) of his grandfather's house in London, and Hamphrey Lytteton was a trumpet player. But the battle was not yet won.

How near he came to becoming an Old Etonian ex-Guards Officer orchestral trumpeter, doomed to obscurity in the anonymous brass section of a symphony orchestra, can be judged from the words of Dr Mervyn Bruxner, the conductor of the Eton School Orchestra, on hearing Humphrey perform the Jeremiah Clarke Trumpet Voluntary within a few weeks of taking up the instrument – 'Good God!' One should mention, too, a later performance, arranged for trumpet, pipe organ and stentorian tenor voice, of the aria 'Sound an Alarm' from Handel's *Judas Maccabeus*, a musical event which is marked by a commemorative metal plaque erected only recently at the approaches to Eton College which reads

'WINDSOR BRIDGE IS NOW CLOSED TO TRAFFIC DUE TO THE DISCOVERY OF A PERMANENT STRUCTURAL FAULT. NO ACCESS TO WINDSOR VIA ETON HIGH STREET'.

The manner in which Himphrey became an Old Etonian ex-Guards Officer jazz trumpeter is now too well-known to need reiteration. The name of historic stepping-stones – the Nuthouse, Regent Street . . . the Orange Tree, Friern Barnet . . . the Red Barn, Bexleyheath – are etched in the annals of jazz history, not to mention his liver. The careful reader will note that as yet the infant Lutterworth's full ambition was unrealized. He had yet to become a *well-known* Old Etonian ex-Guards Officer jazz trumpeter. At this point he met up fortuitously with several people who were to have a considerable influence on his career.

One was Canadian-born jazz clarinettist Wally 'Trog' Fawkes, a member of George Webb's Dixielanders, who persuaded Hphmrey to join the band. Shortly afterwards, on the occasion of the first International Jazz Festival at Nice, Canadian-born *Daily Mail* temporary Foreign Correspondent W. E. Fawkes wrote an article for his paper revealing that the young trumpet player from England who was appearing at the festival was, in fact, an Old Etonian ex-Guards Officer jazz trumpeter whose ancestor, Humphrey Lyttelton, had been an associate of Guy 'Trog' Fawkes in the Gunpowder Plot. Overnight Lyllelton had become well-known.

It wasn't long, however, before Lymington confided in friends that life at the top, as a well-known Old Etonian ex-Guards Officer jazz trumpeter, was far from easy. For one thing, there was the competition. Was not Old Stoic, ex-Navy author-scriptwriter-art critic blues-singer George Melly coming up fast behind him, becoming more well-known every minute. With a ruthless energy unusual in a man of his size (six-foot three in his stockinged feet, slightly smaller in shoes) he threw himself into the task of accumulating hyphens.

Within weeks, thanks to a broadcast on what was then the BBC Home Service entitled 'How I bought my first trumpet', he had become jazz trumpeter-broadcaster. Meeting up fortuitously with Canadian-born clarinettist-journalist-cartoonist 'Trog' of the *Daily Mail*, he became overnight a jazz trumpeter-broadcaster-cartoonist. He started his own band with Canadian-born former George Webb Dixielander cartoonist-journalist-clarinettist Wally Fawkes, thus turning into a well-known Old Etonian ex-Guards Officer jazz trumpeter-broadcaster-cartoonist-bandleader.

There seemed no end to the man's achievements. The purchase of a pair of binoculars, a quick tour of fifty London restaurants, the acceptance of an article by *Punch*, an appearance on 'Any Questions?' and a chat with Michael Parkinson led to his becoming, by 1973, a well-known Old Etonian ex-Guards Officer jazz trumpeter-broadcaster-cartoonist-bandleader-birdwatcher-gastronome-humorist-panellist-TV-personality. It was fantastic, incredible unpreceden . . .

Enough! When the well-known Old Etonian-ex-Guards Officer jazz trumpeter-broadcaster-cartoonist-bandleader-birdwatcher-gastronome-humorist-panellist-TV-personality-corpse is finally laid to rest, let some professional obituarist in need of the gig put the finishing touches. I have given all the help I can and, in the process, outlined the patchwork quilt of a career, as yet only just begun, which this book may well turn out to be about.

Take It from the Top (1970)

Humphrey Lyttelton

4

MUSICIANS ON MUSIC

Jazz musicians take music very seriously. Sometimes it is the only thing they do take seriously. You have to practise long and hard to get as good as they get. They tend to be interested in the way music works and sometimes they will say some quite illuminating things. At other times they will, with equal intensity, discuss the best reeds or strings to use, and where to get them. Most of the writing on jazz, unfortunately, has been done by critics who are always self-appointed and usually not popular with the practitioners. This section quotes no critics, only musicians.

The Book of Chords
(or, The Book of Knowledge)

I REMEMBER my first jazz-piano lesson with Enos Payne. Enos wasn't famous – he had never played with Bird, or anyone who *had* played with Bird. But he personified jazz. Enos talked in syncopation and walked as if a drummer were counting off tunes in his head.

'Jazz isn't music. It's a language. CommunicCAtion,' Enos told me when I sat down. 'To speak it, you have to go to the source. Where's your *Real Book*?' Mine was dog-eared and coffee-stained. 'Damn,' Enos said, grinning as I pulled it from my knapsack. 'You've put that thing to *use*!'

For almost twenty years, *The Real Book* has been the undisputed king of the jazz fake-book industry – five hundred pages of melody lines and chord progressions for 430 jazz classics. I don't know a jazzman who hasn't owned, borrowed, or Xeroxed pages from a *Real Book* at least once in his career. Headliners at the Blue Note wouldn't be caught dead with one, but café-circuit combos unabashedly pull sets from its pages every day.

The quantity of tunes is only part of the allure: *The Real Book*'s an enduring jazz-world mystery. To buy one you need a 'connection' – say, a music-store owner with a stash behind the counter. Depending on how many middlemen stand between him and his 'source', you'll pay $20 to $30. The book has no publisher's page, no copyright – seems no one bothered to pay royalties on the tunes, and people aren't standing in line to take credit.

For years, it's been rumoured that the book originated at Berklee College of Music, the famous Boston jazz school. '*The Real Book* came out around 1971,' says John Voigt, Berklee's music librarian. 'The only material available in print then was crap.' That is, fake books of the day favoured standard dance-band harmonies. And you know how jazz musicians like to futz with chords.

A handful of Berklee professors vowed to fill that harmony gap, Voigt says. They swiped arrangements from recordings like *Kind of Blue*, and Coltrane's *Giant Steps*, ferreted out the jazz harmonies, and bound the tunes into a book. Vernon Duke would have blanched at Charlie Parker's flurry of chromatic changes in the third and fourth bars of 'I Can't Get Started'. But the scribes captured them all.

Eventually, Berkleeites made their way into the world, dropping the books in their paths like Johnny Appleseeds. Unhindered by copyrights, local entrepreneurs reprinted them adding and deleting tunes at will. Voigt has seen hardcover editions, pocket-size editions, editions with lyrics, even Russian editions. Just last year, I ran across *The Real Book Cont'd.*, which contains hundreds *more* tunes. A note in front states that it was penned by the original *Real Book* scribes, whoever they are.

Musicians are forever debating the book's accuracy. A tenor player tells me that 'Sugar', by Stanley Turrentine, is missing a very sweet F sharp 13 chord in the tenth measure. But for me, *The Real Book*'s only flaw is the dime-store plastic binding. Inevitably, pages fall out. My copy has long since shed its cover. Much of the table of contents has disappeared, along with a half dozen of my favourite Y songs (the book has no Zs). I managed to save Rodgers and Hart's 'You are Too Beautiful' – slipped it in with the Ms. But last week 'Yesterdays' up and left me. This morning when I checked, Wayne Shorter's 'Yes or No' was dangling by a thread . . .

Esquire, 7 April 1990
Mark Roman

The Art of Recording

THIS RECORDING engineer was considered one of the greatest geniuses since Rudy Van Gelder. I forget his name right now. I've wiped it from my mind. He put Al McManus, the drummer, in a little house, looked like a dog house. And if I growled, he had this funny little machine that, when it got to playback, the growl would be gone. If I wanted some spittle coming through, or air – phee, phee – it was gone, vanished. I said,

'How would you record Ben Webster? You'd have two sides of silence! You're taking out unique aspects of my playing. So put them back in again!'

Cadence
Kenny Davern

How to Deal with a Jukebox

BUNNY BERIGAN'S custom was to carry several packages of chewing gum in his pocket, not because he was addicted to the vigorous mastication of chicle. He had an even more practical use for the stuff. He'd put three or four sticks of gum in his mouth as we approached a boite with liquor in mind. Once inside, we'd sit at the bar and order our drinks. Then he'd excuse himself, promising to come back in a moment. He would walk purposefully off, to the men's room I assumed incorrectly. Early on I discovered that what he was doing was finding the jukebox, putting a wad of Wrigley's Doublemint through the coin slot, then pushing the slide in to assure the device's inoperability for at least as long as we'd be there enjoying our drinks. He'd return to the bar secure and relaxed in the knowledge that our ears wouldn't be assaulted by bad music. Later on I took to doing that myself.

I Remember Jazz (1987)

Al Rose

How to Win at a Jam Session

STATISTICS HAS proven that nothing stays the same. You either go up or down, so if a guy don't keep up, he is going down because things are going to pass him. Now I play with all kinds of young saxophone players. I was in Paris one time when a young saxophonist told the boss of the club that I refused to jam with him, which was a lie. The boss came to me and asked me why I didn't want to jam with these musicians.

I said, 'I didn't say pro or con,' but I came here to play as an attraction . . . Anyway, it's OK with me. I went on the bandstand and asked the saxophonist what did he want to play and he said in a surfeited way: Oh, anything . . . He was getting on my nerves and I thought – 'You, my boy, you are getting big-headed, but you are not going to fool me . . .'

OK, I answered, let's play 'After You've Gone', what tempo do you want? The guy said: I don't care! – then I decided to give him a lesson so I gave a tempo real fast. After we played the melody, I gave him a sign to take solos. He started playing and it was too fast for him to improvise and so he started fumbling and then went into what we call a 'long-mêtre'; I don't know if you understand what that 'long-mêtre' means. Instead of playing fast notes, you play slow ones . . . That's a trick and good to know it but for musicians of my category, it means that when a guy does that, he can't play fast, he is faking . . . He is ducking so that's how I tricked him by saying 'one more . . . take one more!' He took one more chorus and he tried to play it and he couldn't . . . and I kept on doing that until he fumbled it. So he stopped playing and after that, I just went on and played. What I am trying to tell you, I play with those kinds of guys often but they don't blow me out.

A guy must blow a whole lot to blow me out entirely, anyone . . . even some of those moderns cats. I was jamming right here in London on a riverboat with Sonny Stitt, just last year, last June. Danny Moss was there and Danny's one of the greatest saxophonists here in England. Danny wouldn't play, he had a contract and he thought that he didn't belong in that type of category as Sonny Stitt plays more modern.

So I took my alto and played 'modern' and got just as much applauds as anyone else up there; and when I had finished, Sonny says – in a real rough New York slang – 'See, you've got them, you're the blowdienest old mother fucker I've ever heard! Ha-ha-ha!' You see, I wasn't afraid to blow because I am experienced and I'm sure not afraid of the tempos . . . So I play what I know, that's all . . . My harmonic capacity is just as good as the one of those guys.

The Key to a Jazzy Life (1985)
Benny Waters

Trumpet Battles

THERE WAS a place, where I got wiped out by Rex Stewart, called Greasy's. I was working at Smalls' with Charlie Johnson. Rex had stayed at the house, showed me some of my first riffs, and I had so much respect for him. I even wanted to *be* like the cat, you know? He came down, and he didn't have his horn, and I told him, like you do in New York,

'I'm gonna get you after the show. Go home and get your horn.'

We started to go to the Rhythm Club, but he said, 'No, no, let's go down to Greasy's.'

So we went down there, and I don't know how the word got

around, but before you know it, that joint was packed. There was Gus Aikens and Red Allen, and some other trumpet player, and we started to play. All of Fletcher's cats were in there. They could really load up a cat.

'Roy? Shit, he ain't playin' nothin'! Go get him!' And then when I'd play, 'Yeah, Little Jazz, yeah!'

So he got bigger and bigger, and I made a mistake by coming in on his chorus. I screamed a G and the whole house fell out. He didn't let them other cats in; he jumped in and caught my ass. Hit a B-flat, and I ain't *never* heard a B-flat that high and that loud and big, in my life! I start feelin' around on my horn to see what it is. I said, 'oh-oh.' I took my horn and put it in the case. I told the cats, 'You can't play as high as him. Might as well give it up!' I had tears in my eyes.

I went home and sat on the side of the bed and said, 'Now what did he do that really tore my ass up?' And I dug what it was. He only screamed that note, but he didn't play up to it or back down. Now, if I could get so I could play up to B-flat and back down, make that part of my natural range, then I'd have him.

So that's what I did, and the next time we met, we played 'China Boy', and every time we went to that bridge in A-flat, I was up on that B-flat! and I *played* up there, I didn't just scream it, you know. So that was my round.

The next time we got together, I figured he was going to do the same thing I did, so I'm waitin' on him to see what he's gonna come out with, and he's waitin' on me, and neither one of us played shit! The night was over, and neither one of us did nothin'! That's funny, man.

from the IJS Archive
Roy Eldridge

Practising

IF YOU aren't going to practise, technique arrives in a haphazard way, leaving great gaps of competence. A carrier like a string bag in which only articles of some considerable size are portable. The trick was to collect the right groceries. That took much thought. The process was reminiscent of one of Woody Herman's bands where nearly everyone was on heroin. Herman had some new arrangements done and at rehearsal the musicians would sit reading them snapping their fingers and grinning in appreciation. 'Great, man: these are just great.' No one would play a note.

The McJazz Manuscripts (1979)
Sandy Brown

Bass Players, Phone Numbers and Other Things

ANYBODY WHO gets, professionally or semi-professionally, into the business of assembling groups of musicians for dances, clubs or private functions, builds up a very important, and usually rather eccentric, book of telephone numbers. I'm talking only about jazz, or jazz-related music: the sort of thing that relies a good deal on improvisation and on a set of ideas about instrumentation and repertoire, which all the players who are likely to get booked will have in common. They don't even have to share a common language: I once – in Holland, as it happens – had to play a set of trombone-and-piano duets with an Argentinian trombonist. In spite of the fact that some of his musical colleagues had quite recently been sent out, against their wills, by Galtieri and killed, against my will, by British troops, our only problem of communication was finding an interpreter for the words, 'What are we going to play, then?' For it turned out that he knew the English for 'Misty' and 'Everybody Loves My Baby'. I knew the chords, so we were all set. For both of us, the musical challenge – maybe we met it, maybe we didn't – was the business of working out, as we went along, how to make a reasonable sound out of just a trombone part and just a piano part – a combination which probably neither of us had tried before. It's strange, but had we been put into a full seven-piece band made up of players from seven different countries we would have had a better idea of what to do.

The whole game, in fact, consists of having a reasonable idea in advance of where your particular instrument ought to fit into the general ensemble sound, and then being ready to modify that idea as quickly as possible to match the real sounds you hear around you when the band starts playing. And you do this while the band's playing. Rehearsals are very uncommon; partly because rehearsal fees are even more uncommon, but partly because lifelong buskers get to pride themselves on being able to live a bit dangerously and keep a straight face. I remember once waiting to go on as a member of a band which had been cobbled together to accompany the veteran American cornet-player, Wild Bill Davison. The entire preparation for the performance consisted of his turning and saying, semi-seriously, 'Now listen, let's get all the hellos over back here. No shaking hands with one another on the bandstand; that kinda thing can make the customers feel uneasy.' This brave man had never yet, I think, heard a note from any of us; I have to say that had he done so, he might have been feeling uneasy.

Classical musicians used to have a derogatory term: 'a telephone orchestra'. Just the same sort of thing, but with a necessary added touch of bitterness. This would be an orchestra consisting of all too many substitutes, assembled by phone and often, in effect, providing the conductor of a concert with a quite different ensemble from the one he had rehearsed – and whose absent members, incidentally, had been paid for the rehearsals. In the sort of music I'm talking about, though, the title wouldn't be derogatory; all the bands are telephone orchestras.

And that's where the books of phone numbers come in. I said they tended to be eccentric, and so they do. Mostly they're bottom-heavy. It's the bottom of the band, the drummers and bass-players, who rate the most entries. There'll be a fair number of trumpet-players and saxophonists, quite a few pianists, and even the odd trombonist or two; but there'll be page upon page of bassists and drummers. This isn't because there are more of them in existence. It's because you have to ring up more of them before you find one who's free, and willing to turn out. A lot of wheedling has to go on, and there's call for a variety of techniques. Depending on your nerve, you can either play safe, and book your rhythm team months ahead, when a freelance will accept almost any engagement in order to have something, at least, in an empty diary – the risk you take is that something better will turn up in the interim; or you can go for serious brinkmanship, and delay ringing round until teatime on the day of the gig, in the hope of taking one by surprise while feeding, or at a moment when he's glad of a reason to be out of the house for the evening. That would happen only very rarely; bass-players work so many nights that their wives tend to be particularly tenacious of the nights they have at home. Or so they say.

If your brinkmanship should fail, you're in trouble, of course. Bands designed to have solid underpinning sound thin and helpless without it, so there's a practical reason for all this tyranny from below. I have to say that it's not as severe as it was a couple of decades ago, when the arrival of rock music and the bass guitar opened things up by increasing the supply of people who could play some sort of bass line. But before that it was a perennial burden, a negative, dissuasive element, like a state censorship or a currency export limit. It was like a left-over wartime shortage.

In those days at least, bass-players and, to a slightly lesser extent, drummers, had an image rather like that of the miller in a medieval village. They owned expensive, elaborate and essential items of technology; they knew their worth in market terms and drove hard bargains. They could lift you up, and they could let you down. And they never did anything for nothing. If a band was forming, or rehearsing new material, or preparing for a broadcast, the bassist and drummer would always flatly decline to rehearse, on the grounds that they didn't need to sweat over the parts like the brass and reed players, thank you very much; so long as the pianist was there to vamp the harmonies, that would do nicely. And they always had another job that night, in some dance band or other. In fact, they often had another job on the nights you thought they were booked with you; it would turn up at short notice, and be better paid. They'd send a dep. – no need to rehearse him. No point in rehearsing him, either, in some instances.

For there were two types of bassist. There were bass-players, and there were bass-owners. The bass-owners formed a sizeable, strange sub-class, which outnumbered the bass-players by about five to one. They were people who had bought a double-bass as an investment, and had learned just enough to make a generalized, fairly rhythmic, low humming or thudding noise on it. Not, you must understand, any actually identifiable notes. They could only get away with it on a low-register instrument. On a trumpet or a clarinet, they would have been rumbled at once, if not actually lynched by audiences; but down among the dead notes, they were on to a good thing. They sounded more or less like those home-made broomstick-and-tea-chest basses the Skiffle groups had in the 1950s, but they looked much more acceptably expensive; in fact some of the basses were really handsome instruments, and their owners often had looks to match. They were what you got on the night your bass-player suddenly got a better job. And your gig, in turn, was what they got in return for their investment. They were the millers *par excellence*: they got by without grinding much corn at all. Typical was One-Note-Jack, a tall, doleful man, who hardly moved, once he'd planted his bass and himself at the back of the stand, and was never known to pluck more than the first beat of a four-beat bar.

I talk about these people in the past tense, although there are still quite a few about – even One-Note-Jack, as I was surprised to learn only the other day; I suppose that in the thirty years since I last heard him he's only got through what would be seven-and-a-half years' notes for a proper bassist, so he may still be feeling quite fresh. But the advent of bass-guitar-players did undercut the investment structure somewhat, in that their instruments were rather cheaper to buy and easier to learn to play properly; so they found their way into the dance bands and even into some of the jazz groups, where their comparatively easy-going natures made up in part for the nastiness of the instrument they played. For some reason, too, they were easier to book than either the double-bass-players or the double-bass-owners. I suspect they're a different breed of men; failed guitarists, quite a few of them, and of a lighter temperament than men whose first impulse had been to go in low and strong.

But they do share one characteristic with their colleagues who use what tends these days to be called the Upright Bass. They all lurk in their dens, waiting to be called on; they're very unlikely to provide work for others, in the way that trumpet-players and saxophonists frequently do. And with the towering and troubled exception of the late Charles Mingus, it's very rare for a good bass-player actually to lead a band. Fisher's Fourth Rule of Engagement states that a bassist who offers employment is very unlikely indeed to be proficient, and that the financial incentives must be weighed very carefully against the potential suffering. A splendid example of the sort of man who owns both a bass and a band is the odious Sven Klang, in the film, *Sven Klang's Kvintet*; his way of talking into the microphone while continuing to thud away gives all the warning anyone could need.

Five Radio Talks (1970)
Roy Fisher

Double-bass Strings

BEFORE I left New Orleans I had a couple of sets of strings for my bass that were too light for my instrument, but I thought they were just right for Slow Drag Pavageau's. I hadn't seen Slow Drag so I gave them to Jim Robinson, the trombone player, to give to him. A few years later I was back in New Orleans and I met Slow Drag. I asked him how he liked the strings I'd sent to him, I also told him I was kind of mad he hadn't written and thanked me. He said, 'I don't know, man, I never got them. Who'd you give them to?'

I said, 'Jim Robinson.'

Slow Drag said, 'That dirty bastard, he sold them to me!' They didn't speak for a couple of years after that.

Pops Foster (1971)
Pops Foster

Trombones

ADMIRING THE shine of my trombone's polished brass, I remembered a line by the poet (Eleanor taught it to me) Gerard Manley Hopkins that described something pure 'like shining from shook foil'. We are living in the age of shiny things, we define ourselves by the shiny things we accumulate. The brainwash is reinforced daily. Even those who consider themselves 'liberated' are raped by the shiny things dazzling them continually from all sides. But a trombone is one noble shiny thing. I can think of none nobler. A simple assemblage of tubing with no mechanical equipment of any kind; kiss it and it makes music.

A cruddy instrument makes cruddy music. My trombone is always polished. I am not one to admire Charlie Parker's habit of playing on a cruddy saxophone held together with rubber bands and chewing gum. Bird would have played even better on a shiny saxophone. The shine reflects a certain cleanliness of the soul. It is a sparkle of honour. I love these machines you kiss in order to make music like my father loved the efficient click of calculating machines. Gun-lovers polish their rifles with the same sort of affection I lavish on my slush pump . . .

Monotony is inherent playing classical trombone parts. Richard Wagner, whose music I despise, wrote interesting trombone parts. Mozart, whom I adore, did not. Obviously classical trombone was not for me. But it goes deeper. Classical musicians rehearse and work hard trying to play music like it has been played before. Jazz should be different every time. Orchestra USA was dedicated to uniting those two diametrically opposed streams.

Close Enough for Jazz (1983)
Mike Zwerin

Playing Drums on the Side

I PLAYED drums a couple of times while I was with Count Basie in 1966 when Sonny Payne was late. Basie kept me up there, but, goddam, I could hardly play my trumpet when I got through with that. I don't play drums any more, and I'll tell you what stopped me.

There's a clarinet player on Long Island named Herb Myers, who used to be a policeman. Naturally, he liked Benny Goodman. I did a lot of club dates with him. He got a date playing for the policemen, with an organ player, a singer, and me. Gene Krupa had given me a drum set one Christmas, and after Herb got through playing forty minutes with the tom-toms going, I'd play a thirty-minute drum solo! I knew all Gene's solos, and everything went along nice.

We played about two hours over time, and when we got through I had forgotten how to tear those damn drums down! I'd been juicing and was pretty well out of it by then, but when I used to play drums as a kid, they didn't have stands like they have now. When I played with Gene Krupa, Gene had always set them up. So they were like a jigsaw puzzle to me. Man, I messed around there and couldn't get those drums broken down for nothin'!

'Come on, Roy,' the man said. 'We've got to close.'

Eventually, he got a couple of waiters, picked up the drums just like they were and put 'em in my station wagon. When I got up, and was sober, and remembered how to break 'em down, I put 'em away, and they ain't been out since.

from the IJS Archive

Roy Eldridge

Josh Billings's Suitcase Playing

BILLINGS HAD finally contrived a place for himself in music. In Chicago in a hotel room during a jam session involving a comb and a banjo he had rigged a suitcase to act as a drum. For soft effects he covered the case with wrapping paper, which he wrinkled and then stroked with whisk brooms. For bass effects he kicked the suitcase with his heel. McKenzie, dubious but intrigued, let him try the trick with the Blowers on a party job. It was a success: Billings was a Blue Blower.

At parties everyone wanted to play the suitcase, and sooner or later everyone did, even Mrs Vanderbilt. Billings had a trick of flicking a tip – usually a five-dollar bill – off the suitcase and catching it under his armpit, so that it seemed to disappear. He kicked suitcases to pieces pretty fast. I went with him to the luggage shops to watch the proprietors when Billings tried out their wares.

'I'd like a suitcase,' Billings would say. 'I prefer one made of fibre.'

The man would bring several. 'This is our best,' he would say, pointing to a particular one.

'A very nice bag,' Billings would say. Then he would kick it. The proprietors never said anything – this was during the Depression – but as Billings tapped, slapped, and kicked the bags, listening and muttering to himself, I had the pleasure of observing the effect on a man's face of the gradual discovery that he is dealing with a dangerous lunatic.

'He's harmless,' I whispered to one luggage man who seemed really frightened. 'He just likes to kick suitcases.' The luggage man was willing to be sympathetic.

'Maybe his wife ran away with a salesman,' he suggested.

We Called It Music (1956)
Eddie Condon

Dizzy's Trumpet

THE TRUTH is that the shape of my horn was an accident. I could pretend that I went into the basement and thought it up, but it wasn't that way. I was playing at Snookie's on 45th Street, on a Monday night, 6 January 1953. I had Monday nights off, but it was my wife's birthday so we had a party and invited all the guys – Illinois Jacquet, Sarah Vaughan, Stump 'n' Stumpy, and several other artists – all the people who were in show business who knew Lorraine from dancing. This guy Henry Morgan, who had his own show in New York, invited me to come on his show and be interviewed; he was doing the show from a hotel around the corner. My horn was still straight when I left it on one of those little trumpet stands that stick straight up.

When I got back to the club after making this interview, Stump 'n' Stumpy had been fooling around on the bandstand, and one had pushed the other, and he'd fallen back on to my horn. Instead of the horn just falling, the bell bent. When I got back, the bell was sticking up in the air. Illinois Jacquet had left. He said, 'I'm not going to be here when that man comes back and sees his horn sticking up at that angle.'

When I came back, it was my wife's birthday and I didn't want to be a drag. I put the horn to my mouth and started playing it. Well, when the bell bent back, it made a smaller hole because of the dent. I couldn't get the right sound, but it was a strange sound that I got from that instrument that night. I played it, and I liked the sound. The sound had been changed and it could be played softly, very softly, not blarey. I played it like that the rest of the night, and the next day I had it straightened out again. Then I started thinking about it and said, 'Wait a minute, man, that was something else.' I remembered the way the sound had come from it, quicker to the ear – to my ear, the player. I contacted the Martin Company, and I had Lorraine, who's also an artist, draw me a trumpet at a forty-five-degree angle and sent it to the Martin Company. I told them, 'I want a horn like this.'

'You're crazy!' they said.

'OK,' I said, 'I'm crazy, but I want a horn like this.' They made me a trumpet and I've been playing one like that ever since.

Dizzy (1980)
Dizzy Gillespie

Ornette's Alto

A QUESTION often asked of me is why I play a plastic alto. I bought it originally because I needed a new horn badly, and I felt I could not afford a new brass instrument. The plastic horn is less expensive, and I said to myself, 'Better a new horn than one that leaks.' After living with the plastic horn, I felt it begin to take on my emotion. The tone is breathier than the brass instrument, but I came to like the sound, and I found the flow of music to be more compact. I don't intend ever to buy another brass horn. On this plastic horn I feel as if I am continually creating my own sound.

Sleeve note from *Change of the Century*
Ornette Coleman

Jimmy Maxwell's Bagpipes

WHEN HE left Benny Goodman's band and started playing trumpet for NBC in New York, Jimmy Maxwell went to hear a bagpipe band at Madison Square Garden and was moved to tears by the sound. His wife bought him some pipes, and he found a teacher, Mr Gallagher.

'God, he was a great player,' Jimmy said. 'In the beginning he gave me free lessons. He wouldn't take any money. Then around January one year he said, "Well, it's about time to be measured up for the kilt."'

Jimmy said he didn't want a kilt. Mr Gallagher told him,

'You don't have to march in the parade, but you can't do it without a kilt.'

Jim said he didn't plan to march in the parade.

'Just because I gave you free lessons doesn't mean you're obliged to do it,' said Mr Gallagher.

By insisting on the absence of obligation, Mr Gallagher eventually got Jim into kilts and into the parade.

Jimmy said, 'As I marched down 5th Avenue past NBC, I thought, "Oh, God, I hope nobody comes out and sees me."' He marched every St Patrick's Day for six years.

Plunger Mutes

GARVIN BUSHELL said that Mamie Smith's trumpet-player Johnny Dunn was the first to use a plumber's rubber plunger as a mute. Plungers are made in two sizes, for sinks and toilets. They happen to have just the right diameters for trumpet and trombone bells. After Bubber Miley and Joe Nanton used plungers on recordings with Duke Ellington, arrangers began to write for plungers and they became a standard mute.

While on staff at ABC, trombonist Charlie Small was given something to play that required a plunger, and he didn't have one with him. He ran out to a midtown hardware store and asked for a large regulation toilet plunger. When the man laid one on the counter, Charlie told him, 'I don't need the stick.' Charlie said that the puzzled expression on the man's face was rapidly replaced by one of sheer disgust.

'And to this day, when I go into that store, that man walks away and has a different clerk wait on me.'

Both the above from *Jazz Anecdotes* (1990)

Bill Crow

Girls and the Clarinet

HAVE YOU noticed how many girls take up the clarinet? You don't often see them doing the Mozart, but there's always a few in the second and third chairs of the symphony orchestras. Of course, girls take up all sorts of other instruments too: in the brass-band country round Leeds they play cornets and euphoniums and often turn out quite creditably in talent contests. A memorable confrontation was between one tiny lass who ripped off sixteen bars of triple tonguing on the cornet and was questioned about it by Huw Wheldon, not then Managing Director BBC Television but compère of a kiddies' TV show called 'All Your Own' where youths built dangerous moon rockets, bred tarantulas and generally showed the kind of inventiveness that would foster successful sensationalism in future years. Wheldon's public school English showed encouragingly effusive Welsh inflections: 'Good Heavens, that's really wonderful: I don't suppose many girls your age can play the cornet as well as that. How on earth did you learn?' 'Me Dad plays.' 'But you're still at school: when do you find time to practise?' 'After me dinner.' 'But you must have homework to do – and what about bedtime?' And so on. The interview continued at cross purposes for some minutes, Wheldon plainly unaware that 50 million inhabitants of the UK eat their dinner in the middle of the day: he was marked for high office. He wouldn't have been much good in a low one.

The McJazz Manuscripts (1979)
Sandy Brown

Older Musicians and Critics

ONE TIME I even sat down to read some of my old press write-ups that Dottie had kept. It's funny. All the years on the road I never read them and here I was looking through them with interest. I used to buy *down beat* magazine all the time but once I read that Pee Wee Russell had won a *down beat* poll. That did it. I never read that magazine again. Guys like him and that Frank Teschemacher aren't clarinet players to me. But then I suppose even in those days critics were just as ignorant as they are today. I never, ever, played to please the critics. Not once. I never really cared about them at all. Even today I still don't. I mean you can pick up a music paper and read them knocking all of the old-style New Orleans musicians that are currently out doing their thing. To me it was just beautiful to see those old guys, at their age, coming out on stage and doing a lot of things the youngsters can't do. Most people forget that those guys are the foundations of jazz music. They started it, but naturally everything progresses as it goes along. It's like the Wright brothers' plane. Now you could throw a rock and knock it out of the sky, but for Christ's sake give them credit for building the first. Musicians nowadays have gotten a lot better learning than the old musicians could have had. The kids have every advantage to becoming a good musician, and after they get their learning they try to play on the order of the older men that went before. You see a lot of that. It's not wrong.

With Louis and the Duke (1985)
Barney Bigard

Sandy Brown on Barney Bigard

THE ONE performance I would pick out as the most outstanding of its type is Barney Bigard's thirty-four-year-old classic 'Clarinet Lament' with Duke Ellington. Duke originally wrote the piece for him as 'Barney's Concerto', which describes the form of the piece. Bigard's command of the instrument is complete and mature, and Ellington had recently achieved the orchestral mastery and intention that still seems inexhaustible. The combined effect in the performance is staggering.

You can always tell an Albert system clarinet from a Boehm by the tone. The Albert gives a much fuller sound, particularly in the lower register. This is a result of the instrument having fewer tone holes and having them better sited acoustically than in the Boehm version, the only problem being that you really need tentacles instead of fingers to play anything complex on the Albert clarinet.

Bigard's technique is therefore even more amazing than is apparent at first hearing. He persuades the full tone of the Albert through a series of difficult runs at breakneck speed without ever giving an impression of strain.

Barney had a chequered and not frequently satisfactory musical career before and after his Ellington period, so it's fortunate that there are ten years of recordings of his genius in that most appropriate setting. Woody Herman and Tony Coe owe a debt to Bigard but he influenced only a few later clarinettists probably because his best work was almost contemporaneous with the Goodman era. That was a pity. It seems to me that Barney at his best was unbeatable.

The McJazz Manuscripts (1979)
Sandy Brown

Where 'Mood Indigo' Came From

PIRON'S ORCHESTRA was a New Orleans institution. In these years, the band was at its musical peak with the legendary Lorenzo Tio, Jr, playing the clarinet and Peter Bocage on trumpet, occasionally joining the leader in a violin duet. Old man Louis Cottrell, Sr, played the drums in that band, and Steve Lewis played the piano, with Johnny Marrero and his banjo. 'Dreamy Blues', which was then the band's theme, was to have a devious history, ending when it was published in 1930 as 'Mood Indigo' and carrying the names of Barney Bigard and Duke Ellington as composers. But all of us in New Orleans knew that tune, and we knew it was Tio's.

'She's Cryin' for Me'

SANTO PECORA was the composer of the jazz standard, 'She's Cryin' for Me'. I asked him about the words, since I'd never heard it sung or seen printed lyrics.

'It's got no words,' he assured me. 'I never wrote words to it.'

I said, 'With that kind of a title you'd think it did have words. How come you give it that title?'

He told me, 'I was workin' with Arodin on a job and I says, "I got a new tune I want to try out. You wanna figure out some harmony?" Then I played him the lead on my horn. He says, "That's a nice tune. What's the title?" I said it didn't have no title. Sidney said, "How about 'She's Cryin' for Me'?" I said that was OK, so that's the name I gave it.'

Arodin's been gone for thirty-five years now, so I can't ask him what he had in mind. Pecora died in 1985. I'm sure he never thought about titles or lyrics, though, just where the tailgate licks come in.

Both the above from *I Remember Jazz* (1987)

Al Rose

'Parker's Mood'

O N E   O F the great tracks in jazz is Charlie Parker's 'Parker's Mood'. It begins with a three-note figure contained in a G minor triad – in this sequence: Bb-G-D – and whenever you heard someone whistling those notes in LA, you knew you were in the presence of a friend. It signified you were using but cool, and when you went to buy dope late at night (which was the usual time to cop) if the bell wasn't working or you didn't want to jar the Man out of a sound sleep or there might be someone uncool on the premises, you went *Bb-G-D* in that fast, secret way and the cat would pop his head out the window. When Bird first played his 'Parker's Mood' I think those notes might have been drifting around somewhere in his head and they just flew right out.

Raise Up Off Me (1972)

Hampton Hawes

Whistling in the Bath

FOR SOME reason, Kaminsky's plaintive little introduction to 'Home Cooking' became a common signal, and any of us entering the steam-filled college bath-house would whistle it to see if it was taken up from behind any of the bolted partition doors.

All What Jazz (1985)
Philip Larkin

'Yes, We Have No Bananas!'

AROUND 1923 the delegate of Local 44 got a one-night job over at Beartown, Illinois, for a little pickup band. It was a little coal-mining town where the miners come in and bring a jug to drink on all night. This one big tough guy with a long moustache came carrying a crock jug over his shoulder. He was unshaven, dirty, and chewed tobacco and sat in a chair he'd pulled up right in front of the bandstand. He laid a big pistol in his lap and told us to play nothin' but 'Yes! We Have No Bananas'. We started playing it and the guy who put on the dance came up and told us to do what the guy wanted or he'd break the dance up. All night long we played 'Yes! We Have No Bananas' and the people there danced to it. Sometimes during the evening he'd want us to drink with him and would pass the jug up. None of us wanted to drink behind him, but we did. He'd sit there and sing to the music, twirl the pistol on his finger, and point it at us. Once in a while he'd get up to go to the bathroom. He'd stand up and tell us to stop playing and not to hit a lick until he got back. We didn't care how long he stayed, we waited until he got back. When he came back he'd say, 'All right, fellas, let's go,' and we'd start playing. After all the people left he asked us if we had a good time. We all said, 'Yes.' I never will forget that guy and fifty years later I still can't play 'Yes! We Got No Bananas' without nearly getting sick.

Pops Foster (1971)
Pops Foster

Lazy River

EVERYBODY THINKS of the song 'Up a Lazy River' as a Hoagy Carmichael composition, but that was a melody he wasn't responsible for. Hoagy wrote the words, but the music came from the pen of one of New Orleans's better clarinettists, Sidney Arodin. As Sidney explained the circumstances, Hoagy had come into the Famous Door on 52nd Street in New York to hear Wingy Manone's band in which Arodin occupied the clarinet chair. They played the tune, and Wingy sang it; but, of course, it wasn't yet called 'Up a Lazy River'. The title and words were Arodin's, too. He called it 'Just a Lazy Nigger'. Of course, in our time, such a title would be an atrocity. Even then it was in pretty bad taste – but Arodin didn't have a scintilla of prejudice in him. He had, in fact, been a party to the first mixed record session in the South (The Jones-Collins Astoria Hot Eight). He had, moreover, been the only white musician in the ensemble. Later I asked Hoagy how much cleaning up he'd had to do with the piece, and he said other than the lyric he'd had to make only a minor change in the chording of the verse.

I Remember Jazz (1987)

Al Rose

Louis on Playing High

ERSKINE HAWKINS got some advice from Louis Armstrong about playing in the upper register of the trumpet: 'It didn't come to me too hard, cause I was used to it. I was even doing it through my younger days. My first teacher was called "High-C Foster". It came to me a little easy. I didn't like to puff and act like it was hard for me. That's what Louis explained for me. He said,

"Now you made your point. Now, let them think it's a little hard for you to do it." He said, "You're making it look too easy."'

from the IJS Archive

First-time Conductor

WHEN GARY McFarland turned up in New York fresh from the Berklee School of Music, Gerry Mulligan recorded a few of his arrangements with his Concert Jazz Band. As a result the word got around town pretty quickly that a new talent was in town. Before long Gary found himself writing his own record date. He was slightly awed at the prospect of conducting some of New York's best recording musicians. On the first take Gary did fine all the way to the last chord, which the brass section was holding. A look of doubt crossed Gary's face as he stood there with his arms out and then he made a swooping upward gesture, hoping that was the correct signal for a cutoff. Instead, the entire brass section, still playing, stood up. The ensuing laughter ruined the take, but it was worth it.

Jazz Anecdotes (1990)
Bill Crow

Blues v. Ballads

I DON'T like playing blues too much, maybe I should play more but I feel myself playing more harmony, that's why I play a lot of ballads, I feel the ballads more.

The Key to a Jazzy Life (1985)
Benny Waters

The Blues

MUSICALLY THE blues isn't just a form or a harmonic sequence or an agreed melodic series. It's a method, an approach, a *feel*. Previous definitions have usually started with form/harmony as follows: four bars tonic, two bars sub-dominant, two bars tonic, two bars dominant, two bars tonic equal a twelve-bar blues. If this were the case, the riff tune 'In the Mood' would be the ideal archetype – which it isn't – because it uses only these chords in various inversions and in the correct sequence. The blues scale, so we're told, includes the flattened third, fifth and seventh. So it does. It also includes the major third, fifth, seventh and occasionally the flattened ninth. As these can be related to the tonic of any chord in a blues and as the flattened ninth, like the raised ninth (which is also the flattened third an octave up), may be incorporated for other than blues reasons, it's not unusual to use all twelve semitones in a blues solo. 'In the Mood', of course, doesn't have any of these blue notes: it's still a blues. The frantic virility of blues is now as amazing as ever. Ray Charles, who'd been an effete popular singer, came home to them, as did Berry Gordy, who started the best of all pop–blues productions (Tamla Motown) ten years ago. A cloud somewhat larger than a baseball glove looms, however, in the denial of their Americanism by some of the most gifted black musicians like Archie Shepp. This effectively means not playing blues which have links with slavery. Considering what Americanism has denied Shepp and his race, it's reasonable. But I hope it's only a kind of strike.

The McJazz Manuscripts (1979)

Sandy Brown

~~~~~~~~~

5

PLACES

Jazz, they will tell you, is an international music. Jazz, they will tell you, thrives everywhere. What this really means is that jazz can hide anywhere, get by anywhere, take root and then grow in disguise anywhere. When the German Jewish musician Coco Schumann was interviewed about the jazz group he played in in Auschwitz, and asked how he could bear to play in a place where thousands were being murdered every day, he said, 'Well, when you are a musician, you just play, you know . . . '

What he meant, among other things, was that when he played, he was no longer in Auschwitz. Like air stewardesses, musicians have not much sense of place. Playing is what matters, not where they play, or where they come from. Yet a music that has travelled all round the world does end up in some funny places, and some good places, and some terrible places . . .

New Orleans Today

IT HAD been twenty years since I had been back to New Orleans. I found it to be just as free and easy a town but the people were still the same as fifty years ago. One of the first guys I ran into was Louis

Barbarin, the brother of Paul. Louis is also a drummer and quite good, so we talked a little about old times and I took a walk down to Felix's Restaurant near Canal Street. I practically lived there. I love oysters and they had the freshest and best you could ask for.

I just played the one concert down there but I stayed a whole week and so I got to get around some of the places. I went to where Wallace Davenport was working. There was nobody in there because they charged such ridiculous prices. I ordered a beer and got a 'shorty' for $2.50. Wallace is a good trumpet player to listen to, but at those prices I'm not surprised the place was empty. Another night I went to the Preservation Hall, which is a joke. That's about the worst thing I've ever seen: dirtiest place and nothing exciting happening. The band I heard was Kid Thomas's Band. I don't know what he was doing. He played his trumpet into a derby, and he'd 'wa-wa'. Then he'd sit for another hour and 'wa-wa' again. He wasn't playing nothing. Maybe I was expecting too much, because I had heard that he was supposed to be the nearest thing to Freddie Keppard. I don't know who the hell said that. Whoever it was never knew Freddie Keppard. Hell, no. Kid Thomas's tone was nothing like Keppard. Freddie could take a note and hold it, playing soft, and bring it out and shake up this whole building. I tell you Freddie Keppard was a *musician*. At the end of that week I had done my job and, apart from the oyster restaurant, I decided I didn't miss anything about New Orleans when I was leaving to come back to Los Angeles. I know one thing. People say how the music is still intact down there after seventy years. Shucks, if any of those bands that are in New Orleans today had played at Tom Anderson's Cabaret, where Albert Nicholas and I worked in the early 1920s, the people would have run out.

With Louis and the Duke (1985)

Barney Bigard

Inside South Carolina

BRUCE HAD given us a phone number of Baby Tate, an electric guitarist whom he and his colleague Pete Lowry had recorded in the neighbouring state of South Carolina. I'd written to him tentatively, saying I was a friend of theirs, now I telephoned and left a message that we were coming. We arrived in Spartanburg late in the day, the rain pouring down. We had no idea if we would be welcome, and the taxi driver tried to discourage us from crossing the tracks to the 'Colored' section of town. But a thin, wiry man, very Black, was sitting there on the porch, waiting. 'You looking for Tate?' he queried from behind dark glasses, and we knew we'd hit gold–dust.

With Tate it was another situation right from the start. He was a man who carried himself with dignity, even after a night when the whisky flowed freely. Bruce and Pete were remembered as friends and he produced his own copy of *Crying for the Carolines*. But he'd also been in England during the War and was eager to reminisce about his Service experience. Stationed near Poole in Dorset, he had acquired a local following. He played often in pubs and for dances, travelling back to camp on a hay-wagon. There were other startling tales, too, like the time he was caught off–limits by the military police, *in flagrante delicto* in an air-raid shelter. He drove us to the store to buy hamburgers and whisky, refusing our money, then we settled in for a night with the blues.

If there has to be a 'most unforgettable' night in my life, I suppose this was it. Everyone has their own imaginary picture of what it would be like to experience something they hold most dear as I did the blues. Sitting around with a bottle of bourbon, listening to Tate's rugged music, fulfilled mine. The rain coursed down relentlessly, beating a polyrhythmic patter on the porch outside and seeping through the roof at one point. My copy of *Crying for the Carolines* bears a waterstain to this day, a permanent reminder of the first time I felt the blues in my bones.

Tate and Tillie, his wife, drank heavily, and so did we. She was an extrovert who got us all dancing together as Tate reached into the collective history of Africans in America, the way Black people had been doing for centuries. When he found out that Stevie played drums, he produced a washboard and something to beat with. He even got me playing his harmonica, something I hadn't done since I realized there could only be one Sonny Terry. Whenever Tate laid aside his shiny red instrument, Tillie dropped one of his records on the deck of the battered old record-player. She played 'Late in the Evening' over and over, the grooves turning grey under the light of the single bare bulb in the ceiling. Eventually we settled down for the night, enveloped in a creaking bed that sank to the floor. As we fell asleep, I heard him gently chastizing Tillie to 'leave those peoples alone'. But sleep did not last long. We were wakened several times as the stylus crashed back on the record and they argued, her voice raised, his quiet and firm. Then the door burst open, and the room was flooded with light. The nature of their discussion became clear. Tillie had decided their visitors needed feeding.

She had gone into the kitchen to fix something to eat, and now she swept in thrusting two steaming plates under our noses. We had no alternative but to struggle to a sitting position, not easy in that bed, and eat. It was well past three in the morning but she had prepared pork chops, potatoes and gravy. It was a generous gesture but Tate did not approve of his guests being disturbed. He jumped into his car and drove off. Then, to our astonishment, we heard him return with the local police officer. There and then he had poor Tillie carted down to the cells to sleep it off for the night. He was worried, we heard him say, that in his state of exhaustion, he might get violent. The police officer took it all in his stride, for it was an apparently not uncommon occurrence.

The next morning we found Tate, sobered up, on the porch. He apologized for the disturbances in the night and said he had done his best to see that we slept soundly. We sat there exhausted but happy, to be greeted by an early-morning visitor who dropped by. 'These folks is from *England*,' Tate announced proudly. 'Oh,' said our man, very rural, 'd'y'all come on the bus?'

Mama Said There'd Be Days Like This (1989)
Val Wilmer

Making an Announcement in Japan

ARCHIE SHEPP walked up to the microphone. Someone was going to interpret his conversation. The interpreter said, 'Mr Shepp, they would like to know how do you like Japan?' We're all standing in line, Lee Konitz and his band had played a tune. Archie looks into the camera, front and centre, and says, 'We come here in peace; not like the Americans who dropped the bomb on Hiroshima.'

And Grachan Moncur says, 'Don't remind these motherfuckers!'

This was all on television. I stepped in and said, 'No, we came here to combine the rhythmical blah, blah – ' If I hadn't talked, we'd be in jail.

Cadence
Beaver Harris

On Tour in Russia

I WOKE up a little after sunrise and looked through the window, lying on my stomach. The train was passing through stark primitive countryside which reminded me of Budd Johnson's 1929 Missouri. Ducks, cows, sickly corn, high-tension poles strung out over the brown land. Burgundy-coloured stone houses appeared with increasing frequency alongside the tracks. A work-gang laying rails watched us pass – one strong figure, large back, black cap and knee boots, bushy Stalin moustache.

A small delegation holding eight bouquets of flowers waited for us on the tiny concrete platform. Among them, the director of the Mahatch-Kala Philharmonic Society. He was short, fat, bald, myopic and extremely nervous about the capitalists who would be his responsibility.

He led us to the Caucasus Hotel. Rural types smelling of monthly baths trooped through the peeling lobby dominated by a larger-than-life socially realistic painting of Karl Marx. My room overlooked a small produce market. Two women in oriental robes sliced up a water melon in the back of a shed, looking furtive. I figured I'd better report them to the proper authorities. There's something about this country . . .

Everybody stared at us. We were used to it by now. Getting further into the boondocks, larger and more brazen crowds inspected us with unabashed curiosity. On the train, a policeman had parked himself at the door of the compartment in which Fatha, Budd, Bobby Donovan and Bill Pemberton were continuing their marathon pinochle game and just stared at them. Sasha, our master of ceremonies, chic, in his forties, chivalrous and protective of us, came up to the policeman and said: 'Don't stare, it isn't polite.' The policeman scowled. 'Don't talk to me like that. I could have you put away for fifteen days.' Sasha's habitual ear-wrinkling smile vanished: 'I could have you taken off the force for fifteen years.'

Central versus local power. Sasha would never have been trusted to travel with us had he not been considered reliable. He must have had a power-base somewhere. He could have been KGB; any or every one of our Soviet hosts could have been, just as Bill Dixon may well have been CIA. Bill certainly looked suspicious carrying his enormous short-wave radio that seemed to have enough room for radar in it. But we were so harmless, going to bed early, playing pinochle. Except for me, maybe, and my dispatches to Greenwich Village, there was not a hint of a threat among us and our hosts could see that. They relaxed their guard, leaving Oliver and me, and occasionally Bobby Donovan, free to roam at will.

No trouble, no sir, not from Fatha Hines. Vadim, who took pride in being a good road manager, would fight for better-quality pianos, only to hear Fatha say it was OK, he did not want to cause any trouble. You could see Vadim's respect for Fatha fade. Poor Fatha had been conditioned to submission for too long. He was respected here, a first-class world-quality pianist, and classical musicians were invariably part of our audience. In any case, Fatha could make any old beat-up provincial piano sound like a Bosendorfer concert grand. His large hands covered the keys like tender tarantulas and somehow, within the confines of a fixed and dated style, he would manage to sound totally modern almost despite himself. We all had a lot of respect for Fatha's historic past and lively present. We, particularly some of the other black members of the band, could not understand why he did not have more respect for himself. We were embarrassed by his definition of entertainment. Our show-stopper was 'St Louis Blues', featuring Fatha's six-chorus right-hand octave trill. There would be inevitable cheers, after which he'd pull out a white handkerchief and, to prove how effortless the trill was for him, dust off the piano with his left hand. This may have been entertainment for Fatha but black men blushed over the assumption that the menial role usually reserved for their race was something to laugh about and entertain people with.

If there were political operatives in our Soviet entourage, they were soon lulled by what they must have seen as our naïveté. We were people who only thought about pinochle and jazz (and drinking). The fact that I had no typewriter and was hand-writing the articles to the *Voice* in letter-form may have had something to do with their getting through. And then both sides began to see each other as people rather than representatives of one system or another. Dealing with most people, you sooner or later come to the point where common human denominators dominate. So much for geopolitics.

We had become used to being stared at. Standing outside the hotel in Mahatch-Kala, waiting for the bus to take us to the concert, Money Johnson observed the gathering crowd and said: 'Looks like the circus has come to town.'

Every eye in the early evening street was focused our way. These people may never have seen anybody from the other side of the Caucasus before, let alone non-Caucasians. A little old man looking as though he had been born in the tall brown fur cossack hat he wore despite the extreme heat came up to six-foot Clea and stared at her eyeball-to-Adams apple in Barnum and Bailey juxtaposition.

The concert was held in an outdoor amphitheatre in 'Green Park' by the Caspian Sea. Backstage, long tables covered with red velour cloths held cookies, mineral water, black bread and caviar. This was the land of caviar. It was king here. It was served with every meal. These other Americans considered caviar too salty. 'Pass it this way,' I kept saying. There was always a mountain of caviar on my plate.

It was also the land of vodka. When I asked Herr Philharmonic director to get three bottles before the concert he went into what resembled a *petit-mal* epileptic fit explaining that drinking was forbidden before a concert. I told him this was a special occasion, which it was. He was probably feeling like a New York cop when Castro is in town. He wasn't taking any chances. When I insisted, he spoke to Vadim Petrovitch. Used to us by now, liking us, Vadim shrugged his fat shoulders with a smile, extended thumbs up and arranged for the vodka.

'We're celebrating a wedding,' I announced, pouring it around. We toasted the happy couple. Nobody asked who they were. Maybe they thought I was kidding, or looking for an excuse to get bombed, but the wedding was real enough. Bill Dixon had brought me a telegram from Eleanor in Miami, announcing her marriage, which meant no more alimony payments. Glasses were raised: 'To the bride.'

Fatha played his opening solo number 'Lover Come Back to Me'. In Kiev this had been substituted, by Soviet request, for the original opener, 'I've Got the World on a String', which somebody apparently thought subversive. I peeked through a small hole in the wooden barrier to look at the audience. Student faces mostly, intelligent; total concentration. A girl in large round glasses like Janis Joplin was wearing at the time looked just as pseudo-serious as American girls wearing such glasses. The faces were mystified rather than hostile, but distant just the same. The response was mild; they were thinking too hard to applaud. Our first mild reception. The radio, Bill Dixon had told us, was bombarding them with news of evil Americans bombarding Hanoi; they had heard and read the official view of jazz as 'decadent capitalist' music and were too busy trying to figure us out in relation to all of that to swing.

Close Enough for Jazz (1983)

Mike Zwerin

Dublin University 1961

JOURNAL (NOVEMBER 1961): I wore my US army combat jacket under my gown for a ghastly lecture on Descartes and his candle. 'That the mind is more easily known than the body.' After filling my pipe with the Provost's Mixture I set off in freezing cold for a rendezvous with the Trinity College Jazz Band, at home. They live together as one man in a seedy part of town, sharing a room. I've been asked to join on piano and mouth-harp. I'm reading *Mr Jelly Roll* and *The Country Blues* to get the feel. The band was all in bed together, plus 'free' girl scrubbers including one-eyed Edwina, Dublin's Queen of the Blues. She sports mauve legs and buttered hair. Her dad's an IRA sergeant and she's really been through the blues, green-style. A blanket, hanging out the window to air, was so stiff with the stuff of life that it banged noisily against the wall. A jam session was in progress together with a breakfast of toast 'n' marge. That's all they ever eat, three times a day. Sean Banjo lost his strumming hand years ago in industry but he plays acceptably by sticking a pick in the stump. He manages to keep a rigid rhythm, bleeding a bit on up-tempo stuff. That afternoon we formed up as the Paragon Marching Band under the direction of history student Barold Pilschardson – strapped into bass drum, tishing a tiny cymbal with a kitchen spatula. We weren't playing a funeral but advertising a hurling match. We marched proudly through the rain but nobody much could hear us because chinless-wonder types were out in force too, blowing hunting horns and yelling slogans like 'T-R-I-N-I-T-Y', 'No Popery', 'Pull the Chain' and so forth. We had our revenge, though, that very evening when we turned up to play an Anglo-Irish aristocratic gig. 'I don't think I know your face,' drawled the velvet-jacketed host after creaking open the castle door to Harry Trombone, our tough leader. 'You won't know yours, matey, by the time I've finished with you si vous don't open up sharpish!' slashing mine host with a handy trombone. Next morn Harry woke up in an upstairs chamber and, full of overnight beer, pissed into a nearby Celtic vase which he then politely emptied out the window hoping it might disappear into the moat – only it didn't. It crashed through the plate-glass conservatory roof arriving smartly on the breakfast table to join the scrambled eggs and kedgeree being served to the weekend guests. I'm also reading *Really the Blues* by Mezz Mezzrow.

After the Ball (1973)
Ian Whitcomb

Tokyo

ONE NIGHT after playing at Ray Bass's Harlem Club I was up in Be-bop's second-storey pad with a soldier on R&R. As usual wearing my low quarters instead of boots, because you have to take your shoes off to enter a Japanese house and if I wanted to beat a quick retreat I wouldn't have time to be tying no boots. And this particular house had been staked out before. We were getting into things pretty good when a little kid came tearing by on his bicycle shouting up, 'MP comin', MP comin'!' I think I know why our army had so much trouble with secrecy leaks in Vietnam: those Asian kids on their cycles are bitches as watchouts. Many's the time I've known about the approach of the MPs or CID minutes before they arrived. But this kid tonight was a shade slow. He jumped off his cycle, ran into the house yelling, 'MP comin'!' and no more than ten seconds behind him the door came crashing down. I got into my low quarters and jumped out the window, landing on the roof of the one-storey house next door. Went through the roof thinking, Everybody got to die, all kinds of casualties on the road to truth, and came down in the kitchen with a lot of splintered wood and sawdust. Woman at the stove standing there staring at me like she's thinking, What's it doing raining niggers? I got up, brushed myself off, said 'Go mena si' (sorry) and split.

Raise Up Off Me (1972)

Hampton Hawes

West Hampstead

THIS WAS West Hampstead, or, for Protestant whites (about 50 per cent of the local population), British West Hampstead. The boundaries of the district are vague. Although there is a South Hampstead station no one really accepts that as the name of a district, so the approximate limits would be Boundary Road (with St John's Wood), Finchley Road (with Hampstead proper), Mill Lane (with Cricklewood) and Kilburn High Road (with Brondesbury and Kilburn). The confines of the Maryon-Wilson estate, however, are much smaller, centring on Greencroft Gardens with a number of parallel streets and two cross ones. The streets are long, about half a mile, and while the total population of West Hampstead must be about 20,000, that of the estate itself isn't inconsiderable at about eight thousand, mostly bed-sitters. The largely Jewish developers were surprisingly flamboyant in choice of design, bearing in mind their frugal reputation. Much wrought iron wove in stars of David. Carved brickwork and turreted, gazebo-like structures commanded the heights. The only concession to parsimony was the reversion, once round the corner from the façades, to London stocks from the brilliant red facing bricks shining scrubbedly to the streets. The glowing colour of these bricks – a red often used in illustrations to science fiction literature of just-above-interplanetary Arthur C. Clarke level – is renewed by an automatic meteorological process each year. The bricks are porous and as the water soaks in during the winter and freezes the expanding ice pushes the old faces off: a kind of moulting. The renewal is now in its seventieth year, and on average about half an inch of brick has gone. In some cases much more. But about seven o'clock on a summer evening the colour's worth it. The London stocks are grey and yellow, hard as flints and dependable: great value for money, but there's something heroic about annually reborn brickwork.

Eight thousand people: a not-so-small town. There should be a happy family of tradesmen, a butcher, a baker, a candlestick-maker. There's nothing. Worst of all there are no pubs. Whether the Maryon-Wilsons' religious scruples forbade John Barleycorn or whether the profitability of drink in a largely Jewish community was considered dubious will be hard to establish now. But there it is: a boozer desert. In such circumstances, how did jazz musicians settle here in quantity? This was no place for them in socio/economic terms – high rents, cramped accommodation, insuperable problems practising instruments three-inch-partitions-away from sleeping families. And no boozers for miles. The overriding influences on the choice, so important as to dismiss all other considerations, were being near town and the road North. Getting back to Sidcup or Cheam at four o'clock in the morning after a gig in Birmingham was something only to be undertaken until a bed, any bed, could be found in West Hampstead. At any time during the 1950s and 1960s, 100 jazz musicians would be living in West Hampstead, at least fifty of them seemingly at 4 Fawley Road, or Bleak House as it came to be known.

Outwardly there was little to distinguish the place itself from many other unattractive three-storey terraced dwellings. Well . . . perhaps it had a rather special *dankness*. Its environs were unusual if consistent. There would always be the burnt-out hulk of a motor car outside or across the road or in the near vicinity. The charred remnants changed from month to month: only the story behind the original was partly known. Tony Bayliss, a bass player, owned that and it had just gone on fire. Spontaneous combustion. Efforts to put it out failed, and like everything at Fawley Road it was left alone if no longer of value. Inside the house – the distinction between in and out was blurred by the door panels having been kicked in as inhabitants, lodgers, wayfarers forgot/lost/never had keys – conditions had achieved squalor of a surrealism it would have been hard to invent. The sink was no more than an exemplar. It looked like a microcosmic Mediterranean: azure blue water and peaceful. The calmness remained unchanged for ten months, as if the commune members were too sensitive to drain away this simple beauty. Dishes and cups would somehow be washed elsewhere, perhaps in a dust bath like birds, or more likely – for the Fawley society were ingenious and experimental – in Flash or something that didn't need water or suds, or even, because emergencies often arose in the house, not washed at all, just reused, opening new avenues of flavour leaning towards jugged hare and long-hung game.

The story of the sink was at once less pretty and more complex. Legal Pete had started by being sick in it. While this was an improvement on being sick up the wall and waking everyone up, saying proudly 'Come and look at this: look how far I've got up the wall', Pete's diced carrots and tomato skins had been wolfed down without chewing between pints of Newcastle Brown and the aggregate being larger than usual, was too big to get down the drain. For some weeks dishes were piled in, the top ones being washed when required. It was never understood how, but Tony Coe, writing a score, managed to spill a whole bottle of blue ink on top of everything else. After that you couldn't see below the surface, and it became possible to believe, although only in Fawley Road, that an ever greater evil lurked there. You could get your hand bitten off looking for a plate: no agency disturbed the serene waters. This was a nuisance at parties, which were numerous. Someone had to steal glasses from the nearest pub, which wasn't very near as we've seen.

Some of the great musicians who lived at one time or another at Fawley Road were the pianists Brian Lemon, Colin Purbrook; sax player Tony Coe; trumpet player Jimmy Deuchar. The astonishing leaven of non-musician jazz lovers included Legal Pete, Oxford George, Ray Bolden and Al Babb. Sandy Brown and pianist Keith

Ingham lived round the corner in Greencroft Gardens and Phil Seamen, the best drummer in the UK, in Goldhurst Terrace.

Throughout the crunch and snap of breaking glass, the splintering door panels and the endless regurgitation of overindulged stomachs (singing a rainbow), Tony Coe would flit faultlessly through Bartok or Jimmy Deuchar would write down musical figures to show what brass arranging was about. The musicians would help, correct, encourage. Bleak House was an embodiment of the archaic atelier. Centripetal forces to do with learning the extending musical frontiers were inexorably to be overcome by the centrifugal ones carried by whirling excesses of numerous patrons of Fawley Road, but for four or five years it was a phenomenon unique in academic responsivity. It was more of a freewheel on top of power like a Saab, than an overdrive. It was like an electron accelerator: you got a push every time you came round. Everyone expected the apocalypse to be heralded by some formal dissolution, the event itself to resemble the Fall of the House of Usher in intensity: electric storms, cascading masonry, great rents appearing in walls. Far from Poe's frenzy, rents played a part. The increase was modest, but enough gradually to prorogue the unrepeatable assembly. They stole away one by one.

The McJazz Manuscripts (1979)

Sandy Brown

A Black American Girl at a Leningrad Blues Concert

A FEW weeks ago we were lucky enough to attend a B. B. King concert in the Gorky Palace of Culture in Leningrad. B. B. King, correctly described by his publicity as the best-known blues musician in the world, had been touring the Soviet Union for three weeks, generating waves of enthusiasm among its citizens – who know jazz well but have little exposure to the blues. The tour began with a concert in the capital of Azerbaijan; it moved on to Yerevan and then to Tbilisi, where, according to a State Department aide, the impulsive Georgians nearly started a riot, shoving into the theatre until two people sat in every seat. In Leningrad, the excitement had been building up long before we reached the Culture Palace. There had been absolutely no advance publicity in the city, but all our Russian friends knew about the concert from Voice of America (another, not always facetious, nickname for this broadcast is 'Voice of the Enemy'). The afternoon of the concert, a subtle excitement diffused itself through the crowds on Nevsky Prospekt. On the metro, groups of well-dressed people were eyeing one another and anxiously demanding the time. The horde of ticket scalpers encountered on the way to any Soviet performance extended this time all the way down into the subway. 'Do you have extra tickets?' people were shouting on all sides. Our friend Tolya, who was with us, said that the street tickets were going for between fifty and a hundred rubles apiece.

Inside the performance hall, we found an ample display of Soviet fashion. There were endless pairs of American jeans, which women wore with the skinny-heeled Italian ankle boots that are the *dernier cri* of Russian style. The curious thing about the crowd was that it consisted not mainly of young people, as one might expect, but of people of all ages. There were many middle-aged men and women, dressed in their best baggy suits and polyester dresses. There were small children, and there were some of the oldest *babushki* I had ever seen, walking slowly, with pleased grins, their heads wrapped in shawls.

A slick-haired Soviet MC announced B. B. King ('A great *Negritanski* musician'), and then King was onstage with his well-known guitar – Lucille – and a ten-man ensemble. As King and the ensemble swung into 'Why I Sing the Blues', one could sense the puzzlement of the Soviet audience. 'Negro' music to them meant jazz or spirituals, but this was something else. Also, there was the question of response. B. B. King is a great, warm presence when he performs, and he asks his audiences to pour themselves out to him in return. King teases his audiences, urging them to clap along, to whistle, to hoot their appreciation, like the congregations in the Southern churches in which he grew up. But to Russians, such behaviour suggests a lack of culture and an almost frightening disorder. Though obviously impressed, the audiences at first kept a respectful silence during the numbers, as it might at the symphony. (Only the foreigners shouted and stomped out the beat; we found the Russians around us staring at us open-mouthed.) Then King played an irresistible riff, stopped and leaned toward the audience with his hand cupped to his ear. The audience caught on and began to clap. King changed the beat, and waited for the audience to catch up. Then he changed it again. Soon the whole place was clapping along to 'Get Off My Back, Woman', and there were even a few timid shouts and whistles. King, who has cried the blues to Europe, Africa, and the Far East, had broken the ice one more time.

At intermission we were fortunate enough to talk to B. B. King. He rose when we came into his dressing room, a large dark-skinned man with sweat glistening on his forehead. King is one of the few performers whom it is not a revelation to see close up; he presents himself onstage exactly as he is, and his conversation has the same warmth and intermittent playfulness as his music. We asked him about his experiences in the Soviet Union, and he answered carefully, glancing occasionally at his manager, Sid Seidenberg, who stood by the door, and at an Intourist guide sitting nearby. (The backstage area was bristling with security people and Intourist personnel; Tolya said, 'This place is full of KGB.') King said that although he preferred capitalism, he respected the Soviet system, and that he had been impressed by the cordial hospitality of the Soviet people. Audiences all over the Soviet Union, he said, had received his music enthusiastically. 'The blues is likely something they've never heard before,' he said. 'I like to help them understand.' He told us a bit about touring Georgia and Armenia – his favourite parts of the Soviet Union. His best memory, he said, was driving up to a mountain lake in Armenia, eating a fish dinner, and meeting the local people. 'I grew up working on farms,' he added.

We asked him what he felt he'd learned from touring the Soviet Union and he seemed to give the question serious thought.

'I've learned two things,' he said finally, leaning toward us. 'The first is patience. The Soviet people are very patient. When things don't happen on time – if a plane doesn't take off for three hours, if a meal doesn't come – they wait. I've learned how to wait. The second thing I've learned here is that you can be a great musician and an amateur. I didn't think that was possible before I came to the Soviet Union. But we have listened to – and in one case actually jammed with – some very fine jazz musicians in Baku and Tbilisi. None of them were professionals.'

When we asked him what he thought of Soviet jazz in general, he said he was impressed by what he heard.

'They were good technically – sure, that you'd expect,' he said. 'But these fellows felt the music, and that's what impressed me. I don't know where they got the feeling, but they felt it.'

We said goodbye to B. B. King and left the dressing room to talk with some of his back-up musicians. These musicians were less guarded in their comments. Like King, they were happy about the audience response, and they praised the jazz musicians of Baku and Tbilisi. But they generally agreed that for a touring musician, the Soviet Union is a boring place.

'There's nothing to do here,' said one. 'At home we'd finish up the show and go to some little after-hours joint and listen to some *music* or something. But there's nothing like that here. Everything closes down. It's hard to meet women. It's hard to meet *any*body.'

Another player complained, 'It's like a damn prison here. We go down to dinner in a big group, we go up to our rooms in a group, and there's two, three Russians watching us all the time. Are we followed? Hell, yes. I live in New York. I know the fuzz when I see it. Guides, they call them. They don't like us to do one thing on our own. I like the people, man. The people – especially those Georgians – are something else, if you can just get away from the guides.'

By the second half of the performance, the audience was looser than any other Soviet audience I'd ever seen. People whistled, they hooted with delight, they clapped along, answering King's playful coaxing on the guitar. The guards standing against the auditorium walls looked uneasy. 'This is exactly what they don't like,' whispered Tolya. 'This rowdiness. They're terrified of a riot.' The music, already superb, got better and better. By the time King swung into his final song – the show-stopper – 'The Thrill is Gone', the audience was in love. Following the number, there was tumultuous applause, flowers were flung on the stage, and three Soviet hippies forced their way up on to the stage to kiss King's hands and to get his autograph. They were quickly wrestled away by a combination of American and Soviet security forces. King bent to shake hands from the stage, and the guards frowned some more as the crowd broke out into a roaring chant of 'B. B. King! B. B. King!'

Quickly the guards fanned out through the audience, pushing people toward the cloakrooms and ending the wild applause before it really got going. At one point, during a lull, Tom and I had a chance to talk to our neighbour, a woman who had initially stared at our clapping. She was a well-dressed middle-aged woman who hadn't taken part in any of the 'rowdy' behaviour. Nevertheless, she had seemed deeply moved by the performance, and when we asked her how she had enjoyed it, we saw that she had tears in her eyes. 'I have been studying American Negro music for years,' she said. 'I have listened to hundreds of records. It has been a kind of dream of mine to attend a live performance. Now – all that I can say is that I understand the music. One performance is worth a thousand records.'

In the cloakroom line, we talked to other local people. The reactions were all enthusiastic and emotional. One girl said, 'This is one of the greatest things that ever happened to me in my life! A friend gave me the tickets; I never expected to go. It's almost impossible for an ordinary person like me to see something like this. You have to be special – to have a lot of money or some Party connections – to get to a performance like this.'

An older man in a baggy suit looked thoughtful as we talked to him. 'B. B. King,' he said, pronouncing the syllables distinctly, 'B. B. King astounded me. This blues music – it's not like jazz. He poured his whole heart and soul out there on the stage. Such feeling is very Russian – we believe in emotion, in the soul. I never thought that an American could feel that way.'

Russian Journal (1982)
Andrea Lee

A Strange Encounter with Bechet in Paris

IT WAS a bright crisp winter day, with already the promise of spring in the still air, and the night frost made the pavements sparkle like a thousand glittering mirrored lark-lures. The fountains at the round-about soared high and cascaded down into their basins in crystal chandeliers, sending a fine rainbow spray around. In the surrounding gardens the bare twigs on the trees and bushes quivered with the promise of new growth, of impending bud-burst. People walked unhurriedly, looking at the shop-windows.

'Mademoiselle! . . . mademoiselle, excuse me . . . ' The chance of meeting anyone I knew in the middle of the day on the Right Bank was remote, but I turned my head, and saw an old black man approaching me, smiling. His face was familiar: 'Excuse me, mademoiselle, will you have a cup of coffee with me? I'm Sidney Bechet.' And he held out his hand. I was in too optimistic a mood to refuse – what did it matter, since I was leaving in a couple of days? – besides I liked his music, which was played on juke-boxes everywhere. In the café-bistro opposite the Cité Universitaire where we sometimes took refuge from canteen food, there was always someone pressing the button for 'Petite Fleur', a beautiful tune, and a hit for years, played on clarinet by Bechet. For us students he was a far-away idol whose music resounded in cafés and glided across the busy boulevard to our rooms at the Cité. His picture was everywhere, playing his clarinet, or smiling at the camera, his hooded eyes, squashed nose and round cheeks giving him the expression of a mischievous child. Like Louis Armstrong, he had a far wider appeal than most of the other jazz musicians who played in Left Bank clubs.

Jazz, banned by the Vichy government during the war as an expression of decadence, had consequently become an anti-bourgeois symbol for the young after it ended, and among Left-Bank intellectuals it was fashionable to know about and listen to jazz. Indeed a few became professional players, chief among them being the writer Boris Vian, who was said to have compiled a jazz record collection for Sartre and de Beauvoir. Black players were particularly appreciated, since the struggle for racial equality was on the agenda of the Left, and many famous American jazz musicians were invited to play on the Left Bank in the late 1940s and 1950s. But Bechet had settled down in Paris, where I believe he remained till the end of his life.

He led me to the first café-terrace on the Champs-Elysées, and I told him that I heard his records every day, and that all the students loved his music. But he had more in mind than a fan's admiration, and was not interested in discussing the subtleties of improvisation in jazz, classical and oriental music – he thought he had picked me up, since I had accepted his invitation to coffee. I told him I was thrilled to meet a living legend, but I was just about to leave Europe, and would never again have the opportunity for such a fortuitous encounter. When he realized I was not swayed by his compliments, he changed tactics and offered more: 'You see that Cadillac?' he asked, pointing to an American car as big and slick as a motor-boat. 'I'll buy it for you!' 'I don't like American cars!' I parried. 'Ar' right, I'll buy you a Citroën Déesse,' pronouncing the last word 'day-yes'. Next he offered me a house, trips to America, South America . . .

It was getting late for my appointment, and I was not a little bored, so I said goodbye, leaving him to look for another quarry, and I only remembered this episode recently, when I heard a man in the street say to his toddler daughter: 'Come along, Little Flower . . . ' Memory, like God, works in mysterious ways.

A Girl in Paris (1991)
Shusha Guppy

Edinburgh's Gangland

THE THREE gangs were Golly's, Naz's and the Val d'Or boys. There was actually a Golly, who always smelled of gelignite – it has quite a strong, unmistakable smell – a Naz, a portly little chap called William Nisbet, and the Val d'Or was a café. Sometimes the leadership and even the names would become blurred or changed, but at every dance there was violence. We coined the phrase 'faces are changing at the Jazz Band Balls', some of them, regrettably, almost unrecognizably. We tried a different venue to give the gangs the slip but this attempt, held at the Palace Ballroom at the foot of Leith Walk, generated the most spectacular fracas of all. At one point Golly threw Naz down a flight of steps which ended in the centre of the dance floor. Al Fairweather, Sandy's trumpet player, tried unwisely to separate them and was lucky to escape injury. The Naz lifted Golly and threw him against a mirror that covered one wall. One minute there were these two identical chaps hurtling towards each other back to back with a complete circle of onlookers open-mouthed and with alarmed frozen expressions: then crash! Half of them disappeared and the floor was covered with shards of silver. I found a pocket book before the police came with eight pence and a card proclaiming that a William Nisbet was unfit for army service. I threw it out of the window.

After that we hired two bouncers, both jazz fans, and things got quieter. One was Jackie McFarlane who was five feet tall, insisted on singing 'Frankie and Johnnie' in a nasal Dalkeith accent and learned his brawling in the International Brigade in Spain. The other was Tom Connery, who became Sean. None of his 007 crap years later matched the mayhem available from Golly and Naz.

The McJazz Manuscripts (1979)
Sandy Brown

Bombay

BOMBAY TURNED me around. I'd never seen poverty before. Been hungry in the streets of New York, a junkie, been in jail, but I've never seen anybody as fucked up and pitiful as those people in India. It blew my mind to see babies with bloated bellies, women washing them in the streets from fire hydrants, old ladies and cats with crooked arms from malnutrition coming up to you begging for pennies. Makes you stop and take stock. Here I was thinking about making a big splash, a hit record, going home a hero, and I'm walking the streets with motherfuckers who don't even know what a piece of bread is, let alone Stravinsky or Charlie Parker. If Bird came alive and played for them they wouldn't be able to hear him because they'd be too damn hungry. It tore my mind away from music and the good things that had been happening to me in Europe, from Jackie and myself. I was just one motherfucker trying to make it, but here were millions trying to make it on a simpler level – fighting for a piece of bread – and a whole lot of them weren't doing so good. Made me think I had no right to be worrying about how much my next gig would pay, how cool it would be, maybe I ought to consider myself lucky just making a living as well as anyone else so I can eat and pay my bills and have a house and be with people I love, do my gig and die and get on out of here, maybe that's all I got a right to expect.

Raise Up Off Me (1972)
Hampton Hawes

The Apollo, Harlem

'I saw Coltrane play the Apollo one time,' said Lionel Hampton. 'The place was packed when he went in there. When he left, there wasn't but a handful of people in there. He was playing his piece "My Favorite Things", and he played that piece for about half an hour. He was just giving vent to his feelings. Coltrane figured his music wasn't being accepted by everybody. Then it was the 1960s when there was a lot of trouble in the air. Racism. The black man hollering for freedom. Coltrane got caught up into it. He was taking his feeling out that he had against the happenings of the time, taking it out on his horn. One of the things somebody told me a long time ago was, "When you get on that stage, you're in show business. You be kind to your audience. Try to make communication with them. Give them what they want."'

Leslie Uggams remembers a time at the Apollo when another jazz master failed to communicate with her father. 'My father used to go to the Apollo a lot,' she recalled. 'He went to see Miles Davis, and he was sitting there, and across from him was another man about his age, about sixty. Miles started off with a melody, then he began embellishing it. My father lost the tune Miles was playing. At the same time, he and the other guy turned and looked at each other. And the other guy leaned over and said, "What are we doing here? We're too old for this." And they both got up and left.'

When Thelonious Monk, the continually inventive pianist and one of the jazz world's great eccentrics, played the Apollo in the late 1950s, he wore a pink sequined necktie – his one concession to the demands of show business. And as he was wont to do when his sidemen took solos, he got up and danced around his piano. Monk was the epitome of the far-out jazz musician, and he lived in his own little world. 'Monk was scheduled to play the Apollo,' said Bobby Schiffman, 'and at noon on Friday we couldn't find him. It was time for him to go onstage, and I'm running around frantically trying to find him. I see him standing up on the fire escape backstage, outside the building in the middle of winter with an overcoat on and his hat pulled down over his head. Just standing there peering at a tenement house. Everybody else has a case of nervous disorder, and he's standing out on the fire escape.' . . . Even with the greatest jazzmen on the bill, the Schiffmans found that the jazz shows needed help to make them commercially successful. 'No jazz show was successful unless it had a major female artist headlining,' said Bobby Schiffman. 'If you had Sarah Vaughan, you had a successful jazz show. You had Nancy Wilson, then you could have Cannonball Adderley and any number of major attractions there. But you better have that vocalist, who is gonna express what they had to say in words – rather than on the horn – as the main attraction of the show. I have had some great pure-jazz shows with Miles Davis, Mongo Santamaria, Charlie Parker, Thelonious Monk, Erroll Garner, or Dave Brubeck. But if you don't have Ella Fitzgerald, Sarah Vaughan, or Dinah Washington as the headliner, you can forget it. I can never explain why the great jazz talents of our day – almost all of whom were black, and if they were not black they played the Apollo anyhow – just couldn't make it unless they had a major female vocalist. If you had Betty "Bebop" Carter and you had Miles Davis as the headliner, it was no good. She had to be the headliner. At least that was the pattern.'

Showtime at the Apollo (1985)
Ted Fox

New York, New York

New York, N.Y.

Think you can lick it?
Get to the wicket.
Buy you a ticket.
Go!

Go by bus, by plane, by car, by train . . .
New York, New York
What they call a somethin' else town.
A city of more than eight million people,
with a million people passing through every day.
Some come just to visit,

and some come to stay.
If you scuffle hard enough and you ain't no dunce,
You can always get by in New York City I heard
    somebody say once.
Yeah . . . if you can't make it in New York City,
    man,
You can't make it nowhere.
So where do people come to scuffle?
Right here.
Think you can lick it?
Get to the wicket.
Buy you a ticket,
Go!

New York, N.Y.,
A city so nice
They had to name it twice.
It may seem like a cold town,
But, man, lemme tell ya,
It's a soul town.
It ain't a bit hard to find someone who's lonesome
        or forlorn here . . .
But it's like finding a needle in a haystack to find
        somebody who was born here.
New York, N.Y.,
A somethin' else town, all right!
East side, west side,
Uptown, downtown,
There's one thing all New York City has,
And that's jazz.
A while ago there were cats readin's while cats
        played jazz behind 'em,
But wasn't nothing happening, so the musicians
    cooked right on like they didn't even mind 'em.
I wrote the shortest jazz poem ever heard.
Nothing about lovin' 'n' kissin' . . .
One word . . .
Listen!

BIG CITY BLUES

Yes . . .
If you pay New York dues, you get New York
                blues.
There's a lot of givin' and takin' while you're
                tryin' to get by,
And the buildings got somethin' in common with
                the cost of livin' . . .
They're both sky high.
New Yorkers brag about their buildings bein'
                tall . . .
Hah! As narrow as Manhattan Island is,
You go up or nowhere at all.
And on one thing you can rely:
We got New York's finest.
The finest money can buy.
Some give a little, now, and some lean hard.
But they're all right in general . . .
As long as you ain't the wrong cat,
Tryin' to get a cabaret card.
So cats keep on strugglin' to say their say.
But between them and their audience,
There sits the D.J.
And I'm hip lack of acceptance is a drag . . .
People not diggin' the only thing that's their
                own . . .
Man, that's really in another bag.
But lack of acceptance is less like somethin' to
                hide from
And more like somethin' Bird died from.

MANHATTA-RICO

Ninety-five dollars to get to heaven!
That's what it costs to fly from San Juan, Puerto
        Rico, to New York City.
And, if you're down in your native land
And you're not standin' out on no moonlit veranda
        in a full dress suit
With a long, cool drink in your hand,
And you want to get where it's nice . . .
That's the price.

Ninety-five dollars to get to heaven!
And here comes another kinda soul:
To find that in the hottest part of summer it can
        still get very cold.
A quick look around'll tell you what's goin' on . . .
You dig who's livin' high on the hog,
And who's the underdog.
You dig what shape the underdog was in
'Cause you're livin' where he just been.
So, you dig him and you dig your host . . .

And you dig who it is you resemble the most.
Right on down to the rhythm that moves you.
There may be some slight difference in the way
        you say the word,
But Machito didn't have no trouble cuttin' some
        sides with Bird
They probably had trouble pronouncin' each other's
        name,
But they showed how two things could sound
    altogether different, and yet have a familiar ring,
Because they're the same thing.

All three poems from *The Jazz Word* (1960)

Jon Hendricks

Samois-sur-Seine

I WALKED down to Chez Fernand, where Django used to drink, on the river where Django used to fly-fish, for an interview with Jean-François Robinet, the town's dynamic young mayor. A journalist and jazz fan, he started these yearly homages over the objections of his constituency. 'The people here did not know Django as a musician,' he said. 'Or even as a Gypsy. He was known as a billiard champion. In 1950 he beat the Fontainebleau billiard team single-handedly for the Département championship. And they knew him as a fisherman. One year, it was unlike him, he fished out of season. "I can't wait," he explained. "I'll be dead by the season." He was.'

Robinet told me that certain influential residents detest the festival because it attracts Gypsies, hippies and noisy bearded people: 'They don't have any real respect for Django, this genius who chose to live among them. But I do. And too bad for them; they voted for me.'

It began to drizzle in the late afternoon. France joined us and we moved inside the café. I had reserved a table on the terrace of the nearby restaurant which overlooks the barge where tonight's music would be. The mayor introduced me to a dark-skinned man wearing a jacket capelike over his shoulders with a wide-brimmed white fedora on his head: 'Monsieur Rafael, this is Mike . . . ' he had forgotten my last name. 'He's writing a book about Django.'

'Not exactly.' I started to correct him: 'Actually the book is about . . . '

M Rafael could have been around sixty. He was thin but muscular, one eyelid drooped, and a dandy cigar danced in his mouth. He looked Sicilian, but in these circumstances I doubted it. The diamond in one tooth was perhaps a recompense for the empty space beside it. The missing top tooth and a jutting jaw made him resemble the bulldog on a leash at his feet.

'C'est intéressant, ça.' M Rafael tipped back the fedora. 'Moi, je suis le cousin de Django.'

'Did you know him well?'

'Of course. He was my cousin.' He went behind the bar, came back with a battered guitar and began to strum 'Lover Man'.

'I remember when I first heard he died, it was in a pub in Oxford. Somebody came in with the *Daily Mirror* and said: "Pity about Django dying." I'll always remember that pub, like you always remember where you heard that Kennedy was assassinated.

'I left for Paris the next day to see his brother Joseph. Cousin Joseph was a beautiful guitar player, but Django overshadowed him. Django made him carry his guitar. Joseph was always a step behind, carrying Django's guitar. Joseph considered it an honour.

'Joseph was living in a little caravan on a fairground at the end of the metro line. The caravan was full of cousins, there were big fires outside and dogs prowling about. Django's violin was hanging on the wall, and a couple of his paintings. They were terrible, awful, he was a bad painter. The violin was wrapped in one of Django's silk scarves. Later, Naguine, Django's widow, gave the scarf to Stephane Grappelli. It's got a red border and musical notes on it. Stephane still wraps his violin in Django's scarf before he puts it in the case.

'Stephane and Django didn't get on very well. The quintet would get a job at some posh place and the local Gypsies would hear about it and when Stephane went to their dressing room – Django always made sure they had fancy dressing rooms – all these Gypsies would be in there. They'd been out stealing chickens and they'd pluck and cook them. Once there was no stove so they just started burning the furniture.

'Stephane never liked Gypsies. They loved to give him trouble. Even now, when he plays in the south of Germany a gang of Gypsies is always sitting right down front. There are a lot of Gypsies around the Black Forest. They come to send him up, but also there's some real respect because of his connection with Django. They say hello in the dressing room afterwards. When he sees them coming, Stephane screams, "Lock the door, look out for your shirts."

'Stephane is careful with his money; Django was a spender. He was always ordering rounds of Calvados or apple cider for anybody who happened to be in the café. Also Stephane is, well, uncomfortable around women. Django loved to cat. When he saw a bird he liked from the bandstand, he'd play his guitar right *at* her.'

Rafael said 'cat' and 'bird' in English. What was this Franglais mixture of hipster and Chelsea slang? Why would a Gypsy refer to Gypsies in the third person? And where had he learned to play 'Lover Man'?

'Beautiful, isn't it?' he said, holding up the guitar to admire it. 'Early model Maccaferri. Must be worth five thousand dollars by now.'

Mario Maccaferri was a Sicilian classical guitarist who invented a way of building a special soundboard which curved in two directions enabling the player to get a particularly penetrating tone out of an acoustic instrument. In the beginning he made only a few for himself, then a few hundred of the cutaway type Django used and by now that model has the status of a Guarneri violin. Though Django played a key role in the success of that model, Maccaferri did not have a high opinion of jazz musicians in general and they never met. Later Maccaferri founded a company in the US that manufactured over nine million Arthur Godfrey model plastic ukuleles.

'A lot of people think they have Django's Maccaferri,' Rafael continued. 'Diz Disley over in London. Barney Kessel claims some Gypsies presented him with an old Maccaferri and said, "Here you are, this belonged to Django, he would have wanted you to have it." Les Paul says that some Gypsies came to give him Django's guitar.

'Les came to Paris once and asked me for Django's telephone number. I said, "If you find it let me know; he's disappeared." He gave me half of a $100 bill and said I'd get the other half when I found Django. Two nights later they were jamming together. Django told Les that he could not keep up with the electric guitar, it was driving him nuts, kept running away from him. Les invented the solid-body electric guitar and he felt sort of responsible. Django looked real bad – thin, big bags under his eyes . . . bad. "It's just a different technique," Les said.

'Django had two Maccaferris. One was cracked and they put it on top of his coffin when he was buried. Babik has the other one. So you see this is Gypsies for you. They'll tell you anything. Don't misunderstand, I love my people. But let me give you a tip, you seem like a nice young man; never believe anything a Gypsy tells you.'

There was a moment of silence as he pulled out another Dunhill. 'Basically they are all anarchists. They won't have all this bureaucracy stuck on them. They are outsiders, absolutely free people. I'm going down to Spain this week . . . ' He began to play in Flamenco style on the Maccaferri . . . if indeed it really was one. 'A lot of Gypsies play Flamenco guitar in Spain. They pick grapes and live in old buses sprayed with silver paint with big TV antennas. I can't live that way myself.'

I had been meaning to ask him: 'What were you doing in Oxford?'

'I had a foundation grant to write a history of the Roms. I was doing research. I have a degree from the University of Bucharest. They'll give anybody a grant if you know how to talk to them. You should have a grant for your book. If you want I can tell you how to deal with foundations. My grant was twenty thousand dollars. I will tell you for only two fifty. Cheap, no?'

I said I'd think about it, we talked some more and he wrote down his phone number. It turned out to be a muffler-repair shop in Montreuil. And not too long ago we received a summons from the police to pay the tickets he 'took care of' in Samois.

La Tristesse de Saint Louis (1985)
Mike Zwerin

Denmark, 1973

I CAME to my senses in a nearly horizontal position with my face six inches from a polished timber floor. Bang. No serious injuries, but a number of facial contusions which were embarrassingly difficult to explain: 'I walked into a floor.' I'd been sort of sleepwalking naked. When mopping up the blood it dawned on me where I was: in a largish house in the suburbs of Copenhagen at 5 AM. Later that morning I resolved to have a relaxing day, as I faced yet another six hours of clarinet-playing in the evening. I read the morning paper, noting that *moelk, brod* and *flode prisen* had gone *op*. Snap. As I couldn't understand much else except the tantalizingly repetitious 'Watergate' separated by metres of unpronounceable text, I moved to my host's library, selected some yellowing Danish journals on jazz music, and ambled into a garden. After being reminded of a number of unjustly neglected European jazz players of the 1930s and 1940s (André Ekyan, Hubert Rostaing) and wondering what became of them, I pulled open a page to reveal a poor photo-reproduction of Valaida Snow, the black trumpet-playing lady. This was the woman I'd asked about in my last *Listener* piece, which tried to show that in jazz, as in other creative arts, women *do* count less. It was obvious that the anonymous reviewer –

circa 1948? – thought that her reputation was going *op*, and that she had lived and worked in Copenhagen for a time, as Ben Webster and Dexter Gordon do today, but the details escaped me, so I underlined the bits I wanted my host to translate when he, in turn, got *op*, after an equally heavy night. But in the event Valaida slipped my mind: I was kicking myself on the plane to London of course.

When I arrived I found a highly literate account of Valaida Snow's performance and capabilities in a letter to me written by a *Listener* reader, Ken Stewart, who played drums in a band accompanying Valaida on one of her tours of Europe. In this case it included Holland, Switzerland and the UK. The band was formidable: Johnny Claes on trumpet, Derek Neville on saxes, and Reggie Dare on tenor sax in the front line. Ken explains that 'her playing had "authority" – as they say in the jazz books'. This rather endears Ken to me because jazz books, though plentiful, are usually full of meaningless words like 'authority'. But I quote further from his letter: 'Some of her solos were very well constructed and interesting, with a good attack and fine tone – when she was in the mood.' The last six words try to tell a story which most jazz musicians know very well. In any improvised medium the success–failure ratio will be low, for reasons not susceptible to scientific study at this time. *Any* success should therefore be welcomed because it's pretty easy for a trained musician to play passable Bach/Mozart/Beethoven/Wagner/Schoenberg/Stock-hausen. It's something else to stand in front of 3000 or nearly nobody and compose it.

I'm afraid this brings me back to Denmark. I toured with a Dixie band (what else?) who had laboriously learned some of the numbers I had composed twenty years ago. I couldn't remember them and had to be reminded by listening to records (of mine) which I don't keep. It took me some time to persuade the band I toured with for ten days that jazz is an improvised music, and that I'd rather they played what they were going to anyway: I would fit in. *That* got through, but I still had to play 'Everybody Loves Saturday Night' – an African tune I stole from blacks – twice every night and, understandably, four times on Saturday. Denmark is a banjo-land. No banjo: no good. The rationale – as expressed by an intense young Danish clarinettist – goes like this: mainstream music is a bastard quantity. It's a mixture of traditional and modern jazz. When I put it to him that his hypothesis meant that the late Johnny Hodges would, in 1935 or thereabouts, have had to invent what Charlie Parker did ten years later in order to play what he did, he retired hurt but not convinced. Woolly thinking still goes on in jazz and pop in the same way that Deryck Cook, for the classicists, took up swords for the Beatles without having the faintest idea about their antecedents.

The McJazz Manuscripts (1979)
Sandy Brown

Orange County, New Jersey

PAUL DESMOND, alto saxophonist with Dave Brubeck and winner of countless polls, has been promising for years to write the history of the Brubeck Quartet. This instalment is the first he has ever been persuaded to write.

Dawn. A station wagon pulls up to the office of an obscure motel in New Jersey. Three men enter – pasty-faced, grim-eyed, silent (for those are their names). Perfect opening shot, before credits, for a really lousy bank-robbery movie? Wrong. The Dave Brubeck Quartet, some years ago, starting our day's work.

Today we have a contract (an offer we should have refused) for two concerts at the Orange County State Fair in Middletown. 2 PM and 8 PM Brubeck likes to get to the job early.

So we pull up behind this hay truck around noon, finally locating the guy who had signed the contract. Stout, red-necked, gruff and harried (from the old New Jersey law firm of the same name), and clearly more comfortable judging cattle than booking jazz groups. He peers into the station wagon, which contains four musicians, bass, drums, and assorted baggage, and for the first and only time in our seventeen years of wandering about the world, we get this question: 'Where's the piano?'

So, leaving Brubeck to cope with the situation, we head into town for sandwiches and browsing. Since the sandwiches take more time than the browsing, I pick up a copy of the *Middletown Record* and things become a bit more clear. TEENAGERS' DAY AT THE ORANGE COUNTY STATE FAIR, says the headline across the two centre pages (*heavy move*, in that the paper only has four pages). Those poor folk, especially the cattle-judge type (who was probably lumbered into heading the entertainment committee), thought we were this red-hot teenage attraction, which Lord knows we've never been. Our basic audience begins with creaking elderly types of twenty-three and above.

Nevertheless, here we are, splashed all over this ad, along with the other attractions of the day – judo exhibition, fire-fighting demonstration, wild west show, and Animalorama (which may have been merely misspelled). And right at the top, first two columns on the left, is this picture of Brubeck's teeth and much of his face, along with the following text, which I'm paraphrasing only slightly. HEAR THE MUSIC TEENAGERS EVERYWHERE THRILL TO. It begins. HEAR THE MUSIC THAT ROCKED NEWPORT RHODE ISLAND (an unfortunate reference in that only a few weeks earlier the Newport Jazz Festival had undergone its first riot). HEAR DAVE BRUBECK SING AND PLAY HIS FAMOUS HITS, INCLUDING 'JAZZ GOES TO COLLEGE', 'JAZZ IN EUROPE', AND 'TANGERINE'.

So, now realizing – in Brubeck's piquant ranch phrase – which way the hole slopes, we head back to the fairgrounds where the scene is roughly as follows: there is a smallish, almost transistorized, oval race track. (I'm not exactly sure how long a furlong is, but it seems not too many of them are actually present.) On one side of the oval is the grandstand, built to accommodate 2000 or so, occupied at the moment by eight or nine elderly folk who clearly paid their money to sit in the shade and fan themselves, as opposed to any burning desire to hear the music their teenage grandchildren everywhere thrill to.

Directly across the track from them is our bandstand – a wooden platform, about ten feet high and immense. Evidently no piano has been locatable in Orange County, since the only props on-stage are a vintage electric organ and one mike. Behind us is a fair-sized tent containing about two hundred people, in which a horse show for young teenagers is currently in progress – scheduled, we soon discover, to continue throughout our concert. This is hazardous mainly because their sound system is vastly superior to ours.

So we begin our desperation opener, 'St Louis Blues'. Brubeck, who has never spent more than ten minutes of his life at an electric organ, much less the one he is now at, is producing sounds like an early Atwater-Kent Synthesizer. (Later he makes a few major breakthroughs, like locating the volume control pedal and figuring out how to wiggle his right hand, achieving a tremolo effect similar to Jimmy Smith with a terminal hangover, but it doesn't help much.) Eugene Wright, our noble bass player, and me take turns schlepping the mike back and forth between us and playing grouchy, doomed choruses, but the only sound we can hear comes from our friendly neighbourhood horse show.

'LOPE,' it roars. 'CANTER . . . TROT . . . AND THE WINNER IN THE TWELVE-YEAR-OLD CLASS IS . . . JACQUELINE HIGGS!'

As always in difficult situations such as these, we turn to our main man, primo virtuoso of the group, the Maria Callas of the drums, Joe Morello, who has rescued us from disaster from Grand Forks to Rajkot, India.

'You got it,' we said, 'stretch out,' which ordinarily is like issuing an air-travel card to a hijacker. And, to his eternal credit, Morello outdoes himself. All cymbals sizzling, all feet working (Morello has several. Not many people know this.) Now he's into the triplets around the tom-toms, which has shifted foundations from the Odeon Hammersmith to Free Trade Hall and turned Buddy Rich greener than usual with envy.

The horse show is suddenly silent. Fanning in the stands has subsided slightly.

Suddenly a figure emerges from the horse tent, hurtles to the side of the stage, and yells at Brubeck. 'For Chrissakes, could you tell the drummer not to play so loud? He's terrifying the horses.'

Never a group to accept defeat gracelessly, we play a sort of Muzak for a suitable period and split.

When we return at eight, all is different. A piano has been found, the stands are packed with our geriatric following of twenty-five and above, and we play a fairly respectable concert.

Even so, we're upstaged by the grand finale of the fair – the fire-fighting demonstration. A group of local residents has been bandaged and made-up to appear as if they've just leapt from the Hindenburg and their last rites are imminent. But instead of remaining discreetly behind the scenes until their big moment, they mingle casually with friends and neighbours in the audience during the evening, sipping beer, munching popcorn, casting an eerie, Fellini-like quality over the gathering, and considerably diminishing the impact of their ultimate appearance.

After their pageant come the main events of the fair, which have clearly been planned for months: a flaming auto wreck, followed by a flaming plane wreck, each to be dealt with instantly and efficiently by the Middletown Fire Dept. At one end of the oval is a precariously balanced car; at the other end, a truly impressive skeletal mock-up of a single-engine plane, tail up. Midway, at ground zero, is the Middletown Fire Truck, bristling with ladders and hoses and overflowing with volunteers.

A hush falls over the stands. At a signal given by the fire chief, the car is ignited. The truck reaches it in two or three seconds, by which time the fire is roughly equivalent to that created by dropping a cigarette on the back seat for two or three seconds. It is extinguished by many men with several hoses.

A murmur falls over the stands. The fire chief, painfully aware that his moment of the year is at hand, signals for the plane to be ignited, also instructing the truck to take it easy, so that the fire should be blazing briskly when it arrives. The truck starts, at about the pace of a cab looking for a fare. The plane goes WHOOSH! like a flashbulb, and by the time the leisurely truck arrives, has shrunk to a lovely campfire, just large enough for roasting marshmallows.

Later, four pasty-faced, grim-eyed men pile into a station wagon and drive away. It may not be a bank-robbery, but it's a living.

Punch, 11 April 1970

Paul Desmond

6

A TOUCH OF ACID

Jazz musicians are brilliant at the put-down. There was a female singer who, not so long ago, married the bandleader she worked for, even though her charms were more physical than vocal. 'It only goes to show,' a musician said to me, 'that love isn't just blind – it's deaf as well.' Very little of this appears in interviews with musicians, who are almost superstitiously unwilling to criticize other musicians when the press is around. I once was sent to interview Archie Shepp by *The Times* the first time he came to London as a bandleader and arrived at the Park Lane flat his group was occupying on time, at about noon. I rang and rang. 'Who the hell's that?' I finally heard a voice say. 'Oh,' said Shepp audibly, 'it's some motherfucker from *The Times*, but we'd better see him as we need the publicity.' I felt a little unwelcome when the interview started, but he was as sweet as anything to me, and although he was prepared to deal savagely with capitalism, Western culture, the European white, big business, you name it, he never said anything remotely disobliging about a fellow musician. You have to search far and wide to find people in the jazz world going on record with undiplomatic comments about others, but it can be worth it . . .

Crowd Noises

EDDIE THOMPSON was trying to play a set in a very noisy night club. The roar of conversation made the piano nearly inaudible. A few customers down front were trying to hear the music, and one of them rose in righteous indignation. He loudly went, 'SHHHHH!!'

From the piano, Eddie said, 'I'm sorry, I'm playing as quietly as I can.'

Goodman in Russia

WHEN BENNY took his band to Russia in 1962 he engendered enough strife with his musicians and with Russian officialdom to fill half a book, which the editor has already done elsewhere. When Zoot Sims returned to the States from that infamous tour, he was asked what it was like playing with Benny in Russia. Zoot answered, 'Every gig with Benny is like playing in Russia.'

Going Nowhere Fast

JOHN LA Porta reportedly had a little talk with one of his pupils: 'I have good news and bad news about your playing. The good news is: you've got a lot of technique. The bad news is: you've got a lot of technique.'

Country

WHEN BUDDY Rich checked into a hospital, the admitting nurse who filled out his admission form asked if he was allergic to anything. 'Country and Western music,' said Buddy.

Drummers

MONTY BUDWIG's wife Arlette came up with a motto that might look good on a line of T-shirts: 'So many drummers, so little time.'

All the above from Jazz Anecdotes (1990)
Bill Crow

W. C. Handy

HANDY WAS supposed to get the tune copyrighted for Butts, but he changed the name to 'St Louis Blues' and copyrighted it for himself. Jelly knew all about the deal and every time Jelly would see Handy talking on a corner to some guys, he would get on the other corner and start telling guys all about Butts and Handy as loud as he could so Handy could hear. I never knew Butts, but Jelly claimed he knew all about what happened and he used to cuss Handy out and call him a 'horse thief'.

The Boston Symphony made the 'St Louis Blues' for Handy by playing it and making it popular. The rich people around New York knew about it and Handy, and they used to hire him for society dates. Once you've heard the 'St Louis Blues' you've also heard the 'Memphis Blues' and the 'Beale Street Blues', they're all the same. If you're playing any of those tunes you've really got to watch yourself that you don't play the wrong tune, they're so close. Handy never claimed he was any 'Father of the Blues' around me or any of the coloured – we knew he wasn't.

Pops Foster (1971)
Pops Foster

Four Angry Men

IMMEDIATELY PRIOR to the concert a number of incidents culminated in the creation of a situation which Brubeck had not been called upon to face before. An argument had developed between Paul

Desmond and Dave which was still in full swing when the compere made his opening announcement. When the Quartet filed on to the platform Paul and Dave, while maintaining their outward demeanour for the benefit of the assembled students, continued their argument in a more subtle manner. Each did his utmost to out-play the other and, on the evidence of this record it seems safe to assume that Desmond came off best during the 'on-stage' section of the dispute. Bass player Ron Crotty (pronounced Crow-tee) also had his share of troubles and was in no mood to observe the finer points of his task. Shortly before the concert he handed his notice in to Brubeck and played throughout the Oberlin set with less than his usual efficiency. During the musical proceedings Dave found it necessary to call out to Crotty (as he does here in the second chorus of 'These Foolish Things') because Ron was not observing the correct chord progressions. Perhaps it was because of this that Dave's left hand is well in evidence here as he compensates for the uncertainty of the bass player. Finally to drummer Lloyd Davies; Lloyd was not concerned with the emotional upsets of his fellows because an attack of influenza had given him a temperature of over a hundred degrees. The doctor thought that Lloyd should have remained in bed but, despite any other failings he may have, a jazz musician's sense of loyalty to his group is usually well developed therefore the drummer elected to play that night.

It will be seen then that more emotional tension existed within the confines of the Quartet than ever before and it was in this setting of outspoken disagreement, dark brooding and ill-health that the unit played at Oberlin. Neither Brubeck nor Desmond will now listen to this recorded transcription of the concert due to their unhappy memories of the events; this is a pity for, in many ways, this record contains some of their best work.

Sleeve note from *Jazz at Oberlin*
Alun Morgan

Unwelcome Visitors

ANOTHER VISITOR, trumpeter Wingy Manone, was quite forth-coming but didn't have too favourable an impression of England. 'Too many niggers on the sidewalk' was one of his pronouncements, an odd comment from a man who frequently boasted about his friendship with Louis Armstrong. But he was professional in his approach, and played well.

There were other visitors whose behaviour was extremely unprofessional and who often played very badly.

My dream of meeting so many legendary figures often became a living nightmare and many of the romantic images nurtured over the years were unhappily destroyed after some hair-raising experiences with idols who had feet of clay, and were in some cases over-fond of strong drink.

The tenor saxophonist Don Byas carried an obscene litany which every young lady fortunate enough to know the joy of his passion was obliged to read first. This selection of odes was but one unsavoury feature of an abrupt, aggressive and unlovely person. Don Kingswell, genial and anxious to please, introduced himself. He told Byas that his job was to look after him throughout the tour and mentioned that a previous tour by saxophonist Ben Webster had been spoilt by Ben's excessive drinking. Byas assured Don that he, unlike Webster, could take his drink. Kingswell, relieved, added that Webster had carried a big knife. He was further relieved that Byas appeared to respond with incredulous disbelief. He soon discovered why. 'You don't say!' exclaimed Byas. 'A big knife, huh? You call that thing Ben had a big knife? That was nuthin'. Look at this, man. Now *here*'s a *big* knife,' and as he spoke he drew a fearsome-looking dagger from his belt. Don backed away in understandable fright.

All This and Many a Dog (1986)
Jim Godbolt

Goodbye, Glenn Miller . . .

YEAH. WELL, I don't like to be the revisionist on history, but I think that Glenn Miller's band was like the beginning of the end. It was a mechanized version of what they called jazz music. I still can't stand to listen to it. But that's the one of that period that everybody buys, for some reason.

Dialogues in Swing (1970)
Artie Shaw

. . . And Good Riddance

AL KLINK was being interviewed by a radio disc jockey who was interested in Al's tenure on the Glenn Miller band.

'That band was never really considered one of the swing bands, was it?' asked the interviewer.

'We were all too scared to swing,' Al replied.

After years of hearing Miller's hits revived ad nauseam, Al commented, 'Glenn should have lived, and the music should have died.'

Jazz Anecdotes (1990)
Bill Crow

Yes to Duke, No to Mercer

I WAS a Duke Ellington idolater. I mean, there are no words. I can't describe what I felt for Duke Ellington – on a personal as well as a professional plane. And Duke was a little bit (if I may say this, God rest his beautiful soul, his musical genius soul), Duke was not a perfect person – any more than Judy Garland was. Maybe that's what made them, in their respective fields, the virtual genius performers and talents that they were. Duke on many occasions exhibited pomposity, he exhibited extreme self-centredness, and who's to say that's wrong? He was a god musically; he was not a god personally. But I loved him. And when he passed away, I was determined that all these really rotten pressings that had come over from Italy, that you paid $9.98 for and then you had to buy 'em shrink-wrapped, when you open 'em up and put 'em on, it sounds like they've been mixed with equal parts of vinyl and marble halavah. I mean, it's just terrible. So I called this guy, Dave Coughran of, what was the name of his company? Fairmont Records. I had a big Reco-Cut machine that cut 16-inch transcriptions, and I said, 'I have these, all these Treasury broadcasts.' He said, 'Oh! How could I get 'em?' And I said, 'There's one way: no money, but I want ten copies of every volume you put out. Because they're marvellous and I'd like to be able to give 'em as gifts.' And that's the deal we made.

And I must say that one of the most flagrantly abusive times of my life was when Duke's son, Mercer Ellington, accused me of 'making money on his dead father'. First of all, the company was so tiny, Fairmont, that Dave Coughran said, 'Look, this is a labour of love. It'll cost me more than I can ever make on these albums.' God, what wonderful – the 1946 Duke Ellington band with all the greats in it – so I was hugely insulted and I will probably never forgive Mercer Ellington for that. That was a year in which my salary, even then (and this is a few years ago) was a huge, six-figure salary. Why in God's name would I want to make $204 or something on a set of records that I just wanted to share with people? So, the pettiness of people, sadly, when you try to be a little altruistic, can really get to you. And I'm very open about this. There are no secrets in my life.

Dialogues in Swing (1970)
Mel Torme

Borrowing Clothes from Hot Lips Page

LIPS PAGE had a couple or three fine special suits, and at that time he and I were the same size. So one night we were supposed to go out somewhere, and I said I couldn't go because I didn't have anything to match up, and he said, 'That's all right. Why don't you borrow one of my suits?' And I said OK. I figured that would be great. Because he had three real sharp, truly great outfits. But I didn't know what I was getting myself into. I couldn't get rid of him. Everywhere I went he was right there with me, saying, 'Don't lean on that.'

Or he'd say, 'Hey man, that chair is kinda dirty.'

'Hey, Basie, watch it sitting down.'

He couldn't think of anything else all night but that suit of his I was wearing. That was one of the most uncomfortable evenings I've ever had in my life. I never was so glad to get back home and take off a suit.

Good Morning Blues (1990)
Count Basie

Hines v. Armstrong

THE ONE thing was that they never really hit it off too well, Earl and Louis. I don't know how they got along in those early days, but with our band you could feel the animosity between them. I mean they were both bandleaders to begin with. They had their ups and downs and after they would argue Earl would try to make things right with Louis. On the surface maybe he did, but Louis was like an elephant, he never forgot.

Sometimes Louis would get after Earl because he put too much show into it all and wasn't giving the soloists the support he should have. They didn't really have a good rapport together, personality-wise. It was strange to me, because they made such great music together, and had respect for one another's music. I think maybe that animosity dated back to Chicago. Both of them had been pretty popular then and maybe they were trying to out-do each other. Who knows? You understand, the main thing was that it wasn't a factor to consider too much, because they wouldn't carry it to the stand. That was something between themselves. Sometimes they got along fine, sometimes they didn't. It was one of those deals. All in all it was a great rhythm section to work with, but I think Earl felt that he was big enough to have a group of his own. Which he was.

With Louis and the Duke (1985)
Barney Bigard

Sidney Bechet i

I WENT back to New York and took a six-month leave of absence to go play with Sidney's band. From the time we opened we had trouble with Bunk, but I've already talked about it. Sidney fired Bunk and sent to New Orleans for Peter Bocage. He came and started telling everybody how to play so Sidney fired him and got a kid named Johnny Windhurst to finish the job with us.

Some of the problems we had may have been Sidney's fault. He is the most selfish, hard to get along with guy I ever worked with. I saw him fire one trumpet player five times in one night. You really had to try to get along with him. From the time I played with him in Jack Carey's band in New Orleans to making a bunch of Blue Note records with him, he was a tough baby and all for himself.

Pops Foster (1971)
Pops Foster

Sidney Bechet ii

SOME PEOPLE say Sidney was the most temperamental son-of-a-bitch in music. Others say he was the nicest man you ever met. I don't know. All I see is how a guy treats me and then I judge him on that. I didn't care what anyone said, he was strictly OK with me. See, there's no denying. He wanted a number played just like *he* wanted it, but even so he was always the one doing all the playing anyway. I don't blame him. He had to come up with all the fireworks so why not get the background like you want it?

Sidney was murder on trumpet players. Now he and Louis Armstrong couldn't get along so you know the rest of those horn blowers were going to catch hell. See, Sidney and Louis were both 'The King' on their instrument. They didn't record too much together because of the friction. One would want top billing and so forth and that would be a humbug right there, before they got to the music. They both wanted to play lead. Naturally if you're from New Orleans that's the old way. Trumpet always has the lead and everything else works round it. When they came to make those four sides together that's just about what Louis did. He played lead and kind of forced Sidney down. There was some kind of feud in there. I talked to Zutty Singleton one time about that session Sidney and Louis made and he says, 'Man, I don't want to talk about that session. Don't ask me nothing about it at all.' All the time I played with Louis in later years he never once mentioned Sidney's name. Yet if they met on the street you'd swear they were madly in love with each other.

With Louis and the Duke (1985)
Barney Bigard

Sidney Bechet iii

READING SIDNEY Bechet's autobiography, *Treat It Gentle*, I had to accept the fact that the Bechet he was writing about had little in common with the Bechet I knew so well. His Bechet and mine both played soprano sax and clarinet. The kindly old gentleman in his book was filled with charity and compassion. The one I knew was self-centred, cold, and capable of the most atrocious cruelty, especially toward women.

As much as I admired his artistry, I couldn't help being appalled by his character. Toward his fans, his attitude ranged from indifferent to contemptuous. He could have been the prototype for what is now called 'male chauvinist pig'. I never discovered anything he wouldn't do for money; to my knowledge, he had absolutely no ethics, no principle or loyalty.

I Remember Jazz (1987)

Al Rose

Maurice Chevalier: a Jazz View

THEN WE played a concert with a French guy called Maurice Chevalier. We did the first half of the show and he did the second. When he came on we went into the pit and played accompaniment to his songs, he was all by himself out on the stage. He couldn't sing worth beans, but he was a fascinating man to watch. He'd put that big lip out there – 'Louise' – and he sure charmed all those women right out of their seats. It went so well that we held that job down for four weeks.

With Louis and the Duke (1985)

Barney Bigard

The Worst Clarinettist in the World

BUT IF you searched for a thousand years you would never come across a serious musician (if that's the word) like Claude Luter. He had only one peer, a tiny chap called Joey Clark who tragically died young, owned a brown E-flat clarinet and played with a comedy band called the Alberts. Joey's incredible expertise was never to hit a right note during any performance. Luter, however, was demonstrably a dedicated Dodds man and by all accounts had little international humour in reserve. It's hard to know where to begin describing him. He always played out of tune, usually flat, but when caprice descended upon him, sharp as well. Sometimes the vibrato was so uneven it sounded as if he was both flat *and* sharp. The timing of rhythm sections in his bands was so erratic that criticism of this aspect of his playing was unjust if not impossible. Uncannily he appeared to achieve almost exactly Dodds's tone on record, so occasionally one got the feeling that a badly under-the-weather but real Johnny Dodds was revolving on a turntable that needed urgent attention from the refuse collection service.

The McJazz Manuscripts (1979)
Sandy Brown

The Truth About Preservation Hall

TWICE WEEKLY, he took the bus into the French Quarter where he held down a job at Preservation Hall. The hall was a hangover from a period when art gallery owners made their premises available to keep traditional music alive, following the demise of the famous black dance halls. It features in countless tourist advertisements, but in its contemporary manifestation it was a far cry from the intentions of the music-lovers who had provided the new working environment. For a start it was dirty, with no facilities for musicians or patrons apart from a couple of squalid toilets and a Coca-Cola machine. The musicians sat propped in the steamed-up window, displayed like a bunch of ageing icons for tourists. A handful of chairs along one wall were occupied by some of the musicians' contemporaries, who had followed the music for years, but most of the punters had to sit on the floor. Overcrowding and short sets encouraged a rapid turnover, with equally short breaks for the musicians, many of whom were getting on in years.

Polo introduced me to some of his colleagues, notably the celebrated trombonist Jim Robinson, now pushing eighty, who had played in France with the United States Army during World War One and whom I'd once seen in London. There was trumpeter Dédé Pierce, whose wife Billie played with him and the trombonist, in the city's tradition of fine women pianists; Sweet Emma Barrett, one of the first women musicians in jazz to record, and drummer Cié Frazier, Polo's cousin. At first I was so overwhelmed at coming face to face with such 'legends' of jazz, people I'd known of for as long as I could remember, that I failed to reflect on the circumstances under which they were working. But after a couple of visits realism took charge. I looked at the five- and ten–dollar bills piling up at the door and began to ask questions. Records by the featured artists sold well at the Hall, but Polo said royalties were never forthcoming. The musicians got a session fee for each date, just as a night's work paid union 'scale', the minimum, no matter how many people packed into the room. Occasionally the band got tips for playing requests such as 'The Saints', but it was hot, gruelling and undignified, the 'oldtimey' atmosphere cultivated by the proprietors invidiously rooted in earlier social conditions. The musicians, I learned later, called it 'The Plantation'.

Mama Said There'd Be Days Like This (1989)
Val Wilmer

The Not So Great Buddy Bolden

I ONLY saw Buddy Bolden's band play once at Johnson's Park. That's where the rough people went. I knew all the guys in the band and later on played with them. Buddy played very good for the style of stuff he was doing. He played nothing but blues and all that stink music, and he played it very loud. Buddy got to drinking so bad they had to hire two trumpets and Joe Howard played the other one.

Pops Foster (1971)
Pops Foster

7

DRINK, DRUGS AND OTHER THINGS...

There was a cartoon in the *Evergreen Review* in the 1950s which showed two jazz musicians walking along (saxophones, sun-glasses, hats) and one saying to the other: 'You mean, you *drink* tea?' This obscure joke was entirely based on the fact that 'tea' was one of the many slang words for marijuana, but what is interesting is that it was jazz musicians who were chosen as the characters involved. For many years before the excesses of rock musicians hit the headlines, jazz was meant to be the world of addiction. (In about 1960 I saw a women's magazine feature on the drug habits of Chet Baker entitled 'Ten Thousand Hell-holes in My Arm'.) And it was certainly true that under the strain of the jazz life – strange hours, absence from home, lack of recognition, racial discrimination – many players looked elsewhere for comfort or support. In the 1920s it tended to be alcohol. In the 1940s heroin was the in thing among the modernists. But this was not invariable – in the late 1920s Louis Armstrong was actually briefly imprisoned for the use of marijuana.

Jazz musicians resent the association of jazz and drugs, and many of them have gone to heroic lengths to kick their addiction. Many others will tell you that addiction is higher among other professions, such as medicine. This is true. The fact remains that at no period in history could you have printed a drawing of one doctor saying to another, 'You mean, you *drink* tea?'

Condon First Law of Drinking

I arrived on the job in what I considered to be a perfect state of equilibrium, half man and half alcohol.

We Called It Music (1956)
Eddie Condon

The Arrival of Prohibition

ON 4 July 1919, Louis Armstrong, Johnny Dodds, and me got off the boat and went up a hill in St Louis to Boots Saloon to get a half pint of whisky each until Prohibition blew over. We didn't think it was going to last. On the boats they sold ice cream and soda pop and they had a big freezer to keep it in. After Prohibition came, the bootleggers would keep their whisky in the freezer and sell it on the boat.

The dances on the riverboats were segregated. Monday night out of St Louis was for the coloured. There were as many whites as coloured on Monday nights and you could hardly get on the boats that night. In New Orleans no coloured were allowed on the boats. In Memphis and Pittsburgh sometimes they had coloured on Monday nights. We called Mondays 'Getaway Night' because you could get away with anything. The guys in the band would walk around smoking cigarettes and drinking, and come down off the stand. On 'Getaway Night' we used to nearly wreck the boat when we got to fighting. If a big fight breaks out in any dance hall, it's important you keep playing so the crowd won't panic. On the boats it's very important that the people keep dancing. If they all run to one side of the boat, the boat'll tip over. It seems like most fights break out around the bandstand and a lot of them want to get right up on the bandstand and fight. Usually you have three or four guys around the bandstand just to keep people from getting up on it. When the shootin' starts it gets rough.

On the boats the guys who acted up got put in the freezer with the ice cream and soda pop. One guy started trouble when we were just gettin' goin'. He spent the whole evening there and was blue and stiff when he got out.

Pops Foster (1971)
Pops Foster

A Very Drunken Recording Session

SIDNEY BECHET described the fiasco that occurred when Hugues Panassié came to New York to record some of the jazz greats that he admired. The band included Tommy Ladnier, Mezz Mezzrow, James P. Johnson, and Sidney De Paris:

'The men were supposed to be there pretty early in the morning. But something had got going the night before and when they showed up at the studio they were really out; they'd been drinking all night. That was a session I wasn't scheduled to be at, but I heard about it quick enough. Tommy, he showed up dead drunk. James P. Johnson, he just stretched himself on the piano and passed out. Some of the musicianers didn't know how many fingers they'd got on each hand. But they went ahead and recorded somehow. And after it had all been cut, Tommy knew the records weren't what they could have been and he wanted to say something to appease Panassié, who was sitting in the corner holding his head – something he thinks will fit the occasion. So he pulled himself up and called out "*Vive la France*" and then fell almost flat on his face.'

Jazz Anecdotes (1990)
Bill Crow

Louis Armstrong and Pot Smoking

LOUIS'S SECOND wife Lil sure was good to him. She still loves him after all these years. The reason she took off was Louis's pot smoking. There wasn't any woman or nothin', she just got tired of Louis smoking that stuff. He smoked pot just like you smoke regular cigarettes. The band was playing Jack Sheen's in New Orleans when she left. Jack's was a wide open place in St Bernard's Parish. Louis smoked pot all the time I was with him and as far as I know never quit.

Art Hodes and Drink

WHEN I did get drunk, I didn't do anyone any harm. Mostly I'd want to sleep, play music, or try to cut up and be funny. I think coloured musicians mostly drank booze and the white guys started taking dope. Some young coloured musicians did start taking dope after that. The only real trouble I ever had in my life was the drinking I did around New York and that was all harm to myself.

One time I remember we went over to Rhode Island to play a college date. Jimmy Archey, Art Hodes, me, and a couple of other guys. Art brought a whole suitcase full of whisky. We all got pretty well loaded but Art couldn't even stand up. It was wintertime, so we took him outside and laid him out in a snowbank to cool him off. We forgot him. When we finally remembered him, he was nearly frozen stiff. It took us a long time to thaw him out; we worked on it all the way back to New York. He lived, so I guess it didn't do him too much harm.

Both the above from *Pops Foster* (1971)

Pops Foster

Discovering Pernod

I HAD started to take a liking for Pernod, a French drink with a strong taste of anis, and that the people usually drink before meals as appetizing drink. I had a bottle in my room and enjoyed it. But that Pernod started to affect my behaviour. I became very excitable, jumpy, and after a few days, Bill came into my room and said that he wanted to talk to me and find out what was the matter with me. Although I was doing my job correctly, I was acting foolishly on the bandstand, talking loud when others had their solos. He said that he could not understand why I was so high because it didn't seem that I was drinking that much . . .

'What are you drinking in your room?' he asked me.

'Pernod,' I replied, 'only Pernod.'

'But are you putting enough water in it!' he said.

I was puzzled. I didn't know I had to mix it with water and was drinking it pure . . . After that, everything went smooth and I was myself again.

The Key to a Jazzy Life (1985)
Benny Waters

The Saga of Rubberlegs Williams

RUBBERLEGS WAS a big sissy, you know. Great big guy, about six-four. He weighed about 240. This particular day we were making those records, we were doing some of Bessie Smith's songs. 'What's the Matter Now?', 'You Been a Good Old Wagon, But You Done Broke Down', and some of those things. It was late at night or early in the morning, and we all had about ten cups of black coffee. In those days these benzedrine inhalers were very popular. Charlie Parker, he didn't have any stuff this time, so he broke open a benzedrine inhaler. This thing was equivalent to seventy-five benzedrine tablets, and he put it in his coffee to let it soak.

Rubberlegs was already half drunk. He wanted some coffee, so Teddy Reig – he was running this date – he grabbed the coffee up, and Rubberlegs drank it. Later on Bird went and got his coffee and drank it, and he told us, 'Man, my constitution is getting terrible. This stuff ain't even fazing me.' We didn't know what had actually happened, but Rubberlegs had got hold of it.

He kept saying, 'This is bitter coffee, man.' We're recording along and he's breaking out in a sweat and cussing. He called everybody Miss So-and-so. He told Dizzy, 'Miss Gillespie, you keep playing those wrong notes behind me, I'm going to beat your brains.' He had fists big as hams, so we all was getting kind of frightened because the guy was getting so wild around there.

He got after Teddy:

'Put out these lights; it's too hot in here.'

So Teddy put out the lights. The only light was back in the control room. He told Charlie Parker,

'What are you playing? They're some wrong notes!'

You know how Charlie played flatted fifths. He's getting after Charlie and Dizzy. He sang one of those tunes, I think it's 'What's the Matter Now?' He's going all out of tune and all, and we die, we almost roll on the floor laughing, man, and this is when we found out that he had got Charlie Parker's cup by mistake. This was the wildest record date you ever saw in your life. We never did get through with it. And they put those things out! It was the funniest thing I ever heard.

from the IJS Archive

Trummy Young

Looking for Drugs in Japan

ON MY first legal pass, shoes shined and pants creased like any sharp potato-fed US soldier, I split from the group heading for the town bars (have a beer and ball a Japanese broad was the plan for the day) wondering how I was going to score. All my life I'd heard from junkies that dope in Japan and China was it. (Which shows you how stupid the army is. They knew I'd been strung so why send me to the place where all the best shit is?) Now at the time I wasn't strung. I had a habit when I entered the army, kicked, but every time I was AWOL or home on a pass I'd use. But with the time in the stockades and the boat trip it had been some three months since I'd used.

I started walking into town along some rice paddies trying to figure out a course of action. I knew I couldn't stop some strange cat on the street and ask because – number one, there was the language barrier, and two, I was smart enough to know there were probably some undercover CID people around. My mind was just focusing on the idea of *sin* – where there's one kind of sin there's usually another, *ie*, a whorehouse was the thing – when like a genie out of a bottle a little old cat popped out in the road in front of me. Strange genie wearing a kind of hip hat, funny raincoat and tennis shoes. He said in broken English, 'Hey, where you goin' to?' 'Just goin',' I said. 'You want nice girl?' Okay.

He trotted down the road ahead of me and the next thing I knew I was sitting in a house on a bamboo bench and Mama–san is parading some sharp groovy chicks in kimonos before me, bowing and smiling, doing their part to get me excited. I turned down the first chick and Mama-san brought on two others, equally fine, opening their kimonos and flipping their breasts around so I could appreciate their youthfulness and spring. I said I didn't want them either. By this time everyone's looking at me funny, thinking this dude's got to be in the wrong pad, must be looking for a nice, fat Japanese boy, and I'm losing heart too. But when the sliding door opened to admit the fourth chick I happened to glance down the hall and saw a skinny bitch pushing a broom. I almost fell out. Felt my face break into a big happy grin because even at a distance I could see that this chick's arms look like the Penn Central switching yards. I'd never seen arms with that many scars, could hardly conceive of anyone pumping up their veins so bad. She was emaciated, couldn't have weighed more than eighty pounds; her jaw was sunken, there were dark circles around her eyes and it was understandable why they had her pushing a broom. No soldiers were going to pay any kind of bread for her, so if you can't fuck at least keep the place clean. When I saw that mess of tracks I said to Mama-san, That's it, that's who I want. She looked back at the broompusher, then at me, puzzled because I'm the most unlikely-looking junkie she ever saw; I've been eating three squares a day, plenty of army potatoes, and am coming on fat and sassy. Suddenly she's all in a sweat, batting her eyes and fluttering her fat hands, Oh no, bad girl, not good girl for you – so I figured the ultimate thing to do to close the deal is to bring out my wallet. Mama-san glanced at my bread and I knew if I'd said right there I wanted to screw the bamboo bench I was sitting on she would have given me the bench to screw. Ah-so. She went down the hall to tell the broompusher she's it, and that bitch's eyes lit up; she must have thought Buddha's elevated her back to the good graces and done sent her somebody to love. Dropped the broom, happy as a kid, and went running into a nearby room. You wait, Mama-san said, she'll prepare for you. I didn't need anyone preparing for me, but I didn't want to give my game away. Let her put on the powder and lipstick and whatever else, do the whole thing. I'd waited this long anyway. When she was ready I went down the hall into the room, and even as I pulled her into a corner and whispered in her ear, 'Ahen' (heroin), she kept smiling and bowing, thanking Buddha for relieving her of the broom, putting her back in harness. I had to say again, 'Ahen,' and it must be very hard for an Oriental chick's eyes to get round but suddenly this eighty-pound Japanese bitch is Orphan Annie backing away from me frightened and cowering against the wall, those moon eyes taking in a healthy potato-fed American soldier, wondering since when's the CIA hire nigger undercover agents. I rolled up my left sleeve to show her and now there were moons within moons. Ah-so. Soldier shoot up? You dumb bitch, what do you think I been trying to tell you for the past minute? She took me to the window which looked out on a kind of courtyard and signalled to the little genie in the hip hat and tennis shoes who was squatting down in the dirt doing something to a bicycle. He came over, she jabbered a few sentences at him, slipped him some of my loot and in no time the little guy had cycled off, copped and was back with the shit.

Now this chick who's been on a broom for months, wasted, probably having to steal what little dope she got, is so goddammed happy to have found a friend she's laughing and kidding around, hitting me on the arm, and I'm as happy as her. I've got it, found my source, we're like two kids racing across a meadow with bright balloons and she's getting the accessories out of a bureau drawer, being very careful with the amount of shit she's allotting me, doling the stuff on to a crushed cigarette package shaped to a tiny basin and adding water, she doesn't want to lose me, knows I'll be back, scared I might die in this goddamn place six thousand miles from Central Avenue. 'Aren't you going to cook it?' I ask. She doesn't know what I'm talking about. I'm thinking, How can this bitch have all those tracks and not even know how to cook it? No cookie in Japan, she finally gets across to me, just draw it up straight ahead and shoot. *Use more.* No-no-no, too strong. *Listen, do you think this is the first time I shot shit? I've been shooting shit from Watts to 130th Street* (letting her know what a bad cat I am), *come on, shake it out.* No-no, too much. *Will you listen to me, I'll shoot Unguentine, battery water, don't make no difference – it's my money, if I die, I die, fuck it, Fats Navarro went down, we ain't no super race* . . . Please-no, I like you. *I like you too, baby, but I want to get tore up!* We compromised, she shoot out a little more then squatted down in front of me, her kimono parting – not all that bad, I thought and made a mental note. One of these days I'm going to ball this bitch but for right now let's get high. She tied the tourniquet, looking at me, still fearful and I'm saying, *Bitch, will you please shoot this shit in my arm and stop bullshitting*. She stuck the needle in, jacked it off so the blood came in, shot it, and I'm about to say, 'This shit ain't nothin'.' I looked in those dark-ring almond eyes and said, 'This shit ain't . . . ' And it was all over. Over and out. After all that conniving and pleading, going through all those changes to get a fix. When I woke up, the whole family, Mama-san, Poppa-san who had come in, couple little kids, all the young fine chicks and my bitch were sitting around in a circle fanning me, saying, 'Yes . . . ah-so . . . ' Groovy.

Then and there I became the best damn ambassador for the United States. The American image over there at the time was soldiers balling Japanese daughters, buying beer, drop a kid a quarter for a shoeshine, four-star suckers walking around showing off the stars and stripes and generally trying to lead these Orientals into more affluent ways, right? But I came over with my black ass messed up – just off the boat, my first pass, I go out and make contact – and right away they understood me. Took me into the bosom of their family. See, American soldier fucked up too. That's what gets you across, opens the lines of communication.

The next day when I got my pass and started down the little road past the rice paddies with some pears and candy bars I'd bought, the word had already got around: 'Uma-san's coming.' (They didn't know how to say 'Hawes', it kept coming out 'Horse', so rather than offend me they hit on 'Uma-san', as 'Uma' is Japanese for horse.) 'Uma-san's coming.' Little kids on bicycles met me halfway. Mama-san greeted me at the door saying, 'Ah, ah-so, Uma-san.' I hugged her and said, 'Where's my woman?' She was in back getting prettied up, happily putting on her powder and lipstick. So I lay around the parlour sharing my pears and candy while Mama-san and Poppa-san brought in grapes and other goodies. Here was a house of prostitution and they were treating me like a son, like King Farouk. But you know when the sliding door opened and my queen came in, skinny as a stalk, her little sunken face snow white against ruby lips and dark eyes, I glanced past her down the hall and saw one of those fine sharp bitches I'd turned down yesterday. Damn if they didn't have her on the broom.

Raise Up Off Me (1972)

Hampton Hawes

Failing the Army Medical

THE PSYCHIATRIST had been looking through my papers. He leaned back in his chair, smiled again, and said, 'Mr Condon, I see that you drink. How often?'

'Every day,' I said.

'Why?' he asked.

'I work in a saloon,' I said. 'I'm a musician. My employer is a fellow named Nick. His place is in Greenwich Village and he sells whisky' – you've been there, I thought to myself; I can tell by the look in your eyes – 'and his customers drink. I can't stand the customers when they're drunk if I'm sober, so I drink too. It creates a mutual tolerance.'

He nodded. 'How many highballs do you drink every day?' he asked.

'I don't count the highballs,' I said. 'I occasionally check on the cases or barrels, but that's all.'

'Hold out your hand,' he said.

I stretched my right arm towards him, with the palm of my hand down and my fingers held together. Fairly steady, I thought! this isn't going to be so bad.

'Spread your fingers,' the psychiatrist said.

I did, and the dance was on. My hand shook like an electric washing-machine.

'You could stand a drink now, couldn't you?' he said.

'Doctor,' I said, 'I worked until four o'clock this morning. I haven't had a drink, I haven't had a smoke, I haven't had anything to eat since I came in here. There's a saloon called the Boar's Head at 47th Street and Lexington Avenue. When I get out of here I'm going into it so fast I won't even open the door; I'll tear it off the hinges.'

The psychiatrist smiled again. 'Don't forget Allan's,' he said. 'It's at 46th and Lexington.'

He bent over my papers and wrote a single line on the final sheet. Then he got up and put a hand on my shoulder.

'I'll take you to the orthopaedic room,' he said. 'After that you'll be through except for the classification officer.'

He folded my papers and handed them to me; then he led me past the double line of selectees and into the orthopaedic room.

'You'll be out of here in a few minutes,' he said. 'Don't worry, and have one for me.'

As soon as he had gone I looked to see what he had written on my papers. The single line was in a bold, clear hand:

This man needs a drink right now.

And he had signed it.

He was my guy, all right.

We Called It Music (1956)
Eddie Condon

How I Got Started on Drugs

I GOT hit by an ambulance in 1949. It was going about seventy miles an hour – it drug me for thirty feet. My leg was broken in eight places. My mother said that if it had broken in nine, it would have had to be amputated. I was given morphine and that's probably the first experience of euphoria I ever experienced. You know if you get hit by an ambulance, they're not going to let you just lay there and suffer – even if you are a ten-year-old kid. So if some of these rumours about me are true – about me being a drug addict – I didn't ask to be hit by that ambulance. It was an accident.

Sleeve note from
James Booker

A Strange Death

THERE WAS another guy named Sidney Vigne who was working out good with Tio, but he was killed under strange circumstances. It was on Christmas Eve and all the bands, when they finished work at night, would join up at a place called a 'boudoir'. This was during Prohibition and there would be a pool room downstairs in this place and upstairs they would have food and drinks and whatever. Well, all the guys would meet there after hours and play pool and yap. Whoever lost at pool would have to buy the drinks all around. They would all drink this stuff called 'Pink Lady' which was some kind of bathtub gin mixed with Grenadine. The bar would be lined up with bottles of this Pink Lady stuff by the time dawn came. Anyway, this guy was supposed to go to his mother's house for dinner on Christmas Day, but he kept dogs at this house. Maybe four or five of them. He was drunker than a hoot owl, but all that was on his mind was that he had to go home to feed his dogs before going to his mother's. His wife and kids were all over at his mother's house already when he left to go to the dogs. He got as far as Claiborne Street and was standing on the curb at the corner, waiting to cross, when along comes this big meat truck and one of the legs of a cow carcass was sticking out of the side. He didn't see it and it hooked alongside his head and threw him into the street in front of another truck. He was killed outright.

Somehow or other he had got hold of Albert Nicholas's union card, but that was the only thing he had on him besides his money. No identification at all. So when they took him to the morgue, they saw this card and figured that the guy was Nick. They took the address from the card and went right over to Albert's house. His wife came to the door and the cop told her, 'Are you Mrs Nicholas? Well, I hate to tell you this, but your husband was just killed. I'm sorry.'

'My husband's been killed! Well, it must have happened mighty quick because I just left him in the bed to answer the door to you.' And Nick was there snoring like hell.

With Louis and the Duke (1985)
Barney Bigard

Another Strange Death

OUR FIRST guitar player was a guy named Frank who came from around Fort Barrow, Louisiana. He worked on a dredge in the Mississippi River and he was a sleepwalker. One night he walked off the barge and they never found him. Our next guitar player was June Skinner who worked around the Plantation. He played mandolin too.

Pops Foster (1971)
Pops Foster

German Playwright in Death Plunge from Jazz Musician's Window

THEN HE told Sou a hair-raising story of a time nearly twenty years earlier when I'd called him at the Piccadilly Hotel in New York, where he was living, to ask him to book a room for the weekend for the refugee playwright, Ernst Toller. Toller had fled his native Austria after having been, for a brief period, through a freak of circumstances, the dictator of Bavaria. New York was full of conventions, and there was not a room to be found. I had been delegated by a mutual friend to secure housing for this man who had a hit show on Broadway at the time entitled *Reunion in Vienna*. It just happened that Muggsy was going to be out of town himself that weekend and he generously offered to let the author use his room. He'd warned me that the place might not be too neat, but he said he'd notify the desk clerk to give me the key.

I brought Toller to the Piccadilly, took him up to Muggsy's digs, and left. By the time I got down to the lobby in the elevator, Toller had made it a faster way – jumping the fourteen or so floors from Muggsy's window to the sidewalk below. I saw the mob in the street when I left the hotel, but never suspected that the playwright, whom I had just met that evening, had chosen that moment to end his life. I read about it in the papers the next morning.

Muggsy called me soon afterwards and said, 'Don't bring me any more of your friends.'

I Remember Jazz (1987)
Al Rose

The Tragic Death of Velma Middleton

IT WAS a pathetic thing in Africa. We were on tour, playing one day in one of those big fields. They didn't have a bandstand but had built a big high barrack, or whatever you want to call it: big, big steps going up real high. When her time came to go on she was sick, but she never complained to anyone, so up she came huffing and puffing. Nobody really paid much attention because it was so hot anyway out there. She did her numbers and I had to go to the bathroom but I couldn't find one anywhere. I was scared to go out into the field in back of the band because of the snakes. Anyhow this English guy was backstage and said to use his bathroom as his house was only three blocks from there. We got in his car real quick and as we were pulling out of the backstage area I heard this big commotion, like the tent covering was falling. I remember saying, 'Oh boy! One of the tent poles must have broken.' We went over to the guy's house and when we got back there was Velma, on the ground. There was a doctor with her who was sticking her legs. She didn't have any feeling, was glassy eyed and couldn't talk. She'd had a stroke. Right away they took her to this funny little hospital. They didn't have the facilities to treat someone like that. It was just a funny-type little town, see. I felt sure that they would bring out the fire engines if necessary, to bring her to some place where they could help her.

I'll never forgive Joe Glaser and Louis for that, because they said it would take too many people to lift her on to the plane to France. I said to myself, 'This woman gave her all, and they just leave her here, like that, in some little African town.' She died right there in Africa.

With Louis and the Duke (1985)

Barney Bigard

Premature Obituary

THE AFTERNOON we left Tokyo a crazy thing happened. A Japanese reporter rushed up to me in the airport terminal, said the BBC in London had just reported me killed in a car crash in Switzerland. I said,

Well you're about to see a ghost get on a plane for California. Four days after I got home the BBC phoned at five in the morning. I had checked out the local scene, saw no work in sight and was going to the unemployment office that day to start collecting on the Plain Dave's gig. They said, Is this Hampton Hawes? I said, Yeah, you woke me up. They said, We're trying to confirm your death last week in a motor accident outside Geneva. I said, I'm alive and broke in Los Angeles. Hung up and said to Jackie, Ain't that a bitch, a motherfucker got to die to get some publicity.

Raise Up Off Me (1972)
Hampton Hawes

A Very Premature Obituary

UNFORTUNATELY GAILLARD'S private life became a source of interest for the press and with drug stories and divorce in the air he left the west coast in November 1946 to become yet another entertainer pilloried by an unforgiving and hypocritical Society.

Nevertheless, he continued to make occasional records into the 1950s, and made sporadic appearances on both coasts. He even managed a motel in San Diego, and had a brief reunion with Slam Stewart at the 1970 Monterey Jazz Festival and was booked for a European Tour but could not be found on departure. He seems to be one of the last originals from that frenetic period in jazz when he danced on the edge between the boppers and the mainstreamers. Perhaps it was because he never really committed himself to jazz or entertainment that ultimately he was ignored by both and his career ended as seemingly tragically as do so many in this field.

Sleeve note from *McVouty, Slim and Bam*
Dieter Saleman

8

RACE

Jazz came from American blacks, and even today most of the innovations come from American blacks. Society being somewhat blinkered in its views, American blacks have never had their due credit. One can only imagine what it felt like to be Louis Armstrong in the 1920s and see Paul Whiteman, leader of a pretentious symphonic dance band, be dubbed 'The King of Jazz'. It cannot have been much more fun for Count Basie or Duke Ellington to watch Benny Goodman be crowned 'King of Swing' in the 1930s. At least the black jazz musician of the pre-war era had the comfort of a black audience, but nowadays, ironically, the majority of the audience for jazz is white, as black listeners have moved on to other kinds of music.

Musicians are less racist than most people, and many bands are mixed, yet jazz is still a home to prejudices. It is pro-black, pro-American, pro-heterosexual and pro-male (the rare incidence of homosexuals in jazz is astonishing). To come into jazz as a white, English, lesbian woman would be outrageously difficult, in other words. Yet this is exactly what Valerie Wilmer did, to become one of the best photographers *and* writers in jazz, though predictably she has always received less than her fair due.

Race is not often overtly commented on by musicians – only a Miles Davis would growl at interviewers that white men had no soul, no swing – but it is in the background of a lot of what they say. Occasionally it comes out into the open . . .

Louis Answers Back

ANOTHER TIME he was on a plane and a guy came up to him and said, 'Mr Armstrong. Do you remember me?' Louis must have been woken up by this character because he told him, 'All you white folks look alike to me.'

With Louis and the Duke (1985)
Barney Bigard

My First Sight of Segregation

ON THE ferry boat crossing Chesapeake Bay I was heading into the bathroom when the drummer, an older cat, grabbed my arm, turned me around and pointed me toward a sign in the far corner that said COLORED. Never seen one of those before. And an hour later when it was time for lunch we were told to go to the rear deck where there was an outside counter serving chilliburgers and pop. Had to eat standing up, spray whipping our faces, while looking into a big glass-enclosed room: white people spreading napkins in their laps, two different kinds of forks beside the plates and a little bowl of flowers on each table. I turned to the drummer and said, Man, there's some funny kind of shit going on down here.

Raise Up Off Me (1972)
Hampton Hawes

North v. South

SOMETIME IN the year 1929 I returned to Chicago to work at the Opera Club to work with Zez Confrey and His Orchestra. Since Zez's was not a jazz band I frequented all the places I could find that featured jazz music. One such was Kelly's Stables, where the Dodds brothers, Johnny the clarinettist, and Baby the drummer, had a trio. I can't recall the name of the pianist, I'm pretty certain he never became famous, but he was always impeccably dressed and wore diamond rings and a stickpin. Obviously the ladies fancied him because very few musicians could afford to wear diamonds. I had not seen Johnny and Baby since they'd played in the old King Oliver band in 1923.

I went backstage to say hello and they greeted me very warmly. They asked me about New York . . . were the black musicians treated well there? In return I asked them if they preferred working in Chicago to New Orleans . . . were they treated better in the north? Johnny looked at me for a moment and then said: 'Well, Bud, I'll tell you – in New Orleans a white man might slap you in the face, call you "nigger" and give you five dollars. Here they're nice to you but they don't give you anything.'

If You Know of a Better Life (1982)
Bud Freeman

My Neighbourhood

OUR NEIGHBOURHOOD at 35th and Budlong was a mixture of whites, blacks and Orientals with a few Mexicans around the edges. Negroes were niggers to both whites and themselves, and whites were peckerwood trash to Negroes and themselves. The Mexicans kept to themselves and ate tacos; the Negroes kept to themselves and ate collard greens. Both went to church out of fear and need, hoping the security and sophistication and sense of being part of the country would one day drift through the tall stained windows and warm them like the summer sun. The whites went to church for social and moral reasons; that's a big difference. But the minorities had one weapon, and that was language: if they wanted to turn you off, they just went into their native shit.

The Japanese mowed lawns and I don't know what else 'cause they were as mysterious to me as the Chinese who had laundries and grocery stores and sold dill pickles and big, fat glazed doughnuts to the black and Mexican kids. And the strange thing was, there was a peaceable mood in the country, a feeling of satisfaction and ease that people my age and older think of now as 'the good old days'.

. . . The 'good old days' when Franklin Roosevelt sat by a fire and talked to us through one of those funny little radios shaped like a birdhouse, when Stepin Fetchit and Rochester were it, and the day after my father moved into the neighbourhood at 35th and Budlong someone threw a rock through the window.

Raise Up Off Me (1972)

Hampton Hawes

Confusion at *down beat*

down beat WAS published in Chicago, and as their longtime London correspondent I paid a courtesy call to the office. I wanted, too, to use a typewriter for some stories to send back to England. Long-established, the magazine enjoyed a reputation as the world's leading publication on the music, so I was taken aback when I walked into a dingy office in a creaking old building with decor out of the 1930s. But the owner and publisher were friendly enough until the time came when they asked whom I intended to hear on my visit. I'd noticed that Gene Ammons, one of the grits 'n' greens saxophonists, was making a rare appearance at a place called Roberts. 'Roberts?' echoed the owner. 'Didn't that close down some time ago?' No, I told him, it was on 63rd Street. His face took on a strange, wary look. 'Er, it's . . . er . . . rather *Black* around there,' he ventured. 'I know,' I told him, 'I'm staying on the next block.' And I got one of those looks.

Mama Said There'd Be Days Like This (1989)

Val Wilmer

Andy Razaf Becomes White

FATS WALLER and Andy Razaf wrote 'Honeysuckle Rose' in 1928 for a revue at Connie's Inn. It only gained popularity much later, when it was highlighted in a film short of the same name. When Razaf saw the film he was incensed by its depiction of the song's creation. The screen version showed two white men writing the song while they were in jail. Waller felt that the film treatment was inconsequential and refused to join Razaf in a lawsuit. Razaf then wrote a letter to Louis B. Mayer, president of MGM, expressing his resentment and remarking that the film was an affront to Waller and himself as well as to all their race.

Mayer did not reply directly to Razaf, but wrote in *Variety* that the songwriters were 'poor sports', and should be 'proud to have had their song featured so prominently in a big Hollywood musical'. Razaf wondered 'how they would've placated Irving Berlin if they had presented a scene showing "Alexander's Ragtime Band" as being written by a coloured boy behind bars'.

Fats Waller (1980)
Maurice Waller

Colourless Pianist

WE WERE on an elevated stage. I noticed one couple that kept looking up at us while they were dancing. They danced up to the bandstand and the lady leaned forward and said to me, 'Pardon me, Mr Carter, but is your pianist white or black?' I looked over to Joe, turned to her and said, 'I don't know. I never asked him.' They seemed very surprised.

from the IJS Archive
Benny Carter

Red Rodney Turns Black

THE WEIRDEST road incident came about in 1950, when agent Billy Shaw arranged a southern tour for big money.

'You gotta get rid of that redheaded trumpet player; we can't have a white guy in a black band down south,' Shaw insisted. Bird said,

'No, I ain't gonna get rid of him, he's my man. Ain't you ever heard of an albino? Red's an albino.'

Shaw knew Red was Jewish – he'd heard him speak Yiddish to Parker, much to the delight of the saxophonist, who called Rodney 'Chood'. (Red was born Robert Chudnick.) Shaw raised hell. Bird said,

'Leave it to me.'

Red knew nothing of the conversation. When the band arrived at the first gig, Spiro's Beach in Maryland, he was surprised to see a sign reading, 'The King of Bebop Charlie Parker and his Orchestra featuring Albino Red, Blues Singer'. Bird said,

'You gotta sing the blues, Chood baby.'

'But I don't know any blues.'

'Sing 'em anyhow.'

He did. The other guys chanted behind him like a choir, and the audience loved it. In three weeks, nobody ever questioned the masquerade.

'They were very polite,' Red says.

Celebrating Bird (1990)
Gary Giddins

Safety in Islam i

FOR SOCIAL and religious reasons, a large number of modern jazz musicians did begin to turn toward Islam during the 1940s, a movement completely in line with the idea of freedom of religion. Rudy Powell, from Edgar Hayes's band, became one of the first jazz musicians I knew to accept Islam; he became an Ahmidyah Muslim. Other musicians followed, it seemed to me, for social rather than religious reasons, if you can separate the two.

'Man, if you join the Muslim faith, you ain't coloured no more, you'll be white,' they'd say. 'You get a new name and you don't have to be a nigger no more.' So everybody started joining because they considered it a big advantage not to be black during the time of segregation. When these cats found out that Idrees Sulieman, who joined the Muslim faith about that time, could go into these white restaurants and bring out sandwiches to the other guys because he wasn't coloured – and he looked like the inside of the chimney – they started enrolling in droves.

Musicians started having it printed on their police cards where it said 'race', 'W' for white. Kenny Clarke had one and he showed it to me. He said, 'See, nigger, I ain't no spook; I'm white. "W".' He changed his name to Arabic, Liaqat Ali Salaam. Another cat who had been my roommate at Laurinburg, Oliver Mesheux, got involved in an altercation about race down in Delaware. He went into this restaurant, and they said they didn't serve coloured in there. So he said, 'I don't blame you. But I don't have to go under the rules of coloured because my name is Mustafa Dalil.' Didn't ask him no more questions. 'How do you do?' the guy said.

Dizzy (1980)
Dizzy Gillespie

Safety in Islam ii

WE HAD a guy in the band named Rudy Powell. He changed his name to Musa Kalim. He wore fez and grew a little beard. They got into town after midnight and found everything closed. Having no way to locate the rooming houses that accepted black musicians, they decided to park the bus in front of the theatre and sit there until morning.

Rudy had a better idea. He walks into this white hotel, and the minute he hit the door, the man said, 'I'm very sorry, we're filled up.' Rudy says, 'Where's the manager?' The manager comes out and says, 'Well, it isn't the policy of this hotel to rent rooms to coloured.'

Rudy says, 'I'm not coloured.' He whips this card out, which says, 'My name is Musa Kalim, and I am a descendant of Father Abraham, and the mother, Hagar, and I'm entitled to all the rights and privileges of the Mystic Knights.' He's wearing this fez.

He says, 'Call the State Department in Washington. I want to speak to someone in the State Department right now.' The man got scared to death. 'I'm very sorry, sir,' he says. 'We'll get you a room.'

Rudy says, 'I've got nine of my brothers out in the bus there, and they don't speak English. I've got to have room for the nine.' So the guy claps his hands, says to the bellhop, 'Get this gentleman nine rooms.' And it's Jonah Jones, Shad Collins, Kansas Fields, nine of the guys in the band. Rudy got up the next morning and collected the money from all the guys and paid the bill and walked out. Since then, change, integration started. He's back to Rudy Powell again now.

from the IJS Archive
Milt Hinton

The Black Professor

IN THE early days, a jazz musician who could read music was usually called 'Professor'. Written notes were viewed with suspicion by the unschooled and were considered to be devoid of soul. But men like Eubie Blake could read and write music very well. He said: 'In those days Negro musicians weren't even supposed to read music. We had to pretend we couldn't read; then they'd marvel at the way we could play shows, thinking we'd learned the parts by ear.'

Jazz Anecdotes (1990)
Bill Crow

From Brown to Black

TOWARD THE end of the Los Angeles run of *Jump for Joy*, in which I played a featured role, John Garfield was brought in to groom the show for Broadway. The whole cast was introduced to Mr Garfield and told he was going to make a lot of changes.

I was thrilled to meet him; he was a big movie star and I had heard he was a great liberal. He introduced himself to me and said, 'Mr Jeffries, as we all know, this is an all-Negro show, and the contrast between you and the other members of the cast is so great that I think it would be better for you to wear some dark make-up.'

Well, I said OK, and the next night the make-up man plastered me with all this dark Egyptian make-up.

Duke Ellington had written the music and he and his whole band were in the pit playing the show. So I walked out to do my feature number with Dorothy Dandridge, 'If Life Were All Peaches and Cream', and I saw him look up at me. I kept feeling him staring a hole through me, and by this time I had forgotten that I had the make-up on and kept wondering what was wrong.

At the first intermission he came striding backstage, and he was mortified. He was furious.

'What in God's name are you trying to do?' he said. 'Who do you think you are – Al Jolson?'

Well, as they say, this story has no moral, this story has no end – except, I guess that even with my dark make-up we never did get to Broadway with *Jump for Joy*.

Laughter from the Hip (1963)
Herb Jeffries

Blacker Than Thou

LENA HORNE was appearing at the Liverpool Empire and invited Lonnie Johnson to visit her after he had finished his show. I honestly can't recall if I was invited – I think I was – but three members of the Merseysippi Jazz Band (who had been booked to appear with Lonnie until the MU decreed otherwise) came along at my invitation and four utter strangers presented themselves at Miss Horne's apartment. It was an awful bit of cheek on my part but we were cordially greeted by her husband and musical director, Lennie Hayton.

Hayton had played on records with cornettist Bix Beiderbecke and he came in for some lengthy questioning about Bix and these recordings. He took the eager questioning in good humour but dryly remarked that as we appeared to know more about the records than he did himself, perhaps we could leave it at that.

Lena Horne entered the room. She had a striking beauty, with eyes of quite hypnotic luminosity. She looked so gorgeous that we were spellbound and practically speechless. We forgot about Bix Beiderbecke. She soon excused herself but not before Lonnie had respectfully addressed her as 'Missie Horne'. Lonnie, a coloured man born in New Orleans before the turn of the century, grew up at a time when race barriers were very marked. Lena Horne was an international star, lighter skinned and, being much younger, had pronounced and well-publicized views on racial inequality. The difference between these two of the same race, although neither pure Negro, was quite striking and crystallized in Lonnie's deferential address.

All This and Many a Dog (1986)

Jim Godbolt

Black Heritage

ELEMENTALS

ANYBODY KNOW who 'Tricky' Sam Nanton was? Anybody know who 'Fats' Navarro was? Anybody know who Bud Powell was? Anybody know who 'Bird' was? And the Questions roll on. A cultural quiz? A Black musician's version of the $64 question? More like a cultural indictment of Black students; people new to Blackness; people new to the world; a people still hung off in the intestines of radium clouds or looking for a country with a gun; still sucking a poisonous juice from the mildewed breast of someone else's mama.

It's a sad commentary on the consciousness of Black students and Black people, being perpetrated in the midst of the Black realization-revolution, when these same groups of people have the (unconscious) unmitigated gall to produce and display cheshire cat grins in recognition of the Brubecks, Mulligans, Getzes, Desmonds and other johnny-come-lately non-innovative (well-to-do) white jazz musicians; at the same time, in the same instance, casting blank stares upon the likes of Fletcher Henderson, Louis Armstrong, Count Basie, Duke Ellington, Lester Young, Lady Day, Charlie Parker, 'Fats' Navarro, etc. Can one believe that there are eons of Black people (and/or negroes) who actually give credence to the image of exactly what Louis Armstrong isn't; a grinning coon who appears on TV specials three or four times a year; that there are Black kids who really believe 'Hello Dolly' has something to do, organically, with Louis and themselves; who believe that Duke Ellington is JUST a bandleader; think that 'Dizzy' Gillespie is a clown who just HAPPENS to play trumpet; think that John Coltrane was an exotic saxophonist who ate health food and delved into eastern religious-wisdom disciplines; don't know who Ornette Coleman is; never heard of Black Arthur, John Gilmore, Andrew Hill, Cecil Taylor or even the inimitable Sun Ra!

Sleeve note from *Ain't No Ambulances* . . .
Stanley Crouch

Blackness

GRADUALLY IT led me to realize that there *was* no such thing as 'the Black experience', some imaginary homogeneous state of mind. To suggest so, indeed, was a racist simplification, as I once learned to my own everlasting shame. In 1968 I'd reviewed a Supremes show for *down beat* and taken them to task for not sounding more 'soulful'. 'Get back to church, baby!' I'd castigated Diana Ross – so hip and so clever, I'd thought at the time. But my heart pounded when I stumbled on those words twenty years later in the autobiography of her fellow Supreme, Mary Wilson, and read of their hurt and dismay. How ignorant I had been in my 'hipness', and how intolerant of the expression of humanity in all its beautiful disguises. But I had to move with the Sharrocks and their doo-wop pals to learn this, with Larry Johnson and his waking-up gospel. The lesson was well learned in the end but it didn't come easy.

Mama Said There'd Be Days Like This (1989)
Val Wilmer

Blacks Against Blacks

BUT I'LL tell you, the most prejudiced, jivest, complex, untogether race in the world is blacks. There are so many divisions, so many gradations of colour, that's why it's taken us so long to get anywhere; all those years black, brown, high yeller shovin' each other to get closer to the front of the bus. Survival. My best friend married into a light-skinned family and got nervous. If you saw the bitch's father there's no way in the world you'd think he was Negro, that sucker looks like one of them crackers down there in Georgia raisin' persimmons. When my friend's mother-in-law-to-be saw a picture of *his* mother who is darker than him and beautiful, she phoned up to say she didn't think the marriage would be appropriate. *Appropriate* was the word she used. Survival. Mm-hmm.

Jimmy Rushing, the great blues singer who was singing with Count Basie's band when I was doing things to Ann Sheridan in my dreams and reading Batman comics, hired me a couple of years ago to back him on a gig in San Francisco. We were out of different eras, thirty years apart, and he had never heard me play. Was sceptical of me because he knew I'd been born and bred in Southern California. But you know after he heard me take my first chorus of blues he said, 'Son, you may o' been brought up in LA, but you had to have eaten black-eyed peas in Mississippi somewhere along the line.' What he was doing was the same thing the ofays did. So those inbred prejudices stick like flies in molasses.

The thing the black cats do, the mistake they make is to try to use their skin to say they're cool. Same as cats strutting out with saxophone straps around their necks to look hip so they can score with chicks, reap the fringe benefits. The time I flew to Albuquerque to meet Jackie I sat beside a sucker in silk vines from Georgia. Feeling a draught, you understand. Chill. Daggers. Probably owned a restaurant where he would've poured syrup down my shirt front and then thrown me out of. A hundred miles out of Phoenix we hit an electrical storm, the plane turned sideways, the stewardess fell down, all the shit fell off the shelves, and people started screaming. The sucker turned and said, 'Rough, ain't it?' I said, 'You right.' He say, 'You wanna play some tic-tac-toe?' I say, 'I play any damn thing.' For that one minute *what happened to Georgia, man? What happened to*

me, to him? When the commotion and disturbance had died down
a bit he said, 'You want me to buy you a drink?' I said, 'No, it's
cool.'

Raise Up Off Me (1972)
Hampton Hawes

Blacks Against Blacks ii

THE WHITE and coloured musicians around New Orleans all knew
each other and there wasn't any Jim Crow between them. They really
didn't much care what colour you were, and I played with a lot of
them around New Orleans.

The worst Jim Crow around New Orleans was what the coloured
did to themselves. The uptown clubs and societies were the strictest.
You had to be a doctor or a lawyer or some kind of big shot to get in.
The lighter you were the better they thought you were. The Francs
Amis Hall was like that. That place was so dicty they wouldn't let us
come off the bandstand because we were too dark. They would let the
lightest guy in the band go downstairs and get drinks for all of us.
They hired one guy they called Foster who entertained them all the
time. He was as black as the ace of spades, and he was very smart and
spoke eight different languages. When he finished entertaining he had
to go into a little room and stay there. Some of the societies were so
bad they wouldn't even let black people go in. There was a coloured
church in town that had seating by colour. The lightest ones down in
front and darker and darker as you went back. There was a place over
in Biloxi, Mississippi, where they had albinos. They had white kinky
hair and couldn't see good during the day. We used to play dances for
them, but they wouldn't let you into the dance unless you were an
albino. The Negro race has always been crazy. They're the most
mixed-up race of people you ever saw. You get every colour in the
Negro race, the skin is different, the eyes, the hair is different colour
and kinky or not so kinky.

In Washington, DC, way late I was playing a dance for the coloured
mint workers and the coloured mail carriers. The mint workers were

lighter than the mail carriers. They had themselves roped off and wouldn't allow the carriers on their side. We moved the whole band over to the mail carriers' side and told them this was our kind of people over here. That was the only dance I ever played where the coloured people came on time. Usually coloured don't show up at a dance until eleven or twelve and the band starts at eight or nine. You've played your brains out by the time anyone gets there. That's why by the time the people show up the guys are all drunked up sometimes. The coloured usually stay until three or four in the morning.

Pops Foster, (1971)

Pops Foster

Louis Armstrong and the Darkie Problem

YOU SEE, when we made movies you never knew what Louis would do. He would do practically anything and get away with it. He was recording a thing with Bing Crosby one time for a movie. They were going to do 'Sleepy Time Down South', and it had the word 'darkies' in the lyric. The man in charge didn't want that in there so they changed the word from 'darkies' to 'folks' and did the whole thing over. Louis was so 'teed off' at having to keep re-recording, that finally when the end of the day came, and it still wasn't 'in the can', he told them he wouldn't come back the next day. Of course he did come, but he walked straight up to Bing and said, 'What do you want me to call those black sons-of-bitches this morning?'

With Louis and the Duke (1985)

Barney Bigard

Race in New Orleans

THE MUSIC we have come to call Dixieland made its debut north of the Mason–Dixon line under the leadership of Tom Brown, born in New Orleans on 3 June 1888. He and his Band from Dixieland made their bow at Lamb's Café in Chicago in 1915, and that started it all. Tom played a thoroughly satisfying trombone, and his influence on succeeding sliphorn players was universal. He was not merely an innovator but a protean performer capable of filling every ensemble hole, in and out of his register.

He was also as thorough a bigot as the sunny South ever produced. He provided leadership to a tiny group of peanut-brained musicians, many of whom, I must say in fairness, were among the greatest jazzmen New Orleans ever produced. But this crack-brained coterie effectively kept black and white musicians in the Crescent City from playing together for two generations. Not that there weren't some outstanding white jazzmen, like Johnny Wiggs and Armand Hug, who had no prejudice. Nevertheless some of them refrained from performing with black musicians for fear of being blacklisted by their colleagues. Raymond Burke, Harry Shields, and Boojie Centobie, a trio of super clarinettists, were indifferent personally to the colour line; but except for recording sessions, they refused to work mixed band jobs for me, though Raymond never objected to sitting in informally with black musicians.

I Remember Jazz (1987)
Al Rose

White, Black and Japanese

I STARTED hanging out at the Harlem Club which was run by Ray Bass, an American brother, and Toshiko and I became tight, grooving and playing for each other. She was a big star in Japan at the time; if gospel had been as big as jazz, she would have been Sister Rosetta Tharpe or Aretha Franklin. At first I thought she was only hanging out with me to talk about Bud, to be close to the source. I had recorded, was getting known in the States, and if I wasn't Bud Powell I was maybe two or three grooves removed from him which was the closest she was going to get. What she probably didn't realize was how good she played, so she didn't really need me in that respect. Later on she made it on her own in the States. Anyway I soon discovered she dug me for myself and we developed a lasting friendship. The American consulate arranged for us to play a concert together and the response was so good they contacted the army to see about sending us on tour – Toshiko in her kimono, me in my slick American uniform – figuring it might help improve relations between the two countries which were touchy at the time with the occupation still on. But somebody squashed the idea, probably one of those cracker Texas colonels; which shows you how thin the knife edges are in life. If the scales had tipped a little bit to the left I might have got myself cleaned up and come back a hero, picture on the cover of *Jet* and *Newsweek* (*Soldier singlehandedly cements Orient ties*), instead of as a miserable strung-out prisoner. Might still be in the service today, two stars on my shoulder and going for more, standing on some air base tarmac, tall and proud, razor creases on my pants, raft of ribbons gleaming on my chest, welcoming the POWs back.

Raise Up Off Me (1972)
Hampton Hawes

Black and White Musicians in the Black and White Films

WELL, THAT'S absolutely true. They wouldn't be able to sell it below the Mason–Dixon line. Jack Warner didn't really want to go through with the project when he saw that everyone was black but me. He spoke to Norman Granz about it and asked why he didn't just get a black guitarist. He felt it would be much simpler to do it that way. Norman said no, because the people that were here are not here because they are black or white, they're here because they are the people he (Norman) wanted. They kicked it around for a while, trying to find a solution and finally the solution was that I was in the shadows. It kind of inferred, pictorially, that I might be black.

When they did a close-up of me they did stain my hands with berry juice. Now that might seem far fetched, but this was in 1944 before the civil rights movement and at that time it didn't seem too far out. It was a time, whether you liked it or not, it seemed like that was the thing to do. That was the way it was.

I saw one of the stills and it showed Lester Young and myself sitting there on the soundstage. Now, Lester was a very light complexioned black and he is sitting there with the lights on him and I'm sitting next to him, kind of in the shadows. When I saw this still I turned around to these other black musicians, showed them this picture and I said to them laughingly, 'What's he doing sitting here with us?' He looked much lighter than I did.

Cadence
Barney Kessel

Black America and White Europe

ONE NIGHT Jean Louis Ginibre brought the French pianist and composer Martial Solal into the Cameleon. I had heard Martial's records; his fire and technique and imagination were so heavy he was considered the Art Tatum of France. The only difference was he couldn't get a gig in his hometown, while the American expatriate musicians were jamming those clubs! Martial's sin was that he had become 'local' and was taken for granted in Paris like I was in LA, had to leave the country or go to a town like Nice to get a gig. Jean Louis suggested we record together. I told him there should be a statue of this motherfucker on the Champs Elysées, he can play like six piano players, he doesn't need me. But Martial said, Hamp, we both hit the door and it didn't bust. Let's hit it together and maybe it will give. We rehearsed for a week, grooved together, and cut an album backed by Kenny Clarke on drums and a French bass player. Jean Louis was so excited over the results he had his wife Simone book us as a two-piano trio on a string of concerts in France, Belgium and Italy. It was a beautiful time.

I could understand why so many musicians who had come over here had never gone back, but I wondered how happy they were. When I met brothers I'd known in the States the first thing they said was, 'They built a new freeway, huh?' . . . 'Shelly's still going?' 'What happenin' on Central?' In Amsterdam I saw Don Byas, one of the greatest tenor players in the world; motherfucker's roots go so deep if saxophones were trees he'd be a redwood. He'd been living over there so long he started talking to me in French, then German; when he finally switched to English I still couldn't understand him. I thought, What are beautiful cats like this doing in European capitals? They should be back blowing at Shelly's and the Half Note close to the source where the music was changing and evolving – things happening that might not reach Europe for years. If they stayed over here much longer they were in danger of becoming local like Martial Solal. No need to travel 8000 miles for that. Shit, if I'm going to be local, let me be local at 35th and Budlong where I was born and raised. Sure, blacks are treated better in Europe, but that could be because the Europeans haven't become indoctrinated yet, haven't had us on their backs and consciences for two hundred years. Maybe half the people are treating us nice because we're American so we must have a lot of bread to spend, and the other half because we're *black* Americans and they want to be hip, dissociate themselves from the peckerwoods back home. Well, if that's the case, I don't need that kind of life just so I can work more often, drive on the left side of the road and walk free down a boulevard with a blonde bitch on my arm. I'd rather face the shit at home – at least most of that is sincere.

Raise Up Off Me (1972)

Hampton Hawes

The Race of Jazz Musicians

A s A teenager I liked to say that my race was jazz musician. It was a master race. We were pacifists, outlaws, anarchists. Other people said: 'All politicians are crom the beginning of time were crooked, then there is no crooked.'

This probably explains my admiration for such wrecks as Allen Eager and Squirms. I admired them for the same reason a poor Italian kid, perfectly law-respecting, might have admired Al Capone. I admired their honesty. I, on the other hand, was trying to please all the people I did not respect but feared. I was living like an assimilated Indian, dressing like the white man. I was in the closet. A part of me was ashamed of my race, or frightened of what wrath belonging to that race might bring down on me.

There is room for many tribes within a race, I told myself. We are all family nevertheless. Not all jazz musicians had to be outlaws, and few of them are any more. It was an overly-romantic, unrealistic definition anyway. It has become a myth – like Mexican bandits or Far-West gunfighters. Take Don Ellis. He practised every afternoon in hotel rooms, he neither drank nor smoked anything. Everybody fought to get into the car he drove because he was serious and reliable. There is need for serious and reliable relatives. We would joke: 'Don may be a bore but he's a bitch of a driver.' That may sound like we were making fun of someone who was unlike us, or the way we preferred to see ourselves, but he was still family. Don once typed out a series of exercises for his avant-garde rehearsal band. One of them instructed the musicians to do the opposite of what the conductor indicated. If he requested a slow tempo we played fast, if he indicated piano we played loud, and so on. When Don thought it was time to go to the next exercise, he cut the band off. Obviously we continued to play. He laughed the first time but when he cut us off again, we still continued playing. He lost his already small sense of humour and stomped out of the rehearsal.

My race, my tribe: jazz musicians. Like the Welsh in Britain, the Bretons in France and American Mohawks, we have been assimilated. The assimilation went both ways. *Time* magazine picked up our language, advertising executives began using our drugs. On the other hand we began to be career-motivated, we wanted shiny machines like anyone else. We began to compromise to get them. But still I have more in common with a Russian jazz musician than with an American banker.

In my experience cliques in integrated bands are rarely divided by race. The drinkers stay with the drinkers, the pinochle-players with the pinochle-players and so on. To this extent, the State Department tours were presenting an accurate view of American society. Miles Davis hired Bill Evans, Duke Ellington hired Louis Bellson, Benny Goodman hired Teddy Wilson. Of course there are racists everywhere, but rare, I think, in jazz. We are all of the same race.

Close Enough for Jazz (1983)

Mike Zwerin

Blues: a View from Scotland

AS A teenager in Edinburgh I listened avidly with other young enthusiasts to recordings of the great blues artists: Leroy Carr, Kokomo Arnold, Roosevelt Sykes, Sonny Boy Williamson and a host of others. We understood some of the sexual imagery that formed the largest part of their blues repertoire, but could feel no involvement beyond a musical one in such an alien world. The best a successful Don Juan in our camp could hope for, far from being 'eagle rocked till his face turned cherry red', was to be granted a quick fumble round one of proud Miss Jean Brodie's charges on the Carlton Hill after dark. Whether the bigger misapprehension was that sexual appetites and gratifications aren't pretty evenly spread or that blues are mostly about sex because that's what blacks are mostly about, I don't know. It never occurred to us that sexual censorship was simply easier to buck than anything that was really bugging blacks.

In the 1960s pop's incursion into blues imposed a more stringent censorship, which it brought in from the mass media it depended on. Traces of voodoo, gambling, drugs and sex were permitted only if thoroughly disguised – and camouflage was becoming increasingly difficult. With hallucinogenic banana-skins and LSD about, you don't need much acumen to divine the 'hidden' meaning of 'Mellow Yellow' or 'Sugartown'. At the same time blacks could be more explicit about the consequences of their continuing oppression by whites. All this probably means the end of blues poetry as we know it: I wish it also meant a step in the direction of real emancipation.

The McJazz Manuscripts (1979)
Sandy Brown

White Writing on Black Music

THE HISTORY of white writing on jazz has been filled with misunderstanding and misapprehension. In general, writers considered only those people they had met, mostly musicians. They saw the individual as an 'oddity', evaluating their behaviour against a string of white norms, rather than as a 'type' from within their own culture. Saxophonist Lester Young was a prime example of that, misjudged by white writers to whom he was not anxious to speak, who built up a picture of someone unrecognizable to his everyday companions. A British magazine suggested Louis Armstrong was still a 'country boy' when he turned up in Chicago in the 1920s in a straw hat. Another musician responded immediately to say such assumptions were dangerous. Straw hats, he pointed out, were the 'in' style of the day; Louis was expressing himself as a modish sophisticate.

Few Whites emerge from short contact with Black society with other than superficial burns. Whether there for the music or other sensual attractions, the pervading mood is consumerist. There's an inability to come to terms with anything that fails to fit preconceptions, even if it was that 'outsider' quality of the art that made it attractive in the first instance. An enormous gulf separates those white people who have 'participated' in the 'Black experience' by living and moving with Black people, and those who remain fixed in their own community's spirit and beliefs. Commitment to an alternative way of seeing means a move to another psychological dimension of the cultural self.

Being involved on a one-to-one basis with so many people of colour, I think I escaped sentimentalizing or romanticizing individual and collective needs and demands. As a result, I became out of step with many other Whites I knew. I'd meet other white people who had just had a brush with colour in some shape or form and they'd expect an echo of recognition because of the knowledge they imagined we shared. I couldn't see it that way. I'd think of Stevie and me, and other friends in interracial relationships. We cared for and loved our partners and worked hard to learn from them about their situation. Those others, white women who tell of encounters with 'studs' rather than people, white men with a stable of black starlets to put on parade, they were collectors, the paraders of prized possessions. And there was a history to that.

Among even the most open-minded of Whites, men and women, I've found an unfailing tendency to disbelieve the extent of racism. The psychological dislocation it can create stays unknown. Feeling themselves to be blameless as individuals they can see no need to take on board situations created by 'others'. Tell them that if they're not part of the solution, they're part of the problem and they grow uneasy. Tell them that they, too, are racist because they benefit from an unjust and unequal society, and they go off into paroxysms of protest. Such people cannot conceive that there are others who have challenged themselves and come to terms with the realization that they are participants in the system, that there are some of us who have been torn apart by that realization, that there are those among us who have endeavoured to do whatever we can to change the status quo.

Mama Said There'd Be Days Like This (1989)

Val Wilmer

9

THE LEADERS

I used to be the spare bass player for a band in London, led by an extrovert saxophonist. One night there was a spare pianist as well, who had never played with the group before and, after he had studied the playing of our leader during the first half, he said to me during the interval: 'Isn't it extraordinary how the leader of the group is almost invariably the worst player in it?'

True or not – and it often is – the remark was significant as an expression of deep-seated lack of reverence for one's leader. Jazz is an anti-authoritarian music, yet jazz musicians have to have a leader, if they are not to disintegrate or become an agonized collective. The only way out of this paradox is to have a leader whom you can follow with a total lack of respect and reverence.

Bandleaders: the View from Below

BANDLEADERS ARE right bastards. They steal money from their employees than whom they are very much less talented. They insist on playing repetitious and boring numbers. They hire transport you wouldn't put coal in. But their worst feature is the evil and humiliating use of lies in giving personnel the sack. The classic procedure is as follows. Imagine a cheery Christmassy scene, snow on the ground, all sounds hushed. It's four AM so there's not a great deal going on. Noiselessly a Ford Thames van rounds a nearby corner and stops, windscreen wipers rearranging snow on the glass. A door opens and a figure staggers out blinking. Crump crump of neoprene soles on snow. He is holding an instrument case. 'See you, Dave,' a voice calls from inside the wagon, 'half five at Finchley Road: it's Barnet tomorrow.' Dave weaves unsteadily off. 'See you.' In the morning it seems that things could be worse. At eleven, when Dave wakes, most of the snow has gone and the sun is shining. Good time to get into the Two Brewers: have a few pints with Johnny Kendall, Ray Bolden and the Dobells lot (Doug Dobell has specialized in jazz records in the Charing Cross Road for twenty years). Hullo: a few letters. Two income taxes for Bill who left this address three years ago. Open the other one:

> Dear Dave, Thank you for playing in the band for two years. As a result of a change in musical policy – nothing personal – it has been decided to dispense with your services as from last night. In recognition of your services in the past it has been decided to give you a bonus of £5. As you know you had a sub of £5 on Tuesday, so that makes us even up to date. Thanks again and good luck, Dave.

Almost like a ritual Mafia killing. This victim should be replete with wine and good food before having his brains blown out. 'See you, Dave. 5.30 at Finchley Road.' That method of firing was used a lot, but bandleaders had a lot to put up with. Musicians' habits are so tiresome. They get pissed, take heroin, are extremely vague or inordinately precise – or both vague and precise like Tony Coe. In general they behave badly. Harry Brown, a trombone player, who had been known to raise a glass, worked for Laurie Gold – one bandleader who *didn't* adopt the scurrilous firing methods endemic in the profession. One night Harry turned up so pissed he had to be helped on with his white band uniform jacket. During the first number he rocked backward and forward on his heels but had difficulty in raising his trombone to his lips. It might have helped if he had used his sighting faculties to get the distance of the mouthpiece right, but these were unavailable: unfocused eyes stared out over an undulating sea of dancers. Occasionally a low rasping noise would indicate that momentary contact had been made. Laurie led him off the stage. 'Better have a seat, Harry,' he said. As he returned to play with the depleted band a zombie in a white band coat followed him unsteadily on. Laurie led Harry off again. Same thing. Eventually Laurie took him off and said, 'Harry, you're fired.' As he walked back on stage he was relieved to find Harry wasn't following. Five minutes later a drunk in a white band jacket loomed through the dancers and came to rest directly in front of the bandstand. Harry rocked to and fro in this position staring gloomily at a now thoroughly unnerved Laurie for the rest of the evening.

Next morning Harry phoned Laurie up. He'd inadvertently invented a tongue-twister: 'Does this dismissal still stand?' Laurie was nonplussed.

The McJazz Manuscripts (1979)
Sandy Brown

The Cruelty of Ken Colyer

KEN COLYER blew his last bum note some years ago; I believe the fags got him. He never accepted the normal MU break pattern, but would stop for a third of a fag after each two numbers. He and his band, with no announcement, would have a few puffs, stub out their 'dimps' then carry on. One fag would last for three breaks, typical Colyer ensemble work – all the band smoked, none openly looked at the leader to see when it was time to continue. It was as ingrained as the 'foot-pattern' of the five blind boys.

Colyer was a rottweiler of a man who had a pekinese of a bassist. On one visit to the club, I noticed with surprise a new bass player and asked one of the band what had happened. Looking to see that Ken was out of earshot, he told the tale.

The band were due to be on the bus and away at 7.00 PM. The drummer came haring around the corner, thirty yards away, but was a few seconds late, so Ken gave the order to drive off, complete with drumkit, but minus drummer.

They played the gig, but with poor results. Eventually the bassist offered to play drums instead. Colyer considered this, and growled, 'OK, but no doubling fee.'

At the end of the evening, Colyer turned to him and barked, 'You're sacked!'

The staggered bassist, who'd been with him for years, asked 'Why?'

'Because I didn't know you were such a fucking awful drummer!'

from a letter to Miles Kington

David Fuller

My Entire Career as a Bandleader

I'D ALSO, in that intervening year, tasted blood as a bandleader. I didn't taste much, and it didn't taste good. The band had decided to release me to the public as the leader of a band-within-a-band. The concept followed that of Bob Crosby's Bobcats, Woody Herman's Woodchoppers, Tommy Dorsey's Clambake Seven and the Benny Goodman Sextet; all the big bands had one. But not many four-piece bands did. The Harmonaires, or whatever the quartet called itself, was possibly unique in the audacity by which it transformed itself before the audience's very eyes, into Roy Fisher and his Students of Jazz. This was done simply by removing Auntie Ivy from the piano stool and substituting me, looking suitably studious behind my glasses, and with a black bow in place of my school tie. It all happened as part of the works dance and beano of the drummer's family factory; and I was released from the protection of my family for the evening in the care of Horseface, whose craggy manner and frequent loud protestations made it clear, even to my mother, that he did not Go With Girls. So off we went from the factory gates one autumn evening in a string of coaches to a strange public spot about thirty miles away which I didn't know at all. The Nautical William was one of those Thirties Art-Deco buildings, white, with bevelled corners; it just seemed to have materialized out of the dark, for one night and, not knowing where it was, I never expected to see it again. But driving down the road from Bridgnorth to Kidderminster not long ago, I spotted it; aged a bit, but still having its own strange name, and not, so far at least, retitled 'Naughtys' – or maybe 'Willies'. Or both.

It was quite a heady evening out. My mother didn't go to works beanos, or she would have known that the scenes among which Horseface habitually passed unscathed were even more appalling than Going With Girls; amounting at times even to what would have to be called Going With Grown Women. I'd lived with unblinking eyes through the VE Night party in our street, and I knew I could take it. There was a cabaret, with heavily painted ladies, and a blue comedian in a cream tuxedo; there was dancing, and there was drinking. Our bit, when it came, was quite painless. The Students of Jazz played their unimaginable version of 'Honeysuckle Rose', as heard on record; I played a solo version of Meade Lux Lewis's 'Bear Cat Crawl', but cut it short because I couldn't hear myself for the din of people chattering. Then the Students of Jazz reassembled for their last number ever: 'Big Noise from Winnetka', a piece popular at the time, and consisting only of a simple workout for bass, drums and whistling through the teeth. We had no bass; trumpet, clarinet and piano played the whistling bit; and the drummer went on and on, and up and up. Kazam, Pow, Splat. The End. He was Head of the Drawing Office as well as the boss's son; it went down very well. Somebody gave me a pound note, and I gave up bandleading.

Five Radio Talks (1970)

Roy Fisher

Getting Fats Waller to the Studio

MR ADAMS had a moustache and a problem. The problem was Fats Waller, my favourite piano player. The Southern Music Company had an interest and an investment in Fats; Fats, who was having alimony trouble, had become indifferent to his Victor recording dates – he didn't get what he earned so he didn't care. Either he didn't keep the appointments or he arrived with a band which was unrehearsed. The Southern Music Company was disturbed, Mr Adams said. It had advanced Fats some money.

'Mr Peer has recommended you as a reliable and enterprising young man,' he went on. 'We would like you to undertake the task of finding

Waller and delivering him to the studio on time and with a well-rehearsed band.'

It sounded difficult. I hadn't yet met Waller; why should he let me discipline him for the sake of the Southern Music Company?

'We'll pay you seventy-five dollars if you can do it,' Mr Adams said.

At the moment I would have attempted to produce Herbert Hoover in a soft collar.

'I'll try,' I said.

'Fine,' Mr Adams said. 'We know where you can locate Waller. He's at Connie's Inn in Harlem rehearsing a new floor show. You can find him there this afternoon. The date is four days from now; that will give you time to assemble a band and rehearse it.'

I waited for a pause in the rehearsal; then I introduced myself to Fats. 'Earl Hines told me to look you up,' I explained.

'Ol' Earl?' Fats said. 'Well, that's fine. How's ol' Earl? I'm so glad to hear about him. Sit down and let me get a little gin for you. We'll have a talk about Earl.'

He was so amiable, so agreeable, so good-natured, that I felt almost ashamed of my mission; but I performed it. I asked Fats about making a record? A recording date? He'd be delighted, he'd be proud; just any time. In four days? Fine. At Liederkranz Hall? Wonderful. At noon? Perfect.

I telephoned Mr Adams.

'Very good,' he said. 'We shall expect you at noon on Friday. You had better stay close to Waller.'

I did, but every time I opened my mouth to say something about getting the band together or discussing the numbers to be played, Fats said, 'Fine! Wonderful! Perfect!' and handed me another belt of gin. We were in perfect accord on everything. Nothing happened.

At the end of the first day I was not overly worried except in the matter of my capacity for gin. Obviously it was suicide to match Fats drink for drink. I began to duck and sidestep. All during the second day and the second night I kept trying. 'Fine! Wonderful! Perfect!' Fats said whenever I mentioned the recording date. 'Now, let's have a little gin and talk about it.' The third day I was desperate; as night came on I kept talking and Fats kept handing me drinks. There was still no band. 'After we get the band together what shall we play?' I asked. 'Why, we'll play music,' Fats said. 'Now, let's have a little drink and talk about it.'

Things grew faint and finally dark. When I awoke I was lying on the wall cushions at Connie's Inn, fully dressed. It was half-past ten in the morning. On another cushion Fats was curled up, also fully dressed, asleep. I staggered over to him. He opened his eyes and smiled.

'It's half-past ten,' I croaked. 'We're due at the studio at noon.'

He sat up, stretched, and yawned.

'That's fine! That's wonderful! That's perfect!' he said. 'Now, we've got to see about that band. Look around for some nickels so I can make that telephone go.'

He went to the phone booth and made three calls. By the time we finished washing and straightening our clothes three musicians had arrived: Charlie Gaines, a trumpet player; Charlie Irvis, a trombonist; and Arville Harris, who played clarinet and alto saxophone.

'What are you going to play?' I asked, though by now I figured it didn't matter. Mr Adams would throw me out after the first note.

'You mean what are we going to play?' Fats said. 'Man, you're with us. Where's your banjo?'

'But I'm not supposed to play with you,' I said. 'I only came to make the date and help you get the band together.'

Fats looked hurt. 'You mean you don't want to play with us?' he said.

'I would love to play with you,' I said. 'My banjo is at the Riverside Towers.'

'We'll stop and get it,' Fats said. 'Charlie, get a taxi.'

We piled into a taxi and headed down Seventh Avenue.

'Now here is what we are going to play,' Fats said suddenly. He hummed a simple, basic pattern of rhythm and melody, a blues in a minor key. When we had it memorized he explained what each of us was to do. 'You got that, Charlie?' he said.

Both Charlies said yes. They had it.

We stopped at the Riverside Towers and I got my banjo. At ten minutes before twelve we walked into Liederkranz Hall at 58th Street and Lexington Avenue. Mr Adams was waiting for us.

'I see you are punctual,' he said to me. 'Congratulations.' To Fats he said, 'Well, Mr Waller, what is it to be this morning?'

'Well, Mr Adams,' Fats said, 'this morning I think we'll start with a little thing we call "The Minor Drag". It's a slow number. Then we got a little ol' thing for the other side we call' – he hesitated – ' "Harlem Fuss".'

'Excellent,' Mr Adams said. 'Let's begin with "The Minor Drag".'

We set up our instruments and Fats repeated his instructions. He played the theme for us; as soon as I heard him I knew why we didn't need drums – his left hand would take care of the bass. 'Ready?' Fats said.

'Let's go,' one of the Charlies said.

The warning lights flashed and we took off, every man for himself, with Fats holding us together. When we finished Mr Adams came out of the control room. He didn't say anything. We listened to the playback.

I had a difficult time believing what I heard because it sounded wonderful. I looked at Mr Adams. He was smiling.

'You see,' he said to me, 'what careful rehearsal will do? You have performed your job excellently.'

I walked over to Fats. 'What are we going to play for the other side?' I whispered. 'What is "Harlem Fuss"?'

'It's just a little blues in a major key,' he said.

We made it. When the master was cut Mr Adams was delighted.

'I wonder, Mr Waller,' he said, 'if we could have some piano solos now?'

'Wonderful!' Fats said. 'Perfect! We'll have some piano solos.' Without moving from the bench he made 'Handful of Keys' and 'Numb Fumblin''. 'Handful of Keys' turned out to be the most popular of all his recorded piano solos.

'We must have some more of these dates,' Mr Adams said. 'This is an excellent example of the wisdom of planning and preparation.'

After that the Southern Music Company, with careful planning and preparation, brought out the record on a Victor label with the titles reversed: 'Harlem Fuss' was called 'The Minor Drag' and 'The Minor Drag' was called 'Harlem Fuss'. I got my seventy-five dollars.

We Called It Music (1956)

Eddie Condon

Fired with Enthusiasm

AFTER I was with the band for a while the guys wanted to get rid of Arnold Dupas because he wasn't any good on drums. They were afraid that if they fired Arnold that Dave and Emille would quit. So they fired all three of them. When you got fired in those days they'd shove a letter under your door. All it said was, 'You Are Fired.'

Pops Foster (1971)
Pops Foster

If You Don't Know the Tune . . .

NOWADAYS MOST jazz players can read, but they still may run into situations they aren't prepared for. Saxophonist Jack Nimitz, a Stan Kenton alumnus, had no problem with reading or improvising, but when he took a job with a club date band that fixed harmony to standard tunes, he had trouble. Club date fake bands play long medleys, one chorus of each song. The trumpet or the lead alto will play the melody, and the rest of the horns find harmony parts by ear.

Jack was doing all right with the harmony lines until the band began to play a tune he didn't know. He tried to catch it by ear, but in the process he played a few wrong notes. The leader shouted over the music, 'If you don't know the tune, just play the melody!'

Lester Young and the Drummer

LESTER YOUNG had hired a drummer who wasn't playing what he wanted to hear. During a break, the drummer tried making conversation:

'Say, Prez, when was the last time we worked together?'

'Tonight,' sighed Lester.

Both the above from *Jazz Anecdotes* (1990)
Bill Crow

All Together

NEW YEAR'S Eve, the Red Hill Inn, Camden, New Jersey. We forged a plot on a gospel-type tune called 'Got the Spirit', on which we repeated the same riff over and over behind Maynard's solo until he gave us the cue to take it out. This was New Year's Eve, though, and we decided to celebrate. We moved the figure up a half-tone every time. Maynard found himself playing in such keys as B and F-sharp. He managed pretty well until about the tenth time when he moved up but we didn't. He turned his back to the audience, gave us the arm laughing and shouted: 'You're all fired.'

When It's Hip to Be Late

EVERYBODY KNOWS how hip it is to show up late for the gig. Charlie Parker did it, it must be hip. Starting an hour late after an argument with the promoter creates aggressive energy. Miles Davis did it, it must be hip. Miles is said to believe that if the guys are mad at each other or at him they play more aggressively. Let us examine the American amelioration of the pejorative verb 'to aggress'. To be called an 'aggressive salesman' or an 'aggressive linebacker' is a compliment. They are winners, go-getters, good Americans. Yet aggression involves violence against the bodies and/or minds of others. Hitler was branded 'the aggressor' and thus automatically the bad guy, along with the Japanese who bombed Pearl Harbor with unprovoked aggression. 'Remember, whatever you do, always play aggressively,' I once heard a teacher of jazz instruct his pupils. A lot of saxophone players play more like Adolf Hitler than Adolphe Sax. They say they represent the times, and there is something to that. They consider it survival, aggress or be aggressed. They relate to the art of music as though it was undeclared war. Fuck or get fucked. Come to think of it 'fuck you' as an aggressive expletive misses the same point. Miles sometimes aggressed his personnel by neglecting to list their names on record jackets. Remember who's boss, buddy.

Both the above from *Close Enough for Jazz* (1983)

Mike Zwerin

Miles and Uniforms

MILES REFUSED to be told by anybody what he should wear. Once when he was appearing at Birdland with his sextet, Oscar Goodstein requested that Miles have his band dress in uniforms, as many groups were doing at the time. According to Nat Adderley, Cannonball's brother, the next night Miles kept the group in the dressing room until it was time to go on. When the group went onstage, they were wearing the same disparate clothes they had worn the night before. Miles pulled a rack of uniforms that he had obtained from a nearby clothing store on stage and told the audience,

'Oscar Goodstein wanted to see uniforms onstage so here they are. If that's what you came for, to look at uniforms instead of music, that's what you got. Now we're going to leave so you can enjoy these uniforms.'

Needless to say, Goodstein quickly backed down on his demand, and the group played in their usual clothes.

Round About Close to Midnight (1990)
Boris Vian

Miles and Money

BACK IN the days when he was only getting a thousand dollars for a concert, Miles was booked into Town Hall. The tickets were selling very well, so the promoter suggested doing two shows instead of one. As was customary in such cases, Miles was to get half fee, $500, for the second concert, but when I approached him with this, he looked puzzled.

'You mean I go on stage,' he said, 'pick up my horn, play a concert, and get a thousand dollars. Then they empty the hall, fill it again, I pick up my horn, play the same thing and get only five hundred? I don't understand it.'

I told him that this was how it was normally done, but he was not satisfied. Finally he said he'd do it for $500 if they would rope off half the hall and only sell half the tickets. When the promoters heard this, they decided to give him another thousand for the second concert.

Jack Whittemore

Drug Trouble in the Band

WOODY BEGAN to be aware of what was wrong with his collection of sleeping beauties. And he found that Serge Chaloff was the band's druggist, as well as its number one junkie. Serge would hang a blanket in front of the back seats of the bus and behind it would dispense the stuff to colleagues. This led to an incident in Washington, DC.

The band not only looked bad, it sounded bad. And Woody, furious at what had happened to it, had a row right on the bandstand with 'Mr Chaloff', as he called him, emphasis on the first syllable.

'He was getting farther and farther out there,' Woody said. 'And the farther out he got the more he was sounding like a faygallah. He kept saying, "Hey, Woody, baby, I'm straight, man, I'm clean." And I shouted, "Just play your goddam part and shut up!"

'I was so depressed after that gig. There was this after-hours joint in Washington called the Turf and Grid. It was owned by a couple of guys with connections, book-makers. Numbers guys. Everybody used to go there. That night President Truman had a party at the White House, and afterwards all his guests went over to the Turf and Grid. They were seven deep at the bar, and I had to fight my way through to get a drink, man. All I wanted was to have a drink and forget it. And finally I get a couple of drinks, and it's hot in there, and I'm sweating, and somebody's got their hands on me, and I hear, "Hey, Woody, baby, whadya wanna talk to me like that for? I'm straight, baby, I'm straight." And it's Mr Chaloff. And then I remembered an old Joe Venuti bit. We were jammed in there, packed in, and . . . I peed down Serge's leg.

'You know, man, when you do that to someone, it takes a while before it sinks in what's happened to him. And when Serge realized, he let out a howl like a banshee. He pushed out through the crowd and went into a telephone booth. And I'm banging on the door and trying to get at him, and one of the owners comes up and says, "Hey, Woody, you know, we love you, and we love the band, but we can't have you doing things like that in here." And he asked me to please cool it.

'Well, not long after that, I was back here on the coast, working at some club at the beach. Joe Venuti was playing just down the street, and I was walking on the beach with him after the gig one night, and I told him I had a confession to make, I'd stolen one of his bits. Well, Joe just about went into shock. He was horrified. He said, "Woody, you can't do things like that! I can do things like that, but you can't! You're a gentleman. It's all right for me, but not you!"'

Jazz Letter
Gene Lees

Under Maynard Ferguson

MAYNARD'S BAND would make the perfect soundtrack. It was an air-raid more than music. Maynard slashed and strutted like a lion-tamer. His music accused you of being a sissy for not liking it. Maynard's trumpet is one kissing machine unlike the others. Duck when you hear it. Do not turn your back on it. Playing with that band was like being an American adviser.

But how I loved being in the middle of those twelve-part chords, even as frenetic as Maynard's. I soaked in trumpets above, saxophones below, I felt safe in that warm bath. Twelve human beings kissing their machines in the interest of the collective good. This was the beautiful part, the ease with which even the most stubborn or selfish characters could compromise. Sharp? Pull out. No point pretending you're right. No sense fighting over it. Doesn't matter who's wrong if the total doesn't add up right. Everybody listens. Bullheadedness gives way to universal reason. Everybody becomes interested in what the other person has to say, everybody becomes a pacifist.

Being in the middle is wonderful. It is no spectacular position, only perceptive listeners appreciate it, but a rich trombone section makes the whole band rich. I am here, I am doing something beautiful, it is up to you to find me. I will not oversell you. I do not play the guitar or the saxophone like everybody else. Most trombonists are non-conformists. Here I am, find me.

During my sophomore year at the High School of Music and Art I passed the audition for the senior symphony orchestra. I was proud to announce it when I came home that evening.

'How many trombones are there?' my father asked me.

'Three,' I said.

'And which are you?'

'Second.'

He reopened his paper to the business page without comment. I loved the anonymity of being in the middle. How could I ever explain this to him? How could such an over-motivated person understand? I felt strength in anonymity. I had no desire to be biggest, first, strongest, richest, most famous. I thought I would love living in the country for that reason. My heroes were strong people who did not flaunt their strength. J. D. Salinger retired from public view. He would not puff his chest for Dick Cavett. Sonny Rollins disappeared for a few years. Charles de Gaulle disappeared when he saw it was time. Marlon Brando faded out of focus when that became possible. I am a moving target. Finding myself in a crowd waiting to do something, I automatically lose interest in doing it. I like dark horses, underdogs, lost causes, fallen heroes. Not that I want to follow. I am an unreliable follower. I would not stay out of jail one year in the Soviet Union. I can be counted on not to follow. I'm sort of French that way. I want to lead from a corner – from the middle of the chord. If only my father had been alive so I could have told him how happy I was to be in the middle of the chord.

Maynard on the other hand was a leader, a front man in every sense of the word. He wanted to be on top and bottom at the same time. (In the middle too for that matter.) He could hit a double high C and then without missing a beat drop down to a low G with a fat symphony sound. He had learned circular breathing. He could read fly shit. He could switch between trumpet and valve trombone without a hitch. He was a virtuoso, the complete instrumentalist; even his improvising was not bad for a bandleader. Why then has he left me with so little to remember?

Although Timothy Leary once called Maynard's wife Flo 'the most intelligent woman I've ever met', I don't remember many incisive insights on the part of either Ferguson in a year and a half. Is this their fault, or my faulty memory? It's true, she used to read a lot, or at least she carried books – Sartre's *No Exit* for one – but I recall few conversations worth recalling. There was an attractive complicity between them, however; they were a tight family with four or five kids from previous matings and of their own. When one of them became ill and the best doctor they could find lived in England, they moved there and Maynard had an English band for a few years until the child was healed.

The band of my time has since been called 'legendary'. People often ask me to talk or write about it. Why is there so little to say? It was like a bright shiny package which, when opened, does not fulfil the external promise. It can shake your faith in legends.

Close Enough for Jazz (1983)
Mike Zwerin

Jack Purvis

JACK PURVIS was one of the wildest men I have ever met in my life. He was also one of the greatest trumpet players, certainly head and shoulders above most guys around then. He had great high-note ability and he could play just like Louis Armstrong; but he could also turn around and hold down a chair in a symphony. Jack had been hired to play with Waring's Pennsylvanians when they opened at the Roxy Theatre in New York. The Roxy was then the newest and largest theatre in the country, a truly magnificent place that rivalled the future Radio City Music Hall for sumptuousness. Fred Waring had augmented the band for the occasion and it was to play the 1812 Overture in the huge rising pit.

Now Jack Purvis's pride and joy was a little moustache that he spent hours shaping and waxing to a fine point. It upset Waring, because he tried to project the image of a collegiate-type organization with all the musicians clean-shaven and dressed in sweaters and slacks. So he went to Jack and told him to remove the moustache before the next show.

The 1812 Overture opened with a solo trumpet. Waring had it staged so that the band came up from the pit in the dark. Then a pin spot picked him up and followed him to centre stage. He gave the downbeat and the spot went to Jack Purvis, the only guy who could handle the assignment. At the next show, Waring made his trek across the pit and gave the downbeat. When the spot hit Jack, he had shaved off not only the moustache but every hair on his head, and very uncollegiate he looked. Jack suddenly became available for my band.

Those Swinging Years (1985)
Charlie Barnet

Gerry Mulligan and the Bandboy

WHEN GERRY Mulligan put together the first edition of his Concert Jazz Band in the late 1950s he realized he needed help to get organized. He delegated a lot of the internal responsibility to section leaders Mel Lewis, Bob Brookmeyer, and Nick Travis, got Joe Glaser to handle the booking, and hired a bandboy who said he had worked for Gene Krupa and the Sauter-Finegan band. Gerry mentioned his name to Bill Finegan and his wife Kay and they said he was good. He was.

The bandboy was so efficient that Gerry gave him more responsibility. He was getting Gerry's scores microfilmed for safekeeping and was delivering the cheques from concert promoters to Glaser's office. Glaser was so impressed with the way he took care of business that he let him use his box at Yankee Stadium when he was in town.

During a week when there were no bookings, Gerry called a couple of days of rehearsals at a midtown studio. On the second day the bandboy didn't show up. Phone calls to his hotel room weren't answered. No one could discover what had become of him. Talking to Glaser, Gerry mentioned some money the bandboy was supposed to have delivered and found that Glaser hadn't received it.

When they checked the guy's hotel room they found no sign of the scores he was supposed to be having microfilmed – about half of Gerry's library. And Gerry's favourite horn was missing. About $800.00, the scores and the horn just vanished into thin air. Gerry was stunned by the loss of the horn, since it was an especially responsive old Conn that the factory had modified and adjusted until he was really happy with it.

The next time he saw the Finegans, Gerry told them what had happened with their ex-bandboy. Kay looked crestfallen. She had known the guy had a problem, but hadn't mentioned it because she thought he'd straightened up.

'Son of a bitch!' she said, 'he did it again!'

Jazz Anedotes (1990)
Bill Crow

John Hammond on Signing Up Count Basie

I SPREAD the news of Basie's band to everyone interested in jazz, and I went to Dick Altshuler at the American Record Company to urge him to sign Basie for the Brunswick label. Dick agreed, so back I went to Kansas City to sign the band to its first recording contract. Basie said, 'A friend of yours was here to see me, John.'

'Who?' I asked. 'I didn't send anyone to see you.'

'Dave Kapp.'

Dave, the brother of Jack Kapp, the head of Decca Records, was no emissary of mine, but I knew why he had come to see Basie. 'Let me see what you signed,' I said, fearing the worst.

Basie showed me the contract. It called for twenty-four sides a year for three years for $750 each year. To Basie it seemed like a lot of money. To me it was devastating – for both of us. There was no provision for royalties, so that for the period when Basie recorded 'One o'Clock Jump', 'Jumping at the Woodside', and the rest of those classic hits, he earned nothing from record sales. It was also below the legal minimum scale demanded by the American Federation of Musicians for recording.

Back in New York I called Local 802 to protest these outrageous terms, and did manage to raise the per-side payment scale, but there was nothing the union could do to break the contract. The loss of Basie to Decca was partially my own fault. I had praised the band in *down beat* for months. I had talked about Basie to everybody I knew, and in the music business there are no secrets. Every record executive knew about Basie by the time I went out to sign him. Even Joe Glaser, the head of Associated Booking Corporation, had hurried to Kansas City before me, except that he thought Lips Page was the star and that Basie was no leader; so he signed Page and not Basie.

Glaser's mistake turned out well for Basie. We replaced Lips with Buck Clayton, one of the best – as well as one of the handsomest – trumpet players in jazz. Buck had been playing for Lionel Hampton in Los Angeles, and by accident had burst into a wrong room to the embarrassment of Hampton's wife, Gladys, the real boss of that band. She fired him. Buck joined Basie, and you'll just have to believe me when I say Lips was never missed.

John Hammond on Record (1977)
John Hammond

Firing John R. T. Davies

JOHN R. T. had played with the old Crane River Band, a kind of New Orleans primitive facsimile, and wore a fez. No one ever found out why. He also played an alto saxophone which may or may not have been provided with an octave key: you couldn't find out by listening. This key, if depressed, raises the pitch of the note you're playing by an octave. The way John played it sounded as if the operation of the key was the result of chance rather than deliberate choice, so it was hard to establish any meaningful melody line. Sandy had to stop him playing it. This caused a certain amount of friction and protest in polite public school English, which John always used, but Sandy still wouldn't allow it: it was bad for his nerves, not because he didn't know what was coming next – which jazz is all about – but because he could never be sure what had just happened.

Eventually John left the band at Sandy's request. His trombone playing had been fine, but Sandy was restless to explore some other music and John's devotion to trad was in the way. John was a loss in one respect: he was the kind of person you could phone up and say: 'John, I've got to get to Cairo on Tuesday, can you drive me there?' and he'd be over in ten minutes. Never needed an explanation for that kind of thing. But neither Sandy nor I ever wanted to go to Cairo in haste. John needed that kind of environment, and found it in the Temperance Seven, who *all* seemed to be frantically *en route* to Mandalay or some other suitably John R. T. place.

The McJazz Manuscripts (1979)

Sandy Brown

John Braine at a Rehearsal, Problem of

IAN CHRISTIE was always pressing for rehearsals and Mick [Mulligan] hadn't lost his strong aversion to them. He eventually bowed to Ian's shrike-like (his nickname was Bird) pecking away at the issue and called a surprised band for rehearsal at the Metro Club in New Compton Street, off Charing Cross Road. The persistent campaigner for more rehearsals arrived late and, rather drunk, wasn't in good shape to remember routines, both derelictions inwardly noted by an intensely watchful, testily sober Mulligan.

Halfway through a scratchy rehearsal author John Braine arrived at Ian's invitation and in a broad Yorkshire accent yelled, 'Play "Georgia" in memory of dear old Nat.' (Nat Gonella, the British jazz trumpeter famous in the 1930s, whose signature tune was 'Georgia'.) Nat was (and still is) alive, but Braine obviously thought he'd passed on. Mick, eventually incensed by Braine's repeated cries for 'Georgia', jumped off the bandstand, strode up to Braine and said, 'Look here, cock, we don't tell you how to write fucking *Ulysses*, stop telling us what to play!'

All This and Many a Dog (1986)
Jim Godbolt

Curious Request

I WAS loafing by the bandstand on a break between sets at the Fort Worth Country Club when Claude Thornhill, looking elegant in his tuxedo and giggling into the palm of his hand, walked up to me and pointed to a pale, blue-haired little old lady at a nearby table. She had a carnation in her white gown and eyeglasses with fake jewels on the rim. He said she had just requested 'Chloe'. Claude said he politely answered that we had no arrangement for this composition and thus could not play it for her. She looked disappointed for a minute, but then cheered up, snapped her fingers and said: 'Fuck it. Play "Anthropology".' He looked into my eyes unblinking: 'Do you believe *that*?'

'Sure I do,' I answered. 'I believe it.'

The next set we played 'Anthropology'.

Close Enough for Jazz (1983)
Mike Zwerin

Claude Thornhill at Grand Canyon

GEORGE PAULSON travelled from Connecticut to California with the Claude Thornhill orchestra:

'We stopped at the Grand Canyon in Arizona. Claude asked us to get out our instruments and we all lined up facing the canyon. He called off the chords and we played them and then listened to the echoes. Some very interesting sound effects resulted and we drew quite a crowd of tourist spectators.'

Cadence
George Paulson

Firing Dizzy Gillespie

ONE NIGHT Dizzy sat down in the middle of his solo because he didn't like what the drummer was playing behind him: 'Les Hite *looked* at me, but he was scared to say anything because of my reputation, so he fired the whole band. Les fired the whole band, and then hired back the men he wanted. Bandleaders used to do it like that, and it's a good idea. You say, "I'm breaking up my band, everybody's fired," and then say, "I want you, you, and you in my new band." That's better than pointing at one person and saying, "It's you I want to get rid of." Can you believe Les Hite fired a whole band to get rid of me?'

Dizzy (1980)
Dizzy Gillespie

Zappa, Kirk and the Duke

THE FIRST time we played with Rahsaan Roland Kirk was at the 1968 *Boston Globe* Jazz Festival. After his performance, when introduced to him backstage, I said I really liked what he was doing, and said that if he felt like joining us onstage during our set, he was more than welcome. In spite of his blindness, I believed we could accommodate whatever he wanted to do.

The touring package did not carry its own PA – we had to use whatever speakers existed in each of the venues we were booked into. The hall in South Carolina was rigged with small jukebox speakers, set in a ring around the building. Useless, but there we were – we had to play the show.

Before we went on, I saw Duke Ellington begging – and pleading – for a ten-dollar advance. It was really depressing. After that show, I told the guys: '*That's it – we're breaking the band up.*'

We'd been together in one configuration or another for about five years at that point, and suddenly EVERYTHING looked utterly hopeless to me. If Duke Ellington had to beg some George Wein assistant backstage for *ten bucks*, what the fuck was I doing with a ten-piece band, trying to play rock and roll – or something that was *almost* rock and roll?

I was paying everybody in the band a weekly salary of two hundred dollars – all year round, whether we were working or not, along with all hotel and travel expenses when we did get work. The guys in the band were pissed off – as if their welfare had been cancelled – but at that point I was ten thousand dollars in the red.

The Real Frank Zappa Book (1989)
Frank Zappa

Joining the Ellington Band

I DIDN'T know Wellman Braud that night when he walked into the Nest, and he didn't know me. He had heard about me through King Oliver and that was about it. He just sat there not talking to anyone until intermission came and then he asked me to join him at a table. He introduced himself and right away I knew he was a 'home boy' from the way he spoke. Anyway, he told me that he could get me into the Duke Ellington Band, if I wanted. I just let him keep talking. 'You see,' he said, 'Duke has had this six-piece outfit on Broadway, but he has just landed this deal at the Cotton Club. The man there wants him to expand the band to ten pieces.' I kept listening. 'Duke wants to get a clarinet player to take the place of Rudy Jackson. He is kind of tired of

Rudy.' I just sat there with my drink and let Braud go on talking. 'Rudy came to Duke with this song he called "Creole Love Call" and Duke liked it and recorded it for Mills. Now it turns out that Rudy stole the damned song from King Oliver. Oliver used to call it "Camp Meeting Blues", but Rudy claimed it was his original so Oliver is suing them. Duke has had enough of it all so he wants someone to take Rudy's place.' I guess I couldn't blame him for getting rid of a guy that brought on so much trouble to his band. I mean, nobody needs law suits.

I wasn't interested in all the intrigue of why he was going, but Braud stayed with it and told me about how the band was getting ready to break into the big time and all. He claimed he would bring Duke down after a night or so to hear me. I told him, 'Fine.' That seemed to be that.

I had seen Duke before, but I had never ever met him. They used to have a place at that time in New York called 'Mexico's' which was an after-hours spot that musicians would go to. They used to have music contests – 'Cutting contests' – there between the musicians. One night it would be trumpet players bucking each other, then the next night maybe saxes. The first time I went there it was a piano night. There was James P. Johnson, Willie 'The Lion' Smith, Fats Waller and some others. Well, as the night went on someone pointed out Duke Ellington to me. He never played all night but just sat there writing down music. Those guys were so 'heavy' maybe he just didn't want to get on the piano. Who knows?

Duke was always hanging around Mexico's. In fact the first time that I played there, Luis Russell, bless his soul, told me, 'We're going down there one night, and you are going to break them up.' So he got me to rehearse 'High Society' which nobody had heard too much in New York. We rehearsed it like mad and when we got there we knew exactly what we were going to play. He started to put on. 'Come on, Barney. Take out the horn and play something – anything,' says Russell. So we played out 'High Society' and broke up the joint. They all thought I was a hell of a clarinettist, but that was all I played all night: 'High Society'. Duke must have heard that, I guess. He would come in and go out without much fanfare, because he wasn't like Willie 'The Lion' and them, personality-wise.

It was the same deal when he came over to hear me at the Nest. I didn't even know he had been in there, or left for that matter. The night after he stopped by back came Braud once more. 'Duke wants you to come over to his apartment in the morning to talk. He wants to see you. OK?' said Braud. That's how it all started.

Next morning I went over to where Duke was living. They used to have a theatre in New York called 'The Lafayette' and he lived just about two blocks from there near Seventh Avenue and 128th Street. I wanted to hear what he had to say, so I punched the doorbell.

He came to the door and invited me in. We sat down and he came right to the point. 'I want you to join my band,' he says. 'I don't know how long we're going to stay here, but we are trying to build up a good band. If we can do it, and the boss likes us, then we can stay at this Cotton Club a long time. We'll have a good job there.' I noticed he kept talking in the plural: 'Our band', 'We can stay there', and liked that from the start about him. He thought of a band as a unit and I dug him.

We talked on for a half hour or so and he outlined his plans. He seemed to know what he was about to do and he made sense all the way around. I asked him about the hours and when we'd get off and how long we would play. Also about the money. It turned out to be a smaller salary than I was making at the Nest, but the more the man talked, the more I liked him. He was very ambitious, even then.

He told me that Irving Mills was booking him, and that Mills was also his publisher. He was 'in' at the Cotton Club. You see, a lot of those Broadway show people used to hear Duke's band down on Broadway and they recommended him. That made it even bigger for him at the Cotton Club. I knew all those fine-looking gals that worked there, because they used to come by the Nest after they finished work. They were some real beautiful babies, and that was another incentive right there. You know, the funny thing, he didn't even mention music at all that day. I mean, he knew that I could read, and from being with Russell he knew I could play too. He had heard it for himself. There was just something different about him from other people. For instance, I was much more impressed when Joe Oliver offered me a job than when Duke did, because Joe's band was so much better known, and yet Duke Ellington made you feel so much at ease. Just like he was going to turn the music business upside down and you would be part of it. Anyway, I told him I would join him right then and that I would give Russell my notice that same night. I remember he simply said, 'Good. You won't be sorry. You can start next Friday.' I started that Friday and ended fourteen years later. It must have been my best move in life, I think.

With Louis and the Duke (1985)
Barney Bigard

Duke's Two Bass Players

THERE WERE a couple of times when Duke had two bass players. Billy Taylor, Sr, was in the band when Duke discovered Jimmy Blanton, the young virtuoso who revolutionized jazz bass playing. Duke had to have him, but couldn't bring himself to fire Taylor. The two bassists played side by side until Taylor finally threw in the towel on a job in Boston, walking off the bandstand one night in the middle of the job. He said, 'I'm not going to stand up there next to that young boy playing all that bass and be embarrassed.'

After Blanton's untimely death Duke hired Junior Raglin. He found that his new bassist would often overdo his drinking and miss the job, so he hired Al Lucas as well, hoping to have at least one sober bassist on the bandstand. Lucas and Raglin promptly became drinking buddies. Duke said, 'I'm paying two bass players and neither one of them is here!'

His manipulations didn't always work. When Ben Webster drank too much before a California concert, Duke announced that Ben would play a feature on 'Body and Soul', which was Coleman Hawkins's tour de force. Ben stood up and glared at Duke. 'Play it yourself, you sonofabitch!' he said, and walked offstage. Ben was fearsome when drinking, and quite unmanageable, even by Duke.

Asleep on the Stand

GONSALVES FELL so deeply asleep on the bandstand at a Chicago concert that his lookout man, bassist Jimmy Woode, was just barely able to nudge him awake in time for his solo on 'Take the A Train'.

'Paul, you're on!' Still asleep, he stumbled to his feet and got out to the solo microphone on automatic pilot. Ray Nance had just finished his violin chorus. Paul came fully awake to hear the audience applauding Nance. Thinking he must have already played his solo, Paul took a bow and returned to his seat.

Both the above from *Jazz Anecdotes* (1990)

Bill Crow

Mingus and the Duke

TIZOL WANTS you to play a solo he's written where bowing is required. You raise the solo an octave, where the bass isn't too muddy. He doesn't like that and he comes to the room under the stage where you're practising at intermission and comments that you're like the rest of the niggers in the band, you can't read. You ask Juan how he's different from the other niggers and he states that one of the ways he's different is that HE IS WHITE. So you run his ass upstairs.

You leave the rehearsal room proceed toward the stage with your bass and take your place and at the moment Duke brings down the baton for 'A Train' and the curtain of the Apollo Theatre goes up, a yelling, whooping Tizol rushes out and lunges at you with a bolo knife. The rest you remember mostly from Duke's own words in his dressing room as he changes after the show.

'Now, Charles,' he says, looking amused, putting Cartier links into the cuffs of his beautiful handmade shirt, 'you could have forewarned me – you left me out of the act entirely! At least you could have let me cue in a few chords as you ran through that Nijinsky routine. I congratulate you on your performance, but why didn't you and Juan inform me about the adagio you planned so that we could score it?

'I must say I never saw a large man so agile – I never saw *anybody* make such tremendous leaps! The gambado over the piano carrying your bass was colossal. When you exited after that I thought, "That man's really afraid of Juan's knife and at the speed he's going he's probably home in bed by now." But no, back you came through the same door with your bass still intact. For a moment I was hopeful you'd decided to sit down and play but instead you slashed Juan's chair in two with a fire axe!

'Really, Charles, that's destructive. Everybody knows Juan has a knife but nobody ever took it seriously – he likes to pull it out and show it to people, you understand.

'So I'm afraid, Charles – I've never fired anybody – you'll have to quit my band. I don't need any new problems. Juan's an old problem, I can cope with that, but you seem to have a whole bag of new tricks. I must ask you to be kind enough to give me your notice, Charles.'

The charming way he says it, it's like he's paying you a compliment. Feeling honoured, you shake hands and resign.

Beneath the Underdog (1974)

Charles Mingus

Charles Mingus Addresses the Audience

'YOU, MY audience, are all a bunch of poppaloppers. A bunch of tumbling weeds tumbling 'round, running from your subconscious, running from your subconscious unconscious . . . minds. Minds? Minds that won't let you stop to listen to a word of artistic or meaningful truth. You think it all has to be in beauteous colours. Beautiful, like your "lovely" selves. You don't want to see your ugly selves, the untruths, the lies you give to life.

'So you come to me, you sit in the front row, as noisy as can be. I listen to your millions of conversations, sometimes pulling them all up and putting them together and writing a symphony. But you never hear that symphony – that I might dedicate to the mother who brought along a neighbour and talked three sets and two intermissions about the old man across the hall making it with Mrs Jones' son in the apartment below where the school teacher lives with Cadillac Bill. And how she's thinking of taking up teaching if Mary gets any more minks like that white one she just gave her sister Sal who's in and out on week days and leaves town on weekends with her Rolls Royce full of pretty teachers. And how it's difficult to keep the facts of life from her daughter Chi-Chi. The insurance man got fresh with me too . . . giggle giggle. Just a little kiss . . . and oh! how cute he got he musta thought . . . ?

'I finally asked her to change to a table where she could talk better and let some people sit there who wanted to listen, and the jazzy mother answered me for the rest of the set about how she has to listen to jazz all day long, and don't accuse her of not liking the stuff, she lives on it . . .

' . . . So *I* profit, not her, or most of you, who will leave here tonight and say I've heard Charlie Mingus. You haven't even heard the conversation across the table, and that's the loudest! Have you heard the announcement of a single song title during the night? Or a pause in between tunes, hoping you'd hear yourselves, then quiet down and listen? Joe says he has two very loud bands and he's going for a walk. Maybe the other band has no dynamics, but if my band is loud in spots, ugly in spots, it's also beautiful in spots, soft in spots. There are even moments of silence. But the moments of beautiful silence are hidden by your clanking glasses and your too wonderful conversations.

'Joe tells me: This club is mainly taken over by the artists of the village. Would you like to show your paintings to blind men? Should I like to play my music for blind ears that are clogged up with the noises and frustrations of their own daily problems and egos, carrying on conversations just to be noticed that they are there?

'You haven't been told before that you're phonies. You're here because jazz has publicity, jazz is popular, the word jazz, and you like to associate yourself with this sort of thing. But it doesn't make you a connoisseur of the art because you follow it around. You're dilettantes of style. A blind man can go to an exhibition of Picasso and Kline and not even see their works. And comment behind dark glasses, Wow! They're the swingingest painters ever, crazy! Well, so can you. You've got your dark glasses and clogged-up ears.

'You sit there in front of me and talk about your crude love affairs. You sit there in front of me and push your junky-style glasses up on your noses. You sit there and swing your undulating legs. You bare your loosely covered bosoms in front of me and your boyfriends give an embarrassed look up at the bandstand, so you pretend you don't want us to look down into your unveilings. You stuff in your hankie if you have one, or an old white glove or a dirty dollar bill, or just press your hand to yourself every time you bend forward. All of you sit there, digging yourselves and each other, looking around hoping to be seen and observed as hip. *You* become the object you came to see, and you think you're important and digging jazz when all the time all you're doing is digging a blind, deaf scene that has nothing to do with any kind of music at all . . .

'And the pitiful thing is that there are a few that do want to listen. And some of the musicians . . . we want to hear each other, what we have to say tonight, because we've learned the language. Some of us know it too well. Some of us know it only mechanically. But by listening to others who play it spiritually, soulfully, we can learn to *speak* a little less technically. But imagine an artist of rhetoric, with thinking faculties, performing for an audience devoid of concern for communication . . . imagine his attempting a sensible communicating association even in plain verbal language. Then open your eyes, look around at yourselves posing as listeners to music, which is *another* language, so much more wide in range and vivid, and warm and full and expressive of thoughts you are seldom able to convey . . . '

Someone taped this that night, and the tape breaks off here. Add to this scene most of the audience yelling, 'Bravo!' 'Tell 'em, Charlie!' 'Someone has been needed to say that for years!' 'Most of us want to listen.' 'Tell 'em, Charlie . . . '

The Jazz Word (1960)

Charles Mingus

10

ON THE ROAD

If this were the kind of book that used song titles as chapter headings, this section might well be called 'Travelling Blues'. All musicians get involved in travel, but going out on the road seemed to be a way of life for many jazz players, whether it was the coach and train journeys of the 1930s which took big bands from one dance to another, the boat journeys which took them to and from Europe or even, right at the beginning, the river-boat jobs which took New Orleans men up and down the Mississippi. None of them much enjoyed travelling, but it was a condition of the job, and it still is, with the air flights that take bands from festival to festival or simply van trips up the motorway to the night's gig.

The world of travel seemed also to create a world apart in which musicians were the majority, just for once. A group of musicians can present a united front against the uncomprehending daytime world, where people go to work when it's light and haven't heard of Charlie Parker. No wonder that when musicians get together, it doesn't take much to get them reminiscing about places they have been to, the dreadful time they had getting there and the dreadful things they got up to to relieve the tedium or problems. Maybe footballers tell the same kind of stories and feel the same bond. But jazz musicians seem to be better storytellers.

A Life Apart

As a species, and necessarily confining the subject to music, musicians are open-heartedly dead honest. You can safely take anything they say on the subject absolutely at face value. Straying into other fields, acceptance of any views they care to express would be disastrous. That some of their irrational views on every aspect of human behaviour is due to an apprenticeship served between walls of tin, hurtling through nowhere, five hours a day, over a period of years, is unquestionable. Every member of every touring band (and that means every jazz musician because none escaped a period of wagon-pressure) bears mental scars which never heal.

The McJazz Manuscripts (1979)
Sandy Brown

The Myth of the Road

DAYBREAK. GARE du Nord. Wearing a Lester Young-style porkpie hat and a Dizzy Gillespie goatee, I'm sitting on my horn case, like that famous picture of Bird, waiting for the 3 AM mail train to the Lowlands. It's cold and foggy and I've been on the road so long I don't remember what off is like. I'm sick and tired of waking up tired and sick. My mouth feels as though there are dinosaurs in it. I have to jerk off to get my heart started. My eyes look like road maps.

Actually it was a sunny day and I had the foresight to book in advance, first class of course. I caught an 11 AM train, a sensible hour, and I'd slept eight hours last night in my comfortable apartment in a bourgeois section of Paris. Before that I had lived a sedentary life in the same country house for five years. I was wearing a Swiss suede jacket and a Brooks Brothers turtleneck. I'm told I resemble the French actor Michel Piccoli, a bit kinky around the edges but not enough to scare anybody.

I've always wanted to live like the jazz greats of yore; fearless outlaws travelling the less travelled road, tragic, uncompromising trail-blazers, psychic anarchists with no thought of tomorrow, pulling slick chicks, vomiting in taxicabs, going to sleep at nine in the morning. But I have this awful sensible streak ('Hi there, officer, nice day, isn't it?') which is one reason I am not as great a jazz musician as I would otherwise be. It is not really a sensible thing to do, you have to be crazy to play jazz for a living. Excess is essential, you've got to be eager to spew it out every night, to follow the poet William Blake who said: 'The road of excess leads to the palace of wisdom.'

Close Enough for Jazz (1983)

Mike Zwerin

The Twelve-hour Dice Game

FOURTEEN DOLLARS a day sounded real great. Nobody bothered to tell me I'd have to travel five hundred to six hundred miles on a hot or cold raggedy-ass Blue Goose bus; that it would cost me two or three bucks a night for a room; that by the time I was through having my hair fixed and gowns pressed – to say nothing of paying for pretty clothes to wear – I'd end up with about a dollar and a half a day. Out of that I had to eat and drink and send home some loot to Mom.

Whenever I had a couple of bucks it was always so little I was ashamed to send it home, so I would give it to Lester Young to invest. I hoped he could shoot enough dice to parlay it into a bill big enough I didn't have to feel ashamed to send home.

The first time out we had been riding for three months, and neither Lester nor I had a dime. Both of us were actually hungry. Jimmy Rushing, the blues-singing 'Mr Five by Five', was always the only one who had any loot. We went to him once and asked him real nice for a buck to buy a couple of hamburgers. He wouldn't give us nothing but a lecture on how he saved his money and how we petered ours away.

When we were on the bus coming back to New York from West Virginia, I couldn't stand the thought of coming home to Mom broke. I had four bucks when that crap game started on the bus floor.

'You're not shooting these four,' I told Lester. 'I'm shooting these myself.' I got on my knees, and the first time up it was a seven.

Everybody hollered at me that the bus had swerved and made me shoot it over.

Up came eleven. I picked up the four bucks right there and won the next three pots before someone said something about comfort.

I thought they said, 'What do you come for?' I said, 'I come for any damn thing you come for.' I didn't know the lingo, but I knew Lester did. So I told him I'd do the shooting and he could be the lookout man.

I was on my knees in the bottom of that bus from West Virginia to New York, a few hundred miles and about twelve hours. When we pulled up in front of the Woodside Hotel everybody was broke and crying. I was filthy dirty and had holes in the knees of my stockings, but I had sixteen hundred bucks and some change.

I gave some of the cats in the band enough loot to eat with and for car fare. But not Rushing. I didn't give him back a dime. I took what was left and split on uptown to Mom's. When I walked in she looked at me and like to died, I was so dirty and beat up. I just waited for her to say something, and she did.

'I'll bet you ain't got a dime, either,' Mom said.

I took that money, over a thousand dollars, and threw it on the floor. She salted a lot of it away and later it became the nest egg she used to start her own little restaurant. 'Mom Holiday's', something she always wanted.

Lady Sings the Blues (1990)
Billie Holiday

Late for the Date

THE FINE was that you had to buy booze for the whole band, which cost a lot of bread. Now Buddy Rich was late for the first set nearly every night. But Tommy wasn't there and nobody ever finked on him.

As it happened I was always on time, except about twice. Once I was terribly late and that was when I had a fight with Buddy Rich. When I appeared Tommy stopped the band and said, 'You used to play with us.'

Well, I was late and I had the wrong uniform on. It was Tuesday, after the Monday off, and we changed to the light suits. But I hadn't been home all night and I woke up somewhere uptown of course, so I was wearing the wrong uniform. I was happy to buy the booze.

Anyway, he called the waiter over and made it pretty tough. George Arus and Chuck Peterson drank Canadian Club: a bottle of that. Somebody else had a bottle, and so on. A case of Coca-Cola and, finally, a bottle of wine for Buddy Rich.

'Cancel the wine,' I said. Tommy wanted to know why and I told him, 'Not for that cat. He was late every night when you weren't there. I refuse to buy him wine. Let him pay off first.'

Then a waiter arrived with all the bottles and the wine was there. So I sent it back. Afterwards, Buddy and I went out in the park and beat the shit out of each other. Well, it was a fighting band.

Dorsey came out and tried to stop the fight, which I wouldn't have minded because I was getting the worst of it. But he wasn't worried about us.

'Take the jackets off,' he shouted. 'The jackets! We got another set to play!'

Cadence
Joe Bushkin

A Two-bus Band

WHEN STAN Kenton had the real big band, the Innovations orchestra that made the tour in 1950, there were so many men that we had to be divided up into two busloads. One was what we called the 'balling bus' – you know, everybody living it up. I was on the other bus.

One day a musician from the balling bus visited us for a couple of minutes. He looked around in obvious surprise, then went back and made a report to the fellows in the other bus.

'Do you know what they're doing in there?' he said. 'They're *reading!*'

Laughter from the Hip (1963)
Shelly Manne

A Shake on the Bus

ONE NIGHT when we were down South the bus broke down in a swampy area. Otis Johnson, the trumpet player, and I took off out in the swamp looking for a snake while they fixed the bus. We found one and killed it, then we walked about two miles to a store to get some string. We tied the string on the neck of the snake and propped its head up with a stick. When we got back on the bus we hid it in the front and carried the string to the back of the bus. Finally they got the bus ready to go and the driver turned the lights on and had everybody stick their heads out in the aisle so we could see if everybody was there. We started pulling the snake down the aisle then. Everybody went wild, guys jumped out the windows and climbed in the luggage racks and everything. It was a kick.

Pops Foster (1971)
Pops Foster

A Pullman Life

I WAS in the band for six months before we hit New York. We travelled the road, playing one-nighters mainly, all through the South and Midwest and Southwest. I couldn't get over the band travelling in its own Pullman – strictly first class, all the way. There's never been any band, black or white, that travelled any finer than Cab's band did. Behind the Pullman was the band's baggage car with all the H & M trunks in it. Everybody in the band had the same kind of H & M brand of trunk. When I looked into the baggage car my eyes nearly popped out.

In the middle of all these trunks and instruments was Cab's big green Lincoln. Right in the baggage car. Everywhere Cab went he took that beautiful car with him, and when he got into a town the rest of us would get taxis, but Cab would roll that old Linc down off the train, with his coonskin coat on and a fine Homburg or derby, and drive off into town looking for the action.

from the IJS Archive
Milt Hinton

Hotel Drill

I LEARNED about the day sheet. In those days, if you checked into a hotel at 7 AM you could check out as late as four the following afternoon and pay for only one night. With a little planning and a missed night's sleep here and there, it was possible to check in only three times a week. And ghosting. Ghosting is when two guys check into a double room and some time later four more wander through the lobby looking as though they are checked in somewhere else. By staggering their entrance into the elevator, they could usually get to the room without detection. They slept on a couch or the floor and the cost of the room got split six ways instead of two.

Close Enough for Jazz (1983)

Mike Zwerin

Bad Language in the Berigan Bus

THINGS WERE so rough that the chick with the band reached the point where she just couldn't take it any more. Jane Dover, that was her name. One night there was only one seat left on the bus, and that was next to her. Johnny Napton, the trumpet player, wanted to take it, and she wouldn't let him. So he started cursing her out.

She started to run out of the bus. 'I can't take this any more!' she told Bunny. 'All this rotten language, this foul-mouthed talk, I'm through!'

Bunny, who has had one more for the road and then some, gets back on the bus with her and all the guys are seated in their chairs. He grabs the post beside the driver, starts banging on it with his cane, and just about breaks the cane in half. He's furious.

'I've had it! All this language, and the girl singer wants to quit the band, and you're hanging me up in the middle of a stack of one-nighters without a girl singer! Now I want you to get one thing straight!' (The girl is sitting there while he's saying all this.) 'The first ---- ------ that curses on this bus is automatically through!'

Everybody on the bus starts to laugh, so he catches himself and says, 'Well, I didn't mean to put it that way, but I'm serious! I don't want to hear another foul word out of any of you as long as Jane is sitting in this bus!'

Well, we go about 250 miles, and not a sound out of anyone. The cats were even lighting their cigarettes real quiet because we knew Bunny was flipping.

Along about daybreak, Joe Bushkin, our pianist, is in the back of the bus, and just as everybody's starting to open their squinty eyes Bushkin runs down the bus, and he stops by the driver and turns around facing everybody, including Bunny, and yells:

'I can't stand it any longer! ——! ——!—— ——!' and every other word he can think of.

That was without doubt the most frantic bunch of kids that were ever together.

Laughter from the Hip (1963)
Georgie Auld

A Ghost in the Band

ANOTHER TIME Paul met this girl and he told her he was in the dress business. He took her up to his room at the Douglas Hotel in Philly. My room was right next to his and we listened to them. They decided to go get something to drink and then come back. When they got back we had Albert Nicholas under the bed with a fork to scratch on the bed springs and a string tied to one of the chairs we could pull from the next room. We'd look through the keyhole and make sure the girl could see the chair move. She said, 'Mr Barbarin, Mr Paul, that chair's moving.' Paul said, 'Don't worry, you're with a man, nothing's going to happen to you!' We pulled the chair again and Nick hit the bed springs with the fork. She wet all over the floor, ran out of the room and took off. Paul took off too. When he came back he came to my room and there were nine of us guys in there pretending like we were sleeping. He wanted to fight all of us.

Pops Foster (1971)
Pops Foster

Travelling Baseball

CAB ORGANIZED a baseball team and bought uniforms, gloves, bats, and had a big truck for us to put all the equipment in. When we got into a town a little early, we'd get out the stuff and have a little infield practice or batting and whatnot, and if we got into a town like Los Angeles, we'd play some band out there. We'd play Woody's band sometimes. Oscar Pettiford broke his arm in about three or four places playing baseball in Woody Herman's band.

Cab made Tyree Glenn the manager. Cab was in a batting slump, and Tyree benched Cab. He was furious. It's his team, and his bats and his balls, and Tyree benched him. He got so mad he sold Tyree the whole team for a penny, one cent!

from the IJS Archive
Milt Hinton

Joking with Duke

LOOKING BACK we did some terrible things in that band. Like one of the guys would be trying to sleep it off before the job in the band room and we would sneak up and tie his shoe-laces together and we had a great big bell. We'd hit that bell and yell, 'Fire! Fire!' and the poor guy, whoever it was, would jump up and fall all over his shoes, banging his head on the floor, with his hangover and all. Those guys would be so mad it would be way into the second set before they calmed down. We were like kids really with all that, but it seemed fun at the time. Of course Duke, he would have been up all night writing music and so he'd sleep through the intermissions in a corner somewhere. He never said anything about our crazy pranks.

Another time we put Limburger cheese and cayenne pepper on Freddie Jenkins's mouthpiece. He had a habit of leaving it on the stand before the show started, then putting it to his lips in the dressing room ten minutes before we hit. He jumped like mad. We took Artie Whetsol's valves all out of his trumpet and turned them around. Naturally his horn wouldn't work and he was there on the stand shaking it, and Duke just looking straight at him all the time. Like I said, Wellman Braud he was one of those real old-type of New

244 The Jazz Anthology

Orleans guys that never really saw anything funny in this stuff. He was real serious, but he could play like hell on that bass violin.

The worst prankster of the whole bunch was Juan Tizol. You would never believe it if you met him casually. He always seemed so far above everything, but he was the ringleader of us pranksters. We used to play 'Mood Indigo' and Tricky Sam, Artie Whetsol and I had to come right to the front of the stage for the three-part harmony on the first chorus. It was a real small stage and the curtain made it even smaller, so the three of us were real close up, and Tizol burst a stink bomb right behind us. They had those Klieg lights up full and they hit us full in the face. We had no idea of something thrown in back of us. Pretty soon I started to get a whiff of this thing. So I looked at Whetsol and Whetsol looked at me. I looked at Tricky and he began to giggle. This thing was getting stronger and stronger and the worse it got the more Tricky and I would be giggling. Arthur Whetsol was always the 'prissy' one. Oh so sophisticated. He couldn't laugh if he saw a Charlie Chaplin movie. We had to give up for the laughing, Tricky and I, and went back to our chairs, but not Whetsol. He just kept playing as a solo. We said to Duke, 'You ought to be ashamed of yourself letting something like that happen in your band.' We figured that attack was the best means of defence.

After we came to find out it was Tizol – and we ought to have known right then and there – we fixed him. There was a novelty shop in the next block so we went out and bought some itching powder next day. We got to the dressing rooms early and put this stuff all in Tizol's tuxedo. All over his shirt. Everywhere. Hodges was in on it, in fact everyone in the band was in on it. I guess they had had enough of those pranks and seeing how he was the instigator we were going to give Tizol 'holy hell'.

We went up on the stage and the Klieg lights hit him. After half of the first number, and we were all watching him closely, the itching powder starts to work and Tizol starts moving around. When he started perspiring that made it even worse and after a few more choruses he was really going with that stuff. He couldn't take it and it wasn't funny to him any more. That kind of broke him of that habit and the pranksters in the band cooled off now the ringleader was off it.

With Louis and the Duke (1985)

Barney Bigard

With Humph to Hawick

HUMPH PLAYED an engagement with the Dixielanders at Hawick, in the Scottish lowlands. It was a mystery that the band should have been engaged to play in a place so far remote from any jazz activity, especially as we quoted £75, no small sum for an unknown band in those days.

It was painfully cold. We were in that long, bitter winter of 1946-7 when the fuel crisis was at its worst. My contribution to jazz history that morning was to gather twigs and leaves from the garden to make some sort of fire.

The journey to Hawick was in the aftermath of a snowstorm and took about fourteen hours. On arrival Wally found he had left his clarinet on the train and I spent a couple of sweaty hours tracking it down. It was returned to Hawick and I rushed into the dressing room five minutes before the show was due to begin dramatically brandishing the clarinet. Attendance was sparse. The locals were disappointed although not particularly on musical grounds. One gentleman was quite huffy. 'We thought you were going to be darkies,' he said with a strong Scottish burr, and that possibly explained how the band had obtained the engagement.

All This and Many a Dog (1986)
Jim Godbolt

The Road to England

ONE BAND from Glasgow was called the Clyde Valley Stompers. Their original leader admired and emulated the methods of Chris Barber, whose band had evolved as a breakaway from Ken Colyer's New Orleans fanaticism. The personnel of the band changed from week to week as there was no personal imprint, and it didn't matter who turned up so long as an impostoral Barber band sound was available.

One night I met them playing in Hull. Sandy and I knew most of the chaps from Scotland: the following week we met them in Liverpool. Different chaps. 'See you next week,' they'd said, but you know about firing methods. In the interim no member of the band was left undischarged, some were sacked, many left. A typical itinerary for this band's week was Bristol, Glasgow, Dover, Aberdeen, Penzance, London, Edinburgh: so they lived in the wagon. They had a unique way of retaining sanity: about every three days they would stop the wagon, go into a field and punch each other senseless. By an evolutionary mechanism that requires more study than I can afford, some fine musicians came out of the band. Perhaps it was just that so many played in it over a period of five years. Closely typed, the surnames would have covered ten pages of A4. But the best one was Forrie Cairns, a clarinettist who gave Sandy cause for concern on the occasions they occupied the same bandstand. Forrie's playing was a fierce amalgam of a number of New Orleans originals, notably Ed Hall, but derivative or not it had a grating perseverance that outlived the interminable punch-ups and changes in personnel. Sandy had always assumed he had the edge on any clarinettist in Europe, and Forrie made him more uncomfortable than anyone except Tony Coe. Given the freewheeling, uncommitted atmosphere of Sandy's band Forrie could have been unbeatable: he was never provided that climate, and was consequently under-rated. Everything went by precedent. If a band had become successful it was copied until the sterility of its methods concreted. I was guilty of this too – was it guilt? I insisted that Sandy's band play the African numbers Sandy had written: 'African Queen', 'African Blues', 'Everybody Loves Saturday Night', 'Go Ghana'. These had become popular with the trad crowds and one of them – I forget which – made what was then called the hit parade and was number one in Denmark. As this was pre-1960 and the population of Denmark is five million it didn't mean very much financially, but this and the other African songs kept the band on the road in reasonable financial shape between 1956 and 1966.

The McJazz Manuscripts (1979)

Sandy Brown

Hiring a Plane

I was singing at a club in Las Vegas. One night after work I borrowed Mickey Rooney's plane and flew it to Los Angeles.

The next day I was so tired that instead of flying it back myself I decided to take another pilot with me, and later put him on a commercial plane and send him back to LA. I was really worn out, so I went to sleep on the plane.

When I woke up it was dark.

My God, I thought, where are we? We should have been in Vegas before sundown! The pilot says, 'I think Las Vegas is right over that next range.' I looked at the altimeter: 7000 feet.

'Man,' I said, 'Get this thing up in the air – you're lost!'

He said he wasn't, and gave me the signal, and there it was, *bleep bleep bleep*; as long as you are on a beam you hear that. Well, we were on a beam but it wasn't any Las Vegas beam.

I got on the radio and tried to pick up a reading. Then I looked at the fuel gauge and saw we had just a half hour of gas left. In pitch black dark night, flying over the Sierra mountains, man!

'I've got news for you, Dad,' I said. 'In a half hour we have to have this thing on the ground or she's gonna stop flying.'

'There's a glow over there,' he said. 'Let's head for that; I think it's a city.' We flew to this glow on the horizon, and it was a dam, they were doing night-time construction work on it.

'There it is! Boulder Dam!' he says.

'No, I was at Boulder Dam yesterday and there's no construction work being done on it. Let me see if I can get a tower around here.'

What we had seen was the Davis Dam right out of Needles, California. I couldn't even get a weather signal, so I finally started signalling May Day.

My May Day signal was finally picked up by a ham operator. I don't know to this day who he was, but I wish I could thank him for saving our lives. He quickly lined up a lot of cars and had them form a pattern with their headlights to guide us.

Before long we were entirely out of gas. We sheared off the tops of some trees while we tried to head toward the lights, and finally crashed. I woke up in the Santa Fe Railroad Hospital. The pilot wasn't badly injured, but I had bruises all over my body, and cuts all over my face; I was a mess. And Needles is like the blast furnace of the world – around 120 degrees in the shade by noon the next day.

Eventually my musical director, Dick Hazard, came up and moved me to another hospital in Las Vegas. But the payoff was the Vegas club owner's reaction when I called him from Needles right after the accident. Here I was, feeling and looking like a piece of chopped liver, and after I told him what happened, you'll never guess what he said:

'Look, Needles isn't that far away. Can you try to make the second show tonight?'

Laughter from the Hip (1963)
Herb Jeffries

Johnny Hodges with Duke

JOHNNY WAS scared when he first joined us, I recall. I guess we all were at first because most of us had never before played with a large orchestra that was beginning to get somewhere. Naturally you get a funny feeling, and you're fighting to do good all the time until you can relax yourself. It's kind of a challenge and it scared Johnny plenty. He was a very quiet sort of a guy and everything that he would do would be done in a sincere manner. He and I became the biggest buddies. We'd pool our money and gamble and if one didn't win then the other would take what money was left and try. He was a load of fun, but you'd never guess because he always wore that serious face. Just like he was angry all the time. He wasn't mad or nothing, just shy. He was married at the time he joined the band, and had a baby. Later on he got a divorce from his first wife and married a girl in the Cotton Club show. They had a son somewhere along the line. He wasn't much of a drinker but he loved to play poker, to gamble. That's what we did all those travelling years. Of course we'd drink a little, but when I really started into drinking was later when Ben Webster came into the band. He'd do a lot of things that we wouldn't dare do and Duke would bawl us out. But he was afraid, I think, of Ben Webster. We saw that and we decided, 'He lets

Ben get away with it. We'll do those things. We'll get drinks ourselves.' That's what caused me to start drinking heavy. But Johnny and I never did drink to such excess.

With Louis and the Duke (1985)
Barney Bigard

The Car that Bix Bought

THE BAND at Hudson Lake wore uniforms, with fancy two-tone shoes. Bix was the last to arrive on the job, naturally; he got the last uniform and the last pair of shoes. The uniform was too small for him and the shoes were too big. One night after the dance Pee Wee Russell and Bix went for a row on the lake; the boat upset, and after that Bix's uniform was even smaller for him; the toes of his shoes curled up.

He and Pee Wee, a tall, mournful-looking kid, lived in a cottage near the lake with Riskin, Gabe and Orr. There were three bedrooms, a kitchen, a living room, a tired grand piano, and no housekeeper. The place was always a shambles. The only commodity kept in sufficient stock was a local whisky, purchased in large quantities for five dollars a gallon from three old-maid hill-billies who lived five miles away. Barefoot in a cabin with a brother they were all past sixty and asked no questions.

Bix and Pee Wee were without a car. It bothered them; they couldn't visit the old maids when they wanted to. One day, having received some pay – usually they owed it all – they went to LaPorte to buy an automobile. There were several second-hand Model T Fords available, but Bix had notions of grandeur. He found a 1916 Buick which could be had for eighty dollars. It ran around the block well. 'This is it,' Bix said to Pee Wee. 'Wait until the guys see us with this. We won't have to ride with them any more, they'll be begging to ride with us.' Pee Wee was dubious, but he agreed.

They drove back to the lake and hid the car in a side road. Just before starting time that night they sneaked off, got into it, and drove to the pavilion. As they reached the entrance and caught the attention of the boys on the stand the motor stopped. It refused to start; the owners had to push it to the cottage. Next day they got it going and decided to visit the old maids. They took Charlie Horvath's wife with them – Charlie was managing the band for Goldkette. They got to the cabin, bought a jug, and started back. Half-way home the Buick went dead. They had to find a farmer and hire him to tow it by horse to a garage. Sitting in the car they nibbled at the jug; they arrived at work, loaded, at eleven thirty. A surprise awaited them. Goldkette was there; he had chosen this one night of the whole season to visit the band at Hudson Lake. 'Is this the way things always go – the cornet and clarinet players drunk and mad and missing with your wife?' he asked Horvath. 'It's their birthday,' Horvath said. He could think of nothing else.

The car was delivered next day at the cottage. 'Park it in the backyard,' Bix said to the man who towed it from the garage. It never ran again. It had a fine mirror and the owners used that while shaving. Ten years later Pee Wee was driving to the coast with the Louis Prima band; he detoured to reminisce at Hudson Lake and found the cottage. The car was still in the backyard on its wheels, but groggy with rust. Pee Wee pointed it out to the Prima boys. 'I own half of that,' he said.

We Called It Music (1956)

Eddie Condon

Bix in the Air

HE SENT a telegram to Paul – it was delivered while we were on the train – saying he was going to fly and would certainly be there in time for the concert. When we got into Ponca City, quite a few of us made a beeline out to the airport, such as it was – it looked as though it had until very recently been just another cornfield – to witness his arrival.

Pretty soon this reconverted 'Jenny', 1919 vintage, appears out of a deep blue sky, circles and makes a very good landing. We all rushed up to the plane, an open cockpit job, as Bix and the pilot climbed out. As they both hit the ground, Bix put his arms around the guy and shouted to us, 'He's the best damned pilot in the world!' And with that the pilot took two steps toward us and fell flat on his face. He was so loaded we had to support him to our cars and take them both to the hotel. He and

Bix had been taking alternate sips of corn mash up there, and while Bix was able to hold it, the pilot didn't awaken until seven that evening.

Bix: The Man and the Legend (1985)
Izzy Friedman

Hell-raisers

THERE WERE a couple of celebrated bands in that era that were composed entirely of gays. (They didn't call them 'gays' in those days.) The leader of one of these, who happened to be straight himself and well-known for his unusual trombone solos, explained that it was easier to travel with a gay band. They rarely got in any trouble and usually just hung around in the hotel together. It's no secret in the hotel business that gays don't tip very well as a rule.

But the purveyors of the elemental vices had a field day when Berigan came to town. Then you needed a written pass to get off the elevator at their floor. Some of the most orgiastic nights of my life were spent in this select company in New York and Philadelphia. Those evenings gave me a new slant on living. How the musicians survived through an entire tour, with every night given over to this sort of merrymaking after putting in a gruelling night's work, I'll never know. There were a few other bands that followed this pattern. Wingy Manone's was considered to be runner-up to Berigan's in free-style high jinks. For a brief spell a crew led by Johnny 'Scat' Davis screamed like a comet through the beds of the nation's hostelries. Gene Krupa's band earned an honourable mention from bell captains everywhere. But with *them*, Berigan reigned supreme.

I Remember Jazz (1987)
Al Rose

Jack Teagarden's Private Bottle

THE FUNNY thing was that Jack always drank whisky. Straight whisky. So he always kept a pint in his trombone case to take a nip during intermission. Anyway, Arvell Shaw found out that he had that bottle in there and he was too cheap to buy his own whisky, so every night, just when we would be in the wings about to go on stage, Arvell would run back right quick and take a big gulp. Same thing after intermission was over too. Jack couldn't figure it out. At the end of the every concert the bottle would be almost empty. He would say, 'God! This bottle's almost gone. Someone must be stealing my whisky.' Of course we didn't say nothing, even though we knew who was laying into that bottle. One night Jack got smart, so before the show he half emptied the pint of whisky and took a leak into it. He just put it back in the trombone case and carried on as usual. So Arvell took a drink from it and came out on the stand all mad. 'Somebody done peed in the bottle,' he yelled, right out there on the concert stage. He was mad with everyone in the band, and yet he was the one stealing the whisky. He never stole any more, because he didn't know what in hell would be in that bottle.

Apart from his trombone, Jack's other love was steam engines and miniature trains. I remember once we were just leaving a gig in Washington, DC, and we got out by the wharf and saw this little circus. It was closing down full swing and most of the sideshows had packed up and gone, but Jack spied this little guy holding part of an engine. He watched him walk over to where he had this steam engine stashed away. So Jack went over to the man and asked him if he wanted to sell this whole big engine. The guy was glad to because the circus was going out of business. Jack gave him $200 and all he took was the thing that produced the steam and made the whistle blow. He left the rest of that junk right there.

With Louis and the Duke (1985)

Barney Bigard

A Good Place Not to Go

IN BATON Rouge, Louisiana, there was the Toots Johnson Band. It was very good and Guy Kelly played trumpet with them. They wanted me to go to Montana with them, but I found out it was very cold there and it was wintertime. I told them I wouldn't go because it was too cold, so they wrote a letter to find out. When they got the answer they found out it was, so they didn't go either.

Pops Foster (1971)
Pops Foster

Jazz Fans: an Occupational Hazard

TO MEET and talk with these heroes of mine was a thrill, a dream come true. Don Kingswell mocked this adulation and threw a few barbs about 'fuddy-duddy fan worship'. I had no retort, except to say that I was grateful for those whose playing had given me such deep and abiding pleasure, whose records had changed my life and, indeed, set its very pattern.

When John Chilton and I used to discuss these musicians and their discographies with obvious, perhaps adolescent-like enthusiasm, the Kingswell jowls wobbled in disbelief. '*You* people! You make me laugh! You and your scratchy old 78s!' He mockingly invented his own 'discogaphal' figure, one Matthews, whose instrument Don changed from week to week but who, according to him, recorded for the Regal–Zonophone label in 1926.

'Great player, Matthews! Really socks out the blues. Can't wait to get home and play his 78s. An evening of Matthews really knocks me and the Enemy right out!' The Regal–Zonophone label didn't exist in 1926, but it had sufficiently antique associations to support Don's barbs.

All This and Many a Dog (1986)
Jim Godbolt

Touring: Final Thoughts

OVER THE last five years I had a few good offers and a load of bad offers. It's great to be able to pick your spots. The best feeling on earth. I get guys writing to me or calling me wanting me to do a tour here, a tour there. 'Oh Mr Bigard,' they say, 'it won't be a hard tour.' Well, I've got news for them. There ain't no such thing as an easy tour.

With Louis and the Duke (1985)

Barney Bigard

11

BITS OF LARKIN

Philip Larkin reviewed jazz records for the *Daily Telegraph* for a long time, at the same time as I was reviewing jazz for *The Times*, though as he never seemed to go out and hear any live jazz, our paths never crossed. As Larkin resolutely disliked Miles Davis and John Coltrane and the way jazz was going, he was always ignored by the jazz world. This was a shame, as he wrote much better than any of the rest of them. I have included a selection of brief extracts – one-liners, almost – to give the flavour of his beady-eyed humour, and to remind people that you don't have to have the right opinions to write well.

The Tenor

THERE IS some danger that the tenor sax may become the club bore of jazz, droning on in front of a docile rhythm section for track after track, and nearly every month produces such a session.

Billie Holiday

THIS WAS before Lady Day began to 'use her voice like an instrument' – a fatuous notion for any singer relying so obviously on actual lyrics.

Jazz: a Definition

JAZZ IS always what the young American Negro is playing, and today he is a modernist.

Jazz in Decline

THE EFFETE condition of classical music after 300 years has been reached by jazz itself in under half a century, however, which certainly indicates a superiority of a kind.

Entertainment

I HAVE a weakness for the entertainers of jazz (as opposed to more sombre characters who suggest by their demeanour that I am lucky to hear them), and so for Fats Waller.

Venuti and Lang

VENUTI MADE the blues sound like a novelty foxtrot; Lang made them sound like the blues.

Two Tenors

FEW THINGS wring a groan from my lips more readily than the prospect of another solo tenor team in cliché-ridden conflict.

Duke Ellington

EARLY ELLINGTON records are like vintage cars. They are not as he or anyone else would make them nowadays, but historically they are still important and aesthetically they are still delightful.

Bud Powell

THE MOST moving tract is a solo 'Round Midnight' by Bud Powell; long, painstaking, slow, it is like a confession that omits nothing and excuses nothing, that one hears in silence and can think of no reply to.

Blues and Modernism

BUT FOR all this, popular music today – popular in the real sense of the word, that which makes the most money – is founded squarely on the blues, but the blues of the shouters, not the moaners. It is as if the sudden translation of jazz to the realms of chromatic art-music had called out its most rudimentary elements in compensation – the three-chord trick, as somebody called it, of the twelve-bar blues. From every quarter come whanging guitars, querulous harmonicas, slugging off-beats, and a pretty dreary business it is for the most part. The city Negroes, oscillating between the monotonous Chuck Berry, the lachrymose Ray Charles and the celestial fakery of Ruth Brown, have come perilously near creating a new kind of glossy commercialism out of what originally had been earthy and honest. And of course the whites have followed suit.

Miles Davis

THE FACT that he can spend seven or eight minutes playing 'Autumn Leaves' without my recognizing or liking the tune confirms my view of him as a master of rebarbative boredom.

Sidney Bechet

POSITIVE AS I am that Sidney Bechet is one of the half-dozen leading figures in jazz, I sometimes hesitate when asked to name a record by him that will bring any unbeliever round to my way of thinking. For his particular power resides, after all, in generalities – the majestic *cantabile sostenuto*, the authoritative vitality – and these exist despite innumerable individual records that reveal gobbling irrelevancy, mannered quotes from minor classics, sticky balladry, instant Dixieland, frightful travelling companions.

John Coltrane

HIS SOLOS seem to me to bear the same relation to proper jazz solos as those drawings of running dogs, showing their legs in all positions so that they appear to have about fifty of them, have to real drawings. Once, they are amusing and even instructive. But the whole point of drawing is choosing the right line, not drawing fifty alternatives.

John O'Hara

READERS OF John O'Hara's *Appointment in Samarra* will remember the curious scene near the end where the hero, Julian English, drinks an enormous highball from a flower-vase and plays his favourite jazz records. After a while he goes out to the garage and kills himself. The interesting thing is that the records he plays are not by Armstrong, Ellington or even the Chicago Rhythm Kings, but Whiteman's 'Stairway to Paradise' and Goldkette's 'Sunny Disposish'. Enough to make anyone seek oblivion, you may say, and I thought at one time that O'Hara (who certainly knew his jazz – witness *Butterfield 8)* was being satiric.

Miles Again

I FREELY confess that there have been times recently when almost anything – the shape of a patch on the ceiling, a recipe for rhubarb jam read upside down in the paper – has seemed to me more interesting than the passionless creep of a Miles Davis trumpet solo.

Dizzy Gillespie

DIZZY HAS always been rather emotionless for my taste, and my reply to the sleeve's contention that a tempo of over ninety bars a minute sorts out the men from the boys would be that it is the boys – like Dizzy – who can cope. Technique by itself is as boring in jazz as anywhere else.

Art Tatum

FOR MY taste, Tatum is rather like a dressmaker who, having seen how pretty one frill looks, makes a dress bearing ninety-nine . . .

Miles Ahead

THE PLACING of the sad plangency of Davis's flugelhorn against a shifting background of scored brass, French horns and woodwind produces a much pleasanter surface texture than usual with this soloist, and one can see how, like the companion album *Porgy and Bess*, it won instant popularity. Though only one piece – 'Blues for Pablo' – is actually by Evans, he is the presiding genius, and the album marks a peak of integration of soloist with ensemble. The only trouble from my point of view is that, as jazz, it is practically non-alcoholic.

Luis Russell

IF THE President of Yeshiva University in New York had sent a car for you some five years ago it would probably have been driven by Luis Russell, who at sixty did the job on twenty-four-hour call. This saddening anecdote is not to be found on the sleeve of *The Luis Russell Story, 1929–30* (Parlophone), but then Russell was not a famous chauffeur.

Chick Webb

'STOMPIN' AT The Savoy' (CBS) presents the Chick Webb Orchestra as it was in 1934–5, and I listened in vain for the 'powerhouse drumming' promised on the sleeve. Once I heard a noise like a couple of heavy suitcases being put down, but that was all.

Back to Miles Davis

MILES IS one of the principal figures of present-day jazz, and I'm sure a lot of people like him, but to me he is the Charles Addams of the trumpet – without the humour, of course.

Archie Shepp

I CONTINUE to listen gamely to Archie Shepp (who is wearing a beard now) in the hope that it will one day all cease to sound like 'Flight of the Bumble Bee' scored for bagpipes and concrete-mixer, but *Mama Too Tight* (Impulse) hasn't managed this.

The Blues Boom

I AM getting rather tired of the blues boom. Having for thirty years known the blues as a kind of jazz that calls forth a particular sincerity from the player ('Yeah, he's all right, but can he play the *blues*?'), or as a muttering, plangent lingua franca of the southern American Negro, it gives me no pleasure to hear it banged out in unvarying fortissimo by an indistinguishable series of groups and individuals of both races and nations. Moreover, we may be killing the goose that lays the golden eggs. The blues is tough, resilient, basic, ubiquitous. But it is not indestructible, and if we go on like this the day will come when the whole genre will be as tedious as, say, the Harry Lime theme.

Larkin's Law

I F I were to frame Larkin's Law of Reissues, it would say that anything you haven't got already probably isn't worth bothering about. In other words, if someone tries to persuade you to buy a limited edition of the 1924–5 sessions by Paraffin Joe and his Nitelites, keep your pockets buttoned up; if they were any good, you'd have heard of them at school, as you did King Oliver, and have laid out your earliest pocket money on them. Everything worthwhile gets reissued about every five years.

Billy Banks

S P A C E   I S short, so let's lay it on the line: you are unlikely to encounter a better record this year than *Billy Banks and his Rhythmakers* (CBS/Realm). Or any other year for that matter.

What's good about it? Well, I have written on this subject before, and will try not to repeat myself. These four sessions in 1932, famous as they are, are obscure of provenance: it seems that Irving Mills (Ellington's manager) wanted to record Banks, a young singer he had discovered, and asked Eddie Condon to pick up a supporting group. In fact the groups Condon produced played such exciting jazz that Banks was left off the last session, Henry 'Red' Allen and Chick Bullock doing the vocals instead.

The men who took part were Allen, Pee Wee Russell, Joe Sullivan, Fats Waller, Jimmy Lord, Tommy Dorsey, Happy Cauldwell and Zutty Singleton, and in 1932 they were mostly in the first prime of youth and strength; they picked an assortment of blues, standards and oddities ('Yes, Suh'), and simply jammed them to death in solos and ensembles that for some remain the plainest demonstration of what jazz is – a bunch of Americans, white and Negro, blowing up incandescent versions of a broad spectrum of kinds of tune.

After all, Armstrong is only Armstrong, and Ellington only Ellington, but in the Banks sides you have perhaps a dozen men, all of great individual talent, instinctively combining in a common language to generate a hard-hitting, unaffected excitement, not without humour but utterly without kidding. The last three choruses of 'Yellow Dog Blues', for instance, were reproduced by Wilder Hobson in his book *American Jazz Music* (1938) as an example of what collective improvisation should be.

Goodbye, Johnny Hodges

SINCE I last wrote the demise of Ellington's superb altoist Johnny Hodges has been announced. Hodges brought as much beauty into jazz as Coltrane did ugliness (a large claim, but I'll stick to it), but Coltrane got *The Times* obituary and Hodges didn't: that's the world we live in. Towards the end of his life Hodges's alto tone had become refined to the point at which it hardly seemed like an instrument: more like someone thinking. And, indeed, that's what it was.

Blues and Rock Music

BLUES LIE at the heart of rock, and rock (to quote Mick Farren in the *Melody Maker*) 'today . . . is so powerful a force that it will draw a quarter of a million people to sleep in the open for days on end. It can spread tolerance or invoke violence. It cannot be ignored.' Strong words, but even if one can accept the more philosophical claims that are currently being made for the music ('a source of energy and a means of generating solidarity') it's still only certain elements in the blues isolated, coarsened and amplified. It may affect audiences more strongly but this is only to say that home-distilled hooch is more affecting than château-bottled claret, or a punch on the nose than a reasoned refutation under nineteen headings.

All the above from *All What Jazz* (1985)

Philip Larkin

12

SLEEVE NOTES

Musicians sometimes criticize jazz writers for not knowing what it is like to be underpaid and unrecognized. They obviously forget that jazz writers have sometimes had to make a living out of writing sleeve notes, those long and often well-researched essays that filled up the back of LP covers (and are still found in tiny illegible print on those concertinas of paper that fall out of CDs). Most musicians ran a mile from the idea of doing their own notes, but one exception was Dick Wellstood, the stride pianist, whose sardonic and inventive sense of humour turned the sleeve note into a miniature art form. This section would be worth its presence alone to remind people of his gift.

To an Absent Sleeve Note

Wee, banish'd, cow'rin', starved sleevie,
Wha's happ'nin'? Whaur's thy writer's gravy?
Wi' six a spate o' tunes by Sandy
We couldnae battle!
We wad be laith, O fans, tae haze thee
Wi' murd'ring prattle!

I doubt na, sleevie, thou maun gae:
Baith space an' worrdage hae it so,
The best layoots (an' writings too)
Gang aft tae Hell
An' lae'e us rame for nought tae do
But Personnel.

Sandy Brown,
from *Doctor McJazz*

Sandy Brown

See Obituary on Back

ALBUM LINER notes are like funeral eulogies. They're very very
often misleading. Just as a minister can make the death of a rotten
mother . . . seem like a tremendous loss to society, liner-note writers
often extol the virtues of an inferior album, claiming that listening to
certain cuts from it will cure every disease known to man. However,
after you buy the album and listen to it, you feel like finding the dude
who wrote the notes, putting a gun up to his head and saying, 'Hey,
you jive sucker, you owe me $5.98, I want it now, and I don't accept
cheques!'

from *Franklyn Ajaye – Comedian*

Do Not Read This

IT'S DUMB for liner notes to rave about the music, in view of the fact
that you've presumably already bought the album . . . like those
packages you bring home and the first thing you see when you open
them is 'CONGRATULATIONS!!! YOU HAVE JUST ACQUIRED
THE BEST CASSETTE RECORDER AVAILABLE!!!'.

from *Paul Desmond Quartet Live*

Paul Desmond

On Preposterousness

IT WAS 1856, and Senator James Buchanan was expecting to be nominated for President of the United States by the Democratic Party meeting in Cincinatti, Ohio. Sitting at his home in Washington, he feigned a great indifference to the proceedings, but finally his curiosity and ambition took over, and he dispatched his venerable pompous black butler down to the telegraph office to see whether word had come in from Cincinatti on who had won. The old gentleman left, and an hour later waddled back. 'Senator Buchanan,' he said gravely, 'preposterous as it may seem, you have been nominated for President of the United States.'

The operative word, preposterous. If there is someone reading these notes who figures he'll buy this record or not depending on whether I can authoritatively persuade him to do so, FOR GOD'S SAKE STOP READING.

from *Dick Wellstood and his All Star Orchestra*

Wm F. Buckley, Jr

Miles Davis Speaks

GLEASON ONCE tried to get Miles to suggest what he'd like brought out about his music in some liner notes. No liner notes, Miles said.

'There's nothing to say about the music,' he told Ralph. 'Don't write about the music. The music speaks for itself.'

And on another occasion: 'Critics write whole columns and pages of big words and still ain't saying nothing. If you have spent half your life getting to know your business and the other cats in it, and what they are doing, then you know whether a critic knows what he's talking about. Most of the time they don't. I pay no attention to what the critics say about me, the good or the bad. The toughest critic I got, and the only one I worry about, is myself. My music has to get past me and I'm too vain to play anything I think is bad.'

from *Miles Davis – Dig*

Doug Ramsey

How to Write a Sleeve Note

I LIKED the sound of the bass. I liked the small sounds from the trumpet. I liked it when it went very high, I liked the whole piece, it made me very relaxed, it nearly made me fall asleep when only the bass was playing.

from *Springboard*, entire sleeve note by
Richie Stevens (aged 6)

How to Explain that One of the Instruments on a Record Is Totally Inaudible

IT IS often stated that Steve Brown, later one of the mainstays of Jean Goldkette's and Paul Whiteman's orchestras, was the string bassist on this session. This is not so; Arnold Loyacano was the man responsible, though the crude pre-electric recording, while it worked miraculously with the front line, could not perpetuate the massive tones of Loyacano's instrument, so his bowing and picking can only be felt, rather than heard.

from *Georg Brunis and the New Orleans Rhythm Kings*
Anon

Medical Notes from Sandy Brown

I REMEMBER one occasion at the end of 1973 when he had just been discharged from hospital after an operation for, I think, the removal of varicose veins. He needed two walking sticks and looked pale and drawn. I asked him how the operation had gone and he weighed his words carefully before replying. 'Well, Alun, if you ever have the option to choose either this kind of operation or to be encased for the rest of your life inside an Iron Maiden with extra long spikes, and special attention given to the region of the genitals, then I would advise you to go for the latter.'

from *Splanky*, Sandy Brown
Alun Morgan

Self-portrait

NO MUSICIAN can usefully comment on the quality of his own work. It either communicates or doesn't. But I think I can say how my clarinet playing got to be like it is. I was self-taught from the age of twelve and heard few other clarinettists in person for the first ten years of my career. When I did, it occurred to me that I didn't conform with what were usually considered to be normal clarinet techniques: it seemed a bit late to do much about it except to continue along the same course.

from *Sandy Brown*
Sandy Brown

Heading for Extinction

DURING THIS period Dodo was living alone in a tiny two-storey frame house in West Hollywood, off Santa Monica Boulevard. In it he had installed thrift-store furniture and a good upright piano. The inside of the bath-tub was painted green. Dodo would draw a tepid bath and lie in the tub and luxuriate, watching the rays of sunlight glint through an open window and bounce around the greenish water.

He was a born dreamer, a man enslaved in a universe of sound. Every sound had a secret meaning for him. Certain sounds issued imperious orders. If he were walking down the street and a cathedral began chiming vespers he would stop and listen, rooted to the spot until the sounds stopped and he was released from their spell. One of his favourite things was to stay up all night so that he could stand barefoot on the dewy plot in front of the house, listening to the cries of birds as they awakened to the California dawn. For kicks he continued to whiz through the Bach 'Two-Part Inventions' playing them at perilous speeds, never faltering on a note. And confiding to intimates that he was doomed as a piano player because his hands were too small. The hands that were so quick, sure and equally matched.

from *Dodo Marmarosa*
Ross Russell

On Rhythm Sections

'IF OTHER pianists were as candid as I am,' Lennie once told Bill Coss, 'they would tell you about what they think about rhythm sections. My experience is that if you talk to a bass player, the only good drummer is a dead one. They all talk about Sid Catlett or Dave Tough. And the drummers are the same. My problem has always been to find a bassist and drummer who can play *together*. See, that's the word – together. But nowadays there are no sidemen left. Everyone is a soloist.'

from *Lines*
Lennie Tristano

Lenny Bruce and Jazz

THE JAZZ musician is a rebel with humour, if with a cause, and there is no more effective putdown of the political speeches, the incongruities in the news, the fatuous posing of the tent show religious carnivals than that which goes on in the conversation of the jazz musician and the humour of Lenny Bruce.

It's ribald. Yes, and even sometimes rough. But it's real. You have to earn the respect of the jazz musician, he doesn't give it because he's told to. And this attitude, a modern manifestation of the original American 'show me', is Bruce's strength. He's a verbal Hieronymus Bosch in whose monologue there is the same urgency as in a Charlie Parker chorus and the same sardonic vitality in his comments as in Lester Young's reflections on a syrupy pop tune.

from *The Sick Humour of Lenny Bruce*
Ralph J. Gleason

Coleman Hawkins's Vibrato

AT THIS point, Mr Bernstein required the demonstration of a saxophone phrase played first with vibrato, and then without. Coleman Hawkins, the man who quite literally introduced the saxophone into jazz, did the first part of this beautifully, but couldn't cut out his classic vibrato to save his soul! After a few attempts, Hawk was laughing so hard at himself that he had to give up, so on a subsequent studio date we asked Romeo Penque, a versatile musician with a feeling for jazz, to record these two examples.

from *What Is Jazz?*
George Avakian

My First Good Ballad

CARMEL

I HAVE been composing ballads for some time now and have never liked any of them. To me, there was always something missing – a lack of depth or spiritual quality – or maybe they just were weak tunes, but somehow, all of my ballads sounded stupid to me. As I look back and reflect on these tunes, it came to me that I had tried to plan these tunes into something instead of playing them, and that's what was wrong. In all of my other ballads, I had stifled my creativity with a whole bunch of 'try this chord in this bar' bullshit which just didn't work for me. I didn't plan 'Carmel'. I don't even know how many bars are in it and I don't care. One day, I was playing and it just came out. I left it that way and it's my first ballad that doesn't sound stupid to me.

from *Hampton Hawes*
Hampton Hawes

A Posthumous Sleeve Note

THE OFFICE phone rang just before closing. It was Ben Webster wanting to know if we could bring our equipment to the Renaissance that night and record him. His enthusiasm was hard to resist, and after a quick check with our engineer, Howard Holzer, I said yes.

The next few hours were involved with transporting and setting up our Ampex, mixing console, microphones, and monitor system. The Renaissance, a small club on the Sunset Strip in Hollywood, was a relaxed place to play, but left a good deal to be desired for recording. Howard set up behind the bandstand, just three or four feet from the musicians, separated only by a thin curtain, unable to see them, but so close their sound made it next to impossible to hear the mix through his earphones. The bandstand was small; mike stands and cables were everywhere; it seemed like utter confusion . . . until they started to play. Then, somehow, it all worked. The musicians felt like playing, Ben was in an expansive mood. The audience responded. And we were able to fix some of the music and the mood of the time and the place on tape.

Thinking back to that October night a dozen years ago, it amazes me to realize how much everything has changed. The Renaissance is no more, the Sunset Strip is changed, the music has changed, the mood of the audiences has changed, the musicians have dispersed. It would be almost impossible to bring those times back, or recreate the sounds on this recording.

Those days, before the war in Vietnam turned things around, before rock music and the new life style of the young generation, when black militancy was in its beginnings, before black musicians were deeply committed to the expression of blackness, seem, in retrospect, like the end of a musical era. It was almost the last time jazz musicians would be able to get together to 'swing' and 'have a ball' – to enjoy themselves, and entertain an audience out for a relaxed evening and a good time.

Today even the word 'jazz' is suspect, and the musicians with something to say play for listeners who come to hear the music, not to sit around and relax over a couple of drinks. The jazz club exists as a carry-over from the past, only because we have not yet found a way to bring the new musicians and their audiences together in a better way.

The world is certainly not a better place in 1972 than it was in 1960 but just as certainly we don't want to go back in time. The new music offers new challenges, new excitement, new opportunities. But once in a while it's worth looking back and so this recording is a brief, affectionate return to another time and place. That's the way it was 14 October 1960 . . .

Ben Webster, in 1960, had been living in Los Angeles for a few years, making recordings, playing in clubs, but not really getting anywhere, or even making any money. A warmly sentimental man (you can hear that in the sound of his horn), Ben was really in the area because he was devoted to his old aunt and his grandmother. They were not in good health, he worried constantly about them, and when they died, he moved on to New York, and then to Europe where he now lives, in Copenhagen. Ben wasn't really happy in Los Angeles except for the times, and they were not nearly as often as he wished, when he was playing with some of the superb musicians, who understood him. I remember one afternoon shortly before he left Hollywood, Ben listened to the tape of 'Georgia' in this album, and when it finished there were tears in his eyes. 'Why can't I get to play with guys like that anymore?'

Jimmy Rowles got his start in music through Ben, and they were friends for twenty years. A vastly underrated musician, Rowles seems to have played with everybody in the past thirty years: Benny Goodman, Lester Young, Charlie Parker, Woody Herman, Tommy Dorsey are just a few. Since 1951 he's been much in demand as a studio musician.

Jim Hall has gone on to become one of the handful of . . .

Lester Koenig,
February 2, 1972

Then the pencil broke, and that's all she wrote, like they say in the song.

Somebody must have called Lester Koenig to the telephone to answer some kind of dumb question – that's the way it is when you run an independent jazz record company, and Les was an absolutely quintessential example of the species. Which used to keep him too busy to make all the records he wanted to, and too busy to get right back to finishing a set of liner notes for an album that *should* have gotten out, but, for one reason or another, just stayed stuck in the can.

A lot of us – producers, musicians, engineers, and not a few jazz fans – loved Les because he was a fussbudget who wouldn't let things go out until they were *right*, and because he had the sense to know what *right* was and the ability and determination to get things that way. This was one of the records he was fussing with; he'd play bits and pieces to tease those of us who dropped by to visit while the tapes were up on the machine.

So permit me to complete an unfinished sentence, and a partway-done liner note. When I was a kid, I read that Ben Jonson's tombstone was supposed to read Orare Ben Jonson, using the Latin for 'pray for', but the stonecutter messed it up into O Rare Ben Jonson. O rare Lester Koenig.

from *Ben Webster at the Renaissance*
Ed Michel

What Is 'Good'?

IF THE function of the artist is, as Palinurus said it is, to create masterpieces, then I would never have bothered to conceive this album, for masterpiece I don't intend it to be.

It may not even be 'good', for I don't really know what 'good' is. I know only what I do. For music is something that people *do*, like painting or plumbing or cobbling or butling, not something that is done to people like spanking or air pollution or electronic 'music'.

Since the beginning of my professional career in 1945 the idea of what is good has been stood on its head a few times. 'Stride piano', for instance, was scorned as old-hat but worshipped as a unique art and as 'roots' in 1972. The same pianists who were, in their hipness, playing block chords in 1948 or quoting Myra Hess's transcription of 'Jesu, Joy of Man's Desiring' or 'How High the Moon' in 1953 were adding minor thirds and sevenths to every tonic triad ('funk') by 1960 and playing Jim Webb tunes in 1971. All part of the Dance of Death, and ideas of good or bad have really no part in it.

from *Dick Wellstood and Kenny Davern*

Dick Wellstood

This Is the One

THIS IS it, *This Is the One*. I made this record in October 1975, on one of my days off from an engagement at the Van Dyke restaurant in Schenectady, New York. My playing here is the way I had always wished I could get it on record – free and relaxed. Never thought I'd do it, but I did it and here it is – *This Is the One* is the one!

from *This Is the One*

Dick Wellstood

'I Know That You Know'

SOMEONE HAS said that melody is the layman's key to music. Most lay people listen to the melody and think they're listening to the music (sometimes they'll listen to the rhythm by patting their feet). What do musicians listen to? Things like textures, contours, oddball substitutions, things like that. Sometimes one gets much satisfaction from the small pleasures, such as the special phrasing with which Lambert here jumps into the first chorus, swinging immediately. Very effective, and difficult to bring off so smoothly.

This performance illustrates how the stride players didn't do so much improvising. For instance, the bass line in the turn-around (bars 13–16) is *always* the same, with various licks on top of it (and very complex ones), as in the fourth chorus, where Lambert delays the right hand against the syncopated bass (in such a way as could make your hand fall off at the wrist). So is the bass line at the end of each chorus, bars 23–25 or thereabouts, always the same. Why all this talk about bass lines? What do you think I listen to, the melody?

'Beautiful Love – Sweet Lorraine'

MUCH OF what Lambert does can be explained by the fact that he was usually playing in a bar. Why does he start one song and suddenly go to another? Because he wasn't in concert, and could do what he wanted; or perhaps because somebody started to whistle along with him. Why does he sometimes miss notes? Because the piano was bad or because he had been drinking. (Lambert always drank on duty.) Why does he sometimes play two perfunctory choruses of something and stop? Because he was only fulfilling a request, and was bored. In other words, these recordings are not only not studio recordings of sound quality – they're not studio recordings in terms of intent either. They present a music that was as much *Gebrauchmusik* as a Mozart cassation, music as it was actually made.

Sextet from *Lucia*

THROUGHOUT MUCH of the nineteenth century, up through maybe the first war, a good part of both European and American popular music came from opera and operetta. European piano literature is full of operatic transcriptions for solo piano, and they undoubtedly passed into the ragtime tradition through American tours by such pianists as Anton Rubinstein and Paderewski. It is therefore not at all out of character for Lambert, who was born in 1904, to play a stride version of a piece like the 'Sextet'.

One is struck again by the incredible amount of *patience* it takes to play this way. Lambert's left hand just pumps away unceasingly, never complaining. One must be a very proud man to play like this.

Incidentally, Wolfgang Kunert, one of the Jazz People at North German Radio in Hamburg, once played me a tape of Eubie Blake, recorded at an except-for-Eubie mostly avant-garde intellectual left-wing jazz festival in Berlin in the 1970s. Eubie chose to play the Pilgrim's Chorus from *Tannhaüser* and got a standing ovation. Wolfgang pointed out that absolutely no one else could have gotten away with playing Wagner in Berlin for such an audience. Just think what a hit Lambert could have been in Italy!

All the above from *Donald Lambert II*
Dick Wellstood

Ragtime

RAGTIME IS a fairly simple, straightforward music. Simple, that is, compared to the music of, say, the Beatles, Elliot Carter, Brahms, Ravi Shankar or most 'jazz'. There are ragtime freaks who would have you believe that ragtime is indeed quite complex, perhaps more significant than the stodgy old Beethoven Sonatas. This is not so. Scott Joplin's rags are full of naive harmonizations, simple-assed bass progressions, mock-important interludes and nineteenth-century salon cliché. That they are any good at all is attributable to the lyric gift of Joplin, for his song survives all the above-mentioned faults and many more.

from *From Ragtime on*
Dick Wellstood

'George Sanders'

WE RECORDED this blues in C a day or so after George Sanders committed suicide. I was quite taken that a man who throughout his life gave out that he was bored to death should, in the end, kill himself out of boredom. A peculiar integrity, or perhaps another's triumph. Either way, I felt a common chord.

'Suppertime'

A TUNE Davern taught to me. It was featured by a great singer, Ethel Waters, but Kenny learned it off a record Helen Forrest made with Artie Shaw's band. It was written by a great writer, Irving Berlin, who gave us 'White Christmas' and 'God Bless America'. It was Irving's song of protest against lynching, and he regards it as one of his most interesting songs. That is all I know about 'Suppertime', and I learned most of this information *after* the recording. *You* figure out what it all means.

Both the above from *Dick Wellstood and Kenny Davern*

Dick Wellstood

'Poor Buttermilk'

POOR ZEZ Confrey doesn't fit into any of the fashionable pigeonholes of 'jazz'. He didn't come up the river from New Orleans, didn't jam on 52nd Street, wasn't a junkie, etc. Or if he was I never heard of it. Although he composed the fabulously successful 'Kitten on the Keys', he received a bare mention in Rudi Blesh's book on ragtime. I like 'Poor Buttermilk' anyway. It should properly be played slowly and sweetly by a choir of drunken soprano saxo-phonists. This particular performance was conceived in passion and executed in rage . . . 'Buttermilk' is a tricky piece in its original form and I made it trickier by trading hands in the repeat of the second section, by adding additional material, etc. When I got through I wasted so much tape trying to get a clean performance that I lost my temper and attacked the piano with the idea of destroying Confrey and his damn tune. This performance was the result. I have included it in this album because I felt the spirit of hatred more than made up for a few mistakes.

'Atlanta Blues'

A TUNE I first heard in Greensboro, North Carolina in 1947. I don't know what it's about.

'Carolina Shout'

THIS PIECE was held up to me early as *the* piece one had to cut if one was to play stride piano, and I immediately got so uptight about it that I still have trouble with it. Recently I've started to loosen it up a bit, the way I do here. I knew a piano player named Q. Roscoe Snowden who could play it right.

'Fig Leaf (A Classy Rag)'

ONE OF Scott Joplin's finest. I had originally intended to record more rags for this album but I copped out. Why? Because ragtime is afflicted, not only with the sleeve-garter and straw-hat freaks, but also with the kind of megalomaniac snobs who usually pick nits with each other over things like 'Grand Opera' or eighteenth-century 'melodic' ornamentation. Ragtime suffers much talk of 'inner voices' and 'corrupt editions' these days and has survived the assaults of bar-room piano players (me, for instance) only to find itself in danger of being inflected to death by Juilliard graduates.

'South Amboy Highball'

THE TITLE is heavily ironic. South Amboy is a grimy industrial community in New Jersey, where the Jersey Central trains cross a drawbridge over the Raritan River and change from electric to diesel for the run to the Bay Head loop. The bridge freezes open in the winter, engines are late, things break, etc. The upshot is that nothing highballs through South Amboy. Hence my title. The music itself leans lightly on Wesley Wallace's 'Number 29', a train blues recorded in 1930. I first heard it on Art Hodes's WNYC radio show in 1943. It seemed old then, but it was only thirteen years old. 1943 was twenty-eight years ago. Strange perspectives we have on who and what is old in 'jazz'.

All the above from *Dick Wellstood Alone*

Dick Wellstood

Giant Steps

I LIKE to play pieces such as this one, which is one that gives 'modernists' fits even today. This was my very first public try at it, anyplace. There are many, many pianists who can play 'Giant Steps' but not more than a dozen who can play convincing stride piano.

from *This Is The One*

Dick Wellstood

'Pork and Beans'

'PORK AND BEANS' is a virtuoso piece by the late virtuoso 'Luckey' Roberts, the main point of which is that the third strain imitates the snapping of a rubber band, a conception unique in music so far as I know. I frequently snap better than I did on this take, but life is short and we had to get the record out. It has a nice feel anyway.

'Fucallia'

'FUCALLIA' ('few-sally-uh') is respectfully dedicated to the memory of Proculus of Albengue, who in AD 281 enjoyed one hundred Sarmatian virgins in two weeks. I have been playing piano in bars for twenty-six years, and on this number I sound like a piano player who has been playing piano in bars for twenty-six years.

'Yesterday'

I RECENTLY worked with a drummer, a veteran of the 'progressive jazz' scene of the early 1950s, who was outraged that 'Yesterday' should contain a seven-bar phrase rather than the standard eight-bars. One man's music-of-tomorrow is another man's counter-revolution, I guess. Some Dixieland bands stretch it into eight bars. So it goes.

'Handful of Keys'

'HANDFUL OF Keys' used to be a magic shout piece for me. Willie Gant frequently played it in the Hollywood Café where I used to go in 1946 to hear pianists like Art Tatum, Marlowe Morris, Billy Taylor, Gimpy Irvis and others. I would occasionally play too, and I remember one night an astonished voice exclaiming 'That's a white boy playin'!' God bless you, sir, wherever you are.

All the above from *From Ragtime On*

Dick Wellstood

Stan Kenton

9 April 1956
STAN KENTON
Bandleader

Bartok, Concerto for Orchestra (Amsterdam Concertgebouw/Van Beinum)
'When It's Sleepy Time Down South' (Louis Armstrong and his All Stars)
'The House of Strings' (Stan Kenton and his Orchestra)
'The Blues' (Joya Sherrill/Duke Ellington and his Famous Orchestra)
'Nancy with the Laughing Face' (Frank Sinatra)
Ibert, 'Rome' (from *Escales*) (New York Philharmonic/Rodzinski)
'We All Need Love' (Danny Purches)
'Sixteen Tons' (Tennessee Ernie Ford)

Book: H. L. Overstreet, *The Mature Mind*

Humphrey Lyttelton

3 September 1956
HUMPHREY LYTTELTON
Jazz trumpeter and bandleader

'Café Society Blues' (Count Basie and his All-American Rhythm Section)
'African Queen' (Sandy Brown's Jazz Band)
'Basin Street Blues' (Louis Armstrong and his Orchestra)
'Ain't Misbehavin'' (Louis Armstrong and his All Stars)
'Gone Away Blues' (Mezzrow-Bechet Quintet)
'Rock Island Line' (Stan Freberg and his Skiffle Group)
'Louisiana Blues' (Muddy Waters/Little Walter)
'Panama' (Luis Russell and his Orchestra)

Luxuries: A trumpet and a harmonium

13

DESERT ISLAND DISCS

At my local bookshop, called Ex Libris, in the Shambles at Bradford-on-Avon, the man who looks after it once confided to me that his favourite browsing book when no customers were around was 'Desert Island Lists', which contained the records and books and luxuries chosen by *everyone* who had been on the programme in the Roy Plomley era. Leafing through it I discovered that he was right; it was endlessly fascinating. So much so that I bought his only copy of it, and earned his cordial loathing. Now when I go in there his eyes narrow. Recently he told me he had found another book to browse in, but he wasn't going to tell me what it was, not for any price. Here, anyway, are all the jazz musicians of interest listed in the book. Anyone who raises eyebrows at Sacha Distel's inclusion must remember that he was France's number one jazz guitarist in the 1950s and even recorded a whole LP with the Modern Jazz Quartet. One profound mystery: both Acker Bilk and Ronnie Scott chose the same book for their desert island reading – *Wind in the Willows*.

Jack Teagarden

11 November 1957
JACK TEAGARDEN
Jazz trombonist and vocalist

'Basin Street Blues' (Charleston Chasers)
'You Rascal, You' (Fats Waller/Jack Teagarden and his Orchestra)
'Georgia on My Mind' (Hoagy Carmichael and his Orchestra)
'She's a Great, Great Girl!' (Roger Wolfe Kahn and his Orchestra)
'Knockin' a Jug' (Louis Armstrong and his Orchestra)
'Junk Man' (Jack Teagarden and his Orchestra)
'Rockin' Chair' (Louis Armstrong and his All Stars)
'The Waiter and the Porter and the Upstairs Maid' (from film *The Birth of the Blues*) (Bing Crosby/Mary Martin/Jack Teagarden and his Orchestra)

Luxuries: A trombone, and materials for making a crystal radio set

Earl Hines

16 December 1957
EARL HINES
Jazz pianist

'Cherry' (Bobby Hackett/Jackie Gleason and his Orchestra)
'Makin' Whoopee' (from *Whoopee*) (Nat 'King' Cole)
'You've Changed' (Connie Russell)
'April in Paris' (from *Walk a Little Faster*) (Count Basie and his Orchestra)
'I Hadn't Anyone Till You' (Bob Manning)
'It's All Right with Me' (Lena Horne)
'Somehow' (Billy Eckstine/Earl Hines and his Orchestra)
'Love Is Just Around the Corner' (Les Elgart and his Orchestra)

Luxury: A piano

Chris Barber

9 February 1959
CHRIS BARBER
Jazz bandleader

'Market Street Stomp' (Missourians)
'Right On, Your Time Ain't Long' (Biddleville Quintette)
'Hotter Than That' (Louis Armstrong and his Hot Five)
'Versailles' (from *Suite Fontessa*) (Modern Jazz Quartet)
'Heavenly Sunshine' (Laura Henton)
'Chicago Breakdown' (Big Maceo/Hudson Whittaker/Charles R. Sanders.)
'Automobile' (Lightnin' Hopkins)
'Saratoga Shout' (Luis Russell and his Orchestra)

Luxuries: His sports car and petrol

George Shearing

5 November 1962
GEORGE SHEARING
Jazz pianist

'T'ain't What You Do' (Jimmie Lunceford and his Orchestra)
Debussy, 'La cathédrale engloutie' (*Prelude*, Book 1, No 10) (Walter Gieseking)
Dvorak, 'Humoresque' in G flat (Art Tatum)
Rachmaninov, Piano Concerto No 2 in C minor (Sergei Rachmaninov/Philadelphia Orchestra/Stokowski)
'Lullaby of Birdland' (Erroll Garner)
'Don't Blame Me' (Teddy Wilson)
Bach, 'Widerstehe Doch der Sünde' (Cantata No 54) (Alfred Deller/Leonhardt Baroque Ensemble)
Delius, 'On Hearing the First Cuckoo in Spring' (RPO/Beecham)

Luxury: A metal construction set

Book: Captain Frederick Marryat, *Masterman Ready*

Acker Bilk

10 December 1962
ACKER BILK
Bandleader and jazz clarinettist

'Burgundy Street Blues' (George Lewis's Ragtime Band)
'Diminuendo and Crescendo in Blue' (Duke Ellington and his Orchestra)
'Doctor Jazz Stomp' (Jelly Roll Morton and his Red Hot Peppers)
'Papa Dip' (New Orleans Wanderers)
'You Made Me Love You' (from film *Broadway Melody of 1938*) (Edmond Hall/Lopez Furst)
'Singin' the Blues' (Bix Beiderbecke)
'I Know It Was the Lord' (Famous Ward Singers)
'Stompin' at the Savoy' (Ella Fitzgerald/Louis Armstrong)

Luxury: Apple seeds

Book: Kenneth Grahame, *The Wind in the Willows*

Annie Ross

26 July 1965
ANNIE ROSS
Jazz singer and actress

'Teddy the Toad' (Count Basie and his Orchestra)
'Just Friends' (Charlie Parker)
Villa-Lobos, Bachianas Brasileiras No 5 (Bidu Sayao/8 cellos/Villa-Lobos)
'Chelsea Bridge' (Duke Ellington and his Orchestra)
'Last Night When We Were Young' (Judy Garland)
Weill, 'Surabaya Johnny' (from *Happy End*) (Georgia Brown)
J. Strauss, 'Adele's Laughing Song' (from *Die Fledermaus*) (Florence Foster Jenkins/Cosmo McMoon)
'Good Morning, Heartache' (Billie Holiday)

Luxury: False eyelashes

Book: Marguerite Steen, *The Sun Is My Undoing*

Louis Armstrong

5 August 1968
LOUIS ARMSTRONG
Jazz trumpeter, bandleader and entertainer

'Blueberry Hill' (Louis Armstrong and his All Stars)
Weill/Brecht, 'Mack the Knife' (from *The Threepenny Opera*) (Louis
   Armstrong)
'People' (from *Funny Girl*) (Barbra Streisand)
'Bye Bye Blues' (Guy Lombardo and his Royal Canadians)
'New Orleans' (Bobby Hackett's Band)
Gershwin, 'Bess, You Is My Woman Now' (from *Porgy and Bess*) (Ella
   Fitzgerald/Louis Armstrong)
'Stars Fell on Alabama' (Louis Armstrong and his All Stars)
'What a Wonderful World' (Louis Armstrong Orchestra and Chorus)

Luxury: A trumpet

Book: His autobiography

Sacha Distel

2 January 1971
SACHA DISTEL
Vocalist, guitarist and composer

Weill/Brecht, 'Mack the Knife' (from *The Threepenny Opera*) (Louis
   Armstrong)
'Parker's Mood' (Charlie Parker and his All Stars)
Ravel, 'La valse' (LSO/Monteux)
'Israel' (Miles Davis and his Orchestra)

'Georgia on My Mind' (Ray Charles and his Orchestra/Burns)
'People' (from *Funny Girl*) (Dionne Warwick)
'To Wait for Love' (Sacha Distel)
'Only the Lonely' (Frank Sinatra)

Luxury: A guitar

Book: An illustrated English dictionary

Stephane Grappelli

12 August 1972
STEPHANE GRAPPELLI
Jazz violinist

Beethoven, Symphony No 6 in F major (Pastoral) (Berlin Philharmonic/von Karajan)
Debussy, 'Prélude à l'après-midi d'un faune' (French National Radio Orchestra/Münch)
'In a Mist' (Bix Beiderbecke)
'I Can't Believe That You're in Love with Me' (Louis Armstrong and his Orchestra)
Dvořák, 'Humoresque' (Art Tatum)
'My One and Only Love' (Art Tatum–Ben Webster Quartet)
'Body and Soul' (John Coltrane/ensemble)
'Gary' (Stephane Grappelli/Marc Hemmeler/Jack Sewing/Kenny Clarke)

Luxury: The Koh-i-noor diamond

Book: An atlas

George Melly

17 March 1973
GEORGE MELLY
Writer, film critic and blues singer

Lennon & McCartney, 'Sergeant Pepper's Lonely Hearts Club Band' (The Beatles)
'Auntie Maggie's Remedy' (George Formby)
'Potato Head Blues' (Louis Armstrong and his Hot Seven)
Vivaldi, 'Spring' (from *The Four Seasons*) (Robert Michelucci/I Musici)
Kern, 'Yesterdays' (from *Roberta*) (Billie Holiday)
'At the Ball' (Douglas Byng)
'Winin' Boy Blues' (Jelly Roll Morton's New Orleans Jazzmen)
'Hustlin' Dan' (Bessie Smith)

Luxury: A piano

Book: Marcel Proust, *A la recherche du temps perdu*

Ronnie Scott

31 January 1976
RONNIE SCOTT
Saxophonist and jazz club impresario

'The Look of Love' (Stan Getz/Orchestra/Ogerman)
Puccini, 'Si, mi chiamano Mimi' (from *La Bohème*, Act 1 (Elisabeth Schwarzkopf/Philharmonia Orchestra/Rescigno)
'Invitation' (Joe Henderson/Don Friedman/Ron Carter/Jack DeJohnette)
Ravel, 'Lever du jour' (from Daphnis and Chloe Suite No 2) (Orchestre de la Suisse Romande/Ansermet)
Borodin, 'Stranger in Paradise' (from *Kismet*) (Charles McPherson Quartet)

'In a Sentimental Mood' (John Coltrane/Duke Ellington and his Orchestra)

Ponce, 'Scherzino Mexicano' (John Williams)

'For All We Know' (Billie Holiday)

Luxury: His saxophone

Book: Kenneth Grahame, *The Wind in the Willows*

Philip Larkin

17 July 1976

PHILIP LARKIN

Poet

'Dallas Blues' (Louis Armstrong/Luis Russell and his Orchestra)

'Dollia' (Louis Killen)

Tallis, 'Spem in Alium' (40-part motet) (King's College Chapel Choir/Cambridge University Musical Society/Willcocks)

'I'm Down in the Dumps' (Bessie Smith)

'The Coventry Carol' (St George's Canzona)

Elgar, Symphony No 1 in A flat (LPO/Boult)

'These Foolish Things' (from *Spread It Abroad*) (Billie Holiday)

Handel, 'Praise the Lord' (from *Solomon*) (Beecham Choral Society/RPO/Beecham)

Luxury: A typewriter and an unlimited supply of paper

Book: The plays of George Bernard Shaw

Mel Torme

24 July 1976
MEL TORME
Singer and songwriter

'Westwood Walk' (Gerry Mulligan and his Ten-Tette)
Grainger, 'My Robin Is to the Greenwood Gone' (Eastman-Rochester
    Pops Orchestra/Fennell)
Chopin, Prelude No 7 in A major (Jimmie Lunceford and his
    Orchestra)
'The Christmas Song' (Nat 'King' Cole)
Delius, 'On Hearing the First Cuckoo in Spring' (RPO/Beecham)
'The Carioca' (from film *Flying Down to Rio*) (Artie Shaw and his
    Orchestra)
'Reminiscing in Tempo' (Duke Ellington and his Orchestra)
'Dusk' (Light Music Society Orchestra/Dunn)

Luxury: An air conditioner with solar batteries

Book: *The* New York Times *Film Directory*

Dizzy Gillespie

19 January 1980
DIZZY GILLESPIE
Jazz trumpeter

'Rockin' Chair' (Roy Eldridge/Gene Krupa Band)
'Body and Soul' (Art Tatum)
'Lament' (Miles Davis/Gil Evans Orchestra)
'Deep Purple' (Sarah Vaughan)
'Daahoud' (Clifford Brown Ensemble)
'You Don't Know What Love Is' (Billy Eckstine/Eddie Fraser Bebop
    Band)
'Parker's Mood' (Charlie Parker All Stars)
'Passion Flower' (Ella Fitzgerald/Duke Ellington Orchestra)

Luxury: His trumpet

Book: His Baha'i prayer book

Earl Hines

25 May 1980
EARL HINES (2ND APPEARANCE)
Jazz pianist

'Chant of the Weed' (Don Redman and his Orchestra)
'Have You Met Miss Jones?' (from *I'd Rather Be Right*) (Sam Browne/Jack Hylton and his Orchestra)
'Sleep' (Fred Waring and his Pennsylvanians)
'East of the Sun' (Tommy Dorsey and his Orchestra)
'It Isn't Fair' (Bill Farrell)
'It Happens To Be Me' (Ben Webster/ensemble)
'Trust in Me' (Dinah Washington/Quincy Jones and his Orchestra)
'Satin Doll' (Duke Ellington and his Orchestra)

Luxury: Physical culture equipment

Book: Stanley Dance, *The World of Duke Ellington*

Buddy Rich

9 May 1981
BUDDY RICH
Bandleader and drummer

'Tiger Rag' (Ray Noble and his Orchestra)
'The Good Life' (Tony Bennett)
'Willow, Weep for Me' (Ella Fitzgerald)
Gershwin, 'I Loves You, Porgy' (from *Porgy and Bess*) (Miles Davis/ Gil Evans Orchestra)
'In the Wee Small Hours of the Morning' (Frank Sinatra)

'Mission to Moscow' (Benny Goodman Band)
'The Girl on the Rock' (from *Seven Dreams*) (Soloists/Ralph Brewster
   Singers/Orchestra/Gordon Jenkins)
'The Kid from Red Bank' (Count Basie Band)
Luxury: A Ferrari

Book: *The Story of O*

All the above from *Desert Island Lists* (1984)

Roy Plomley

AND SO WE
SAY GOODBYE . . .

When I was a teenager in New York in 1960, a man slouched against the wall in Greenwich Village said: 'English', as I passed by. Infuriated by such perceptiveness, I went back to ask him how he knew. 'Your trousers,' he said. We got talking. I said I was in New York to work, and to hear all the jazz I could. 'Jazz is dying,' he said. 'There is only one man in jazz I can listen to and not know what he is going to play next. One man!'

I asked him who.

'Thelonious Monk. Everyone else is finished.'

It was a depressing experience for me, because I was still finding out about this magic music, and digging deeper into it. To be told it was dead on its feet was not good news. It was the first time I had been told that jazz was finished. The first of many. In the 1960s it was to be finished off by rock music, by Arts Council grants, by apathy, by academic approval . . . In the 1970s it died because of contamination with rock (to produce fusion music) and because the young were no longer interested . . . In the 1980s it was dying because the young *were* interested again, but misunderstanding it – because the jazz revival was turning it into a museum music, a sort of heritage sound – because all the real people had died or were dying . . .

Personally, I was most convinced that jazz was dead in about 1980. Much to my relief, this conviction has faded since then. But some good stuff has been written about the death of jazz, and it seems apt to finish at the end, even if it is only a false curtain, especially as it gives me the chance to disinter some material from a forgotten but fascinating collection of essays on music by Colin Wilson.

My feeling, for what it is worth, is that jazz died some time ago but that the body is in remarkably good condition.

Beyond Jazz

IN NEW York City Criminal Court recently, Charlie Mingus was referred to as 'a great jazz musician'. Mingus, who had or had not punched his trombonist, Jimmy Knepper, was quick to resent this. 'Don't call me a jazz musician,' he retorted. 'To me the word jazz means discrimination, second-class citizenship, the whole back-of-the-bus bit.'

This revealing anecdote suggests that what is happening in the Southern States of America today is not without significance for the present and future state of jazz. The American Negro is trying to take a step forward that can be compared only with the ending of slavery in the nineteenth century. And despite the dogs, the hosepipes and the burnings, advances have already been made towards giving the Negro his civil rights under the Constitution that would have been inconceivable when Louis Armstrong was a young man. These advances will doubtless continue. They will end only when the Negro is as well housed, educated and medically cared-for as the white man.

There are two possible consequences in this for jazz. One is that if in the course of desegregation the enclosed, strongly characterized pattern of Negro life is broken up, its traditional cultures such as jazz will be diluted. The Negro did not have the blues because he was naturally melancholy. He had them because he was cheated and bullied and starved. End this, and the blues may end too.

Secondly, the contemporary Negro jazz musician is caught up by two impulses: the desire to disclaim the old entertainment, down-home, give-the-folks-a-great-big-smile side of his profession that seems today to have humiliating associations with slavery's Congo Square; and the desire for the status of musical literacy, for sophistication, for the techniques and instrumentation of straight music. I should say Mingus's remark was prompted by the first of these, and much of his music by the second. The Negro is in a paradoxical position: he is looking for the jazz that isn't jazz. Either he will find it, or – and I say this in all seriousness – jazz will become an extinct form of music as the ballad is an extinct form of literature, because the society that produced it has gone.

All What Jazz (1985)
Philip Larkin

The Death of a Music

I ATTENDED a jazz concert at Lambertville, NJ, at which both Duke Ellington's orchestra and the Johnny Dankworth band from England performed. The audience were generous to the visitors without apparent insincerity and Cleo Laine was splendid, never better, much applauded; I had a small, ridiculous moment of relish when she sang 'I don't stand a ghost of a chance with you' using the long British A in 'chance'. And the Ellington band were a national institution. And yet . . . My feelings were crystallized by a visit to Birdland not long before we sailed for home. I have tried to blot out of my mind most of what they played, but the sound of Miles Davis's trumpet, introverted, gloomy, sour in both senses, refuses to go away. I had heard the future, and it sounded horrible.

In 1961 the American musicologist Henry Pleasants published a short book, *Death of a Music?* (Gollancz), which demonstrated to my satisfaction that when a music, or a kind of music, loses all connection with song and, in the second place, with dancing, it also loses its audience and is doomed. The music of Pleasants's title was serious music, classical, whatever you like to call it. The last third of his book consists of a substantial rider arguing that jazz, or American music as he would prefer to have it known, having retained its links with song, was the music of the future and would take over the kind of audience that modern serious music had lost. When I ran into Pleasants some twenty years later in England I asked him, 'In the light of what's happened since, you wouldn't say that about jazz any more, would you?' 'No,' he said, 'absolutely not,' and we went on to agree that it had gone the same way as its elder brother and was lost.

Totally. Only the name survives (I am leaving out more or less worthy pastiches of what we once had). Good going in a sense, to have got from Monteverdi to John Cage in – what? Forty years? The Hot Five to Ornette Coleman? Nothing makes me feel more thoroughly old than to realize that there is nothing but a bloody great hole where quite an important part of my life once was. I mean, poetry, the novel and much more besides have gone off all right, but they have not *vanished* (except as it might be for pastiches of bygone writers).

One of the last jazzmen, the once-great Wild Bill Davison, turned up in London in May 1989, a little old man of eighty-three who when I went to see him was sitting in a kimono eating a bowl of what looked like chop-suey. He was at the start of a UK tour with Art Hodes, an eighty-four-year-old pianist who was terrible forty years ago (Philip Larkin remarked of him that he sounded as if he had three hands and didn't know what to do with any of them). With them there was to be a presumably British group called John Petters' Dixielanders in a show called *The Legends of American Dixieland*. I stayed away, probably wisely in view of the sadly dull record of some of his recent work he presented me with. In the November of the same year Davison died in California.

I never heard in the flesh or met my great hero, Pee Wee Russell, when I had the chance in 1959. But that was no doubt just as well too, because he had 'adapted' or at any rate gone off, as records of his had shown.*

On my newish equipment I can hear the notes of the music on the Banks sides at least as well as ever, but not the things I used to hear.

Memoirs (1991)

Kingsley Amis

*   He had never recovered his old fire after a serious illness half a dozen years before.

Jazz: the Wrong Turn

BOP HAS produced its classics – many of the recordings of the Parker–Davis combination, of Powell and Navarro, of Parker and of Gillespie and Roy Eldridge – but the question that strikes the listener is whether this music is an individual and organic expression of its mood, or whether it is an uncomfortable hybrid that one must judge by intention rather than by achievement. In certain ways it reminds us of twelve-tone music; not that they sound alike, but that both are clearly a reaction, a kind of 'anti-mask' (to use Yeats's phrase), the complex response of over-sensitive men to a world that they are afraid would reject the natural expression of their emotions. Parker's most brilliant solos do not convey any direct emotion – not to this listener, at least; one recognizes that they are a complex expression of a personal intensity, that their complexity is a mask of impersonality. The true Parker emerges in a technically poor solo like that in *Lover Man* (which Parker made on the verge of a nervous breakdown, and after drinking a pint of whisky); the voice here is honest and compelling and proves that the complexity was not necessary to impress the listener.

Gillespie, of course, is a different case. Emotionally, he seems to have little in common with Parker. He belongs to the other jazz tradition – the extrovert, the entertainer. He can play an excellent 'straight trumpet', as in some of his big band recordings such as 'Stormy Weather' or 'Jealousy'; or an exhibitionist bop trumpet, as in the big band recordings of the late 1940s with Chano Pozo. In recent years, he seems to have determined to go 'farther out' than most jazz men in sheer technical virtuosity, and has had whole concertos written for him that seem as dry and lifelessly complex as anything by Hindemith. The result of all this is to make one wonder whether Gillespie ever really had anything to 'say', or whether he would not be a better artist if he expressed his good nature and high spirits less pretentiously, like Cannonball Adderley.

The truth would seem to be, then, that jazz took something of a false direction in bop. Bop aroused legitimate enthusiasm because it seemed to announce jazz's coming of age, a new level of seriousness. But the reactionary Hugues Panassié saw penetratingly that it was a dead end. Jazz is essentially rhythmic expression of exuberance or of melancholy; and sometimes of both at the same time, which gives it its peculiar flavour. But it lacks the foundation to become anything more complex. It can legitimately be argued that a fine improvisation is as truly a musical creation as any 'serious' composition. But the technical apparatus of the serious composer is designed to allow him to build large musical structures if he feels so inclined, and to concentrate his musical thinking. If Sonny Rollins or Jimmy Giuffre improvises with the Modern Jazz Quartet, the result may be interesting and agreeable, but one feels instinctively that, in spite of all attempts at complexity, it can never be more than musically light-weight. And when Rollins and Gillespie get together on 'Sunny Side Up', one feels that this music has lost all contact with the kind of jazz played by King Oliver and Jelly Roll Morton and Fats Waller, or sung by Bessie Smith or Billie Holiday. It is no longer expressive; it has moved closer to the Bach fugue. But jazz began as a romantic idiom, and this return to classicism seems as artificial as Stravinsky's. Even so Stravinsky was better at hiding in a cloud of theory. Jazz is an altogether simpler form of self-expression, and it shows clearly when an artist simply 'wants to be clever'.

Colin Wilson on Music (1967)

Colin Wilson

Jazz: Death by Rock Music

WHY SHOULD rock have almost killed jazz for twenty years? Initially there seemed to be no hostility or incompatibility between jazz and rock, even though attentive readers of *The Jazz Scene* will register the note of gentle contempt with which critics and, above all, the musical professionals of jazz, then treated the early triumphs of rock-and-roll, whose public seemed unable to distinguish between a Bill Haley ('Rock Around the Clock') and a Chuck Berry. A crucial distinction between jazz and rock was that rock was never a minority music. Rhythm-and-blues, as it developed after the Second World War, was the folk music of urban Negroes in the 1940s, when one and a quarter millions of Blacks left the South for the northern and western ghettoes. They constituted a new market, which was then supplied chiefly by independent record labels like Chess Records, founded in Chicago in 1949 by two Polish immigrants connected with the club circuit, and specializing in the so-called 'Chicago Blues' style (Muddy Waters, Howlin' Wolf, Sonny Boy Williamson) and recording, among others, Chuck Berry, who was probably – with Elvis Presley – the major influence on 1950s rock-and-roll. White adolescents began to buy black r&b records in the 1950s, having discovered this music on local and specialized radio stations which multiplied during those years, as the mass of adults transferred its attentions to television. At first sight they seemed to be the habitual tiny and untypical minority which can still be seen on the fringes of black entertainment, like the white visitors to Chicago ghetto blues clubs. Yet as soon as the music industry became aware of this potential white youth market, it became evident that rock was the opposite of a minority taste. It was the music of an entire age-group.

The Jazz Scene (1989)
Eric Hobsbawm

Modern Pop and Jazz: the Great Divide

MODERN POP songs don't suit the improvising habits of jazz musicians. There just aren't enough harmonic changes per mile and the ones that do occur are so determinedly triadic that the kind of extension jazz players insist on would destroy the character of the piece. One result is that there is now a widening formal gap between pop and jazz. I find this sad because shedding public involvement always seems to herald the adoption of a course perilously close to the antics of the oozalem bird; and I'm not so daft as to imagine that it's only a matter of time before the butchers' boys' lips purse in anticipation of a programme of Stockhausen and Albert Ayler.

The McJazz Manuscripts (1979)
Sandy Brown

Artie Shaw and the Avant-garde

I GOT out to a few avant-garde jazz concerts. One of them in particular I remember vividly was at the Beverly Theatre, and I went and listened to some of the cats who were playing – some very modern, sort of abstract, expressionist music. Several critics were there, and our erudite friend Leonard Feather (*Los Angeles Times* jazz critic) said he didn't know if I would like it. And I said, 'Leonard, I don't go to music to hear if I like it. I go to hear if the musicians know what they're doing. And if they know what they're doing, I try to make myself hear whether they succeeded in doing it. Whether I like it is beside the point. We're not talking about me; we're talking about the music.' Anyway, I heard a guy named John Carter play clarinet and another fellow named Muhal Richard Abrams, another guy, Anthony Braxton, and they played some pretty interesting, amazing stuff, some of it very humorous, although the audience was listening very solemnly – almost too solemnly, because serious is one thing, solemn is silly. After it was over, I ran into Patricia Willard and she said, 'Why don't you go backstage? I'm sure the guys would like to meet you.' And I said, 'Well, they probably don't know who I am.' I didn't want to intrude, so I went home. She called me the next day and said, 'You know, Artie, I went back there and they flipped out when they heard you were in the audience. John Carter said, "My God – Artie Shaw was in the audience listening to me? He's the reason I'm playing clarinet."'

Dialogues in Swing (1970)
Artie Shaw

A Jazz Revival?

JAZZ HAS always been a minority interest like classical music but unlike classical music the taste for it has not been stable. Interest in it has grown by spurts and, conversely, there have been times when it was in the doldrums. The later 1930s and the 1950s were a period when it expanded quite strikingly, the years of the 1929 slump (in the

USA at least) when even Harlem preferred soft lights and sweet music to Ellington and Armstrong. The periods when interest in jazz has grown or revived have also, for reasons obvious to publishers, been the times when new generations of fans wanted to know more about it.

But we are once again in a period when interest in jazz is reviving quite dramatically in both Britain and the USA. For shortly after *The Jazz Scene* appeared, the golden age of the 1950s came to a sudden end, leaving jazz to retreat into rancorous and poverty-stricken isolation for some twenty years. What made this generation of loneliness so melancholy and paradoxical was that the music that almost killed jazz was derived from the same roots that had generated jazz: rock-and-roll was and is very obviously the offspring of American Negro blues. The young, without whom jazz cannot exist – hardly any jazz-fan has ever been converted after the age of twenty – abandoned it, and with spectacular suddenness. Three years after 1960, when the golden age was at its peak, in the year of the Beatles' triumph across the world, jazz had been virtually knocked out of the ring. 'Bird Lives' could still be seen painted on lonely walls, but the celebrated New York jazz venue named after him, Birdland, had ceased to exist. To revisit New York in 1963 was a depressing experience for the jazz-lover who had last experienced it in 1960.

The Revival, Continued

WHAT SEEMS to have happened is a growing musical exhaustion of rock in the course of the 1970s which may or may not be connected with the retreat of the great wave of youth rebellion which reached its peak in the late 1960s and early 1970s. Somehow, insensibly, the space for jazz seemed to become a little less cramped. One began to observe that intelligent or fashionable fifth- or sixth-formers once again began to treat parents of their friends who possessed Miles Davis records with a certain interest.

By the late 1970s and early 1980s there were undeniable signs of a modest revival, even though by then much of the classical repertoire of jazz had been frozen into permanent immobility by the death of so many of its great and formative figures, ancient and modern: the jazz life has not favoured longevity. For by 1980 even some of the formative 'new music' stars had disappeared: e.g. John Coltrane, Albert Ayler, Eric Dolphy. Much of the jazz which the new fans learned to love was thus incapable of further change and development, because it was a music of the dead, a situation which was to provide scope for a curious form of resurrectionism, by which live musicians reproduced the sounds of the past; as when a team under the direction of Bob Wilber reconstituted the music and sound of the early Ellington band for the film *The Cotton Club*. Moreover, initially a very high proportion of the live jazz the new fans could hear came from musicians ranging from the rather middle-aged to the very ancient. Thus at the time I wrote a similar introduction for an Italian reprint of *The Jazz Scene* which appeared in 1982, jazz-lovers in London had the choice of listening to a variety of veterans: to Harry 'Sweets' Edison, Joe Newman, Buddy Tate and Frank Foster, who had been enrolled in the Basie band of long ago; to Nat Pierce, known since the days of Woody Herman; Shelly Manne and Art Pepper, familiar from the 'cool' days of the 1950s; Al Grey, who went back to the swing bands of the 1930s, Trummy Young of 1912 vintage, who had spent long years with Louis Armstrong, and other members of the older generation. Indeed, among the important players performing that week perhaps only the pianist McCoy Tyner (born 1938), known for his work with Coltrane in the 1960s, would not have been immediately familiar to most jazz-lovers in 1960.

The jazz revival has continued since then. It has, inevitably, benefited the diminishing band of survivors, some of whom, returning from exile in Europe or in the anonymity of television, film and recording studios, have reconstituted groups dissolved long since, at least for occasional engagements and tours, such as the Modern Jazz Quarter, the Art Farmer–Benny Golson Jazztet. It has been a particular blessing for the survivors of the first jazz revolution, for it is bebop that has emerged or re-emerged as the central style of 1980s jazz and the basic model for youthful musicians. Conversely, the new revival has left out the old, the first 'return to tradition' of those who wanted to recapture the music of New Orleans, and the 1920s. 'Trad', 'Dixieland' or whatever it may be called, the longest-lasting of jazz styles, the one which, based on the happy nostalgia of white middle-class and increasingly middle-aged amateurs best resisted the cavalry charge of rock, but also the one which, it has been said, created nothing of musical value, has not felt the new wind in its sails.

Both the above from *The Jazz Scene* (1989)

Eric Hobsbawm

Forgotten by the Young

I DON'T read as much jazz journalism as I should, but of what I did read in 1969 it is *down beat*'s account of the Rutgers Jazz Festival that has stayed with me most vividly.

down beat, as you know, is the principal magazine of the American jazz music profession; it has been going thirty-five years, and has correspondents in every land from Denmark to Japan. Its policy is a comfortable, middle-of-the-road tolerance: whatever is, generally speaking, is right. And the man they sent to Rutgers was clearly cast in the same mould: let 'em all come, Dizzy, Herbie Mann, Jethro Tull, B. B. King, the Adderley Brothers – the more the merrier. He sat patiently in his seat and tried to hear good in everything, even sermons from Stones had they been present, and on the whole he succeeded, though there is the occasional wince ('I was beginning to wish I wore a hearing aid so I could turn it down').

The flashpoint, if one can call it that, came on the Sunday evening. Our man arrived late, to find the Miles Davis Group launched into what proved their final number, or, as he puts it, 'in the throes of what I most deplore, a free-form free-for-all' that 'degenerated into a musical catfight'. One must salute his honesty: here was one of the groups he was most anxious to hear, and it was terrible, and he admits it was terrible. But then – and this is the point – there followed the Newport All-Stars Braff, Norvo, Tal Farlow, and good old George Wein on piano, and the reporter's relief was so enormous that his encomia became almost pathetic in their hyperbole. Braff and his friends were sparkling spring water, they were *Macbeth* and *David Copperfield*, they were incomparable, they were as eternal as sex and sunlight: 'man, this is what it's all about'. In his enthusiasm he asked a seventeen-year-old girl what she thought of them. She said: 'It's music to go shopping at Klein's by.'

Now the point of this anecdote is two-fold: first, all kinds of jazz are not equally good, no matter what editorial policy may be; some of it is ravishingly exciting, and some a musical catfight scored for broken glass and bagpipes, and you have only to hear the two in succession to grab the one and reject the other. Secondly, jazz (that is, the form of Afro-American popular music that flourished between 1925 and 1945) means nothing to the young. This should strengthen us in our devotion to it. True, we must give up any notion we may have been cherishing that beneath our hoar exteriors lurk hearts of May; we may dig jazz, but the kids want something else. Our passion for this extraordinary and ecstatic musical phenomenon that lasted a mere twenty or thirty years in the first half of our century must now take its place alongside similar passions for Hilliard miniatures or plain-chant.

All What Jazz (1985)
Philip Larkin

Killed by Perfection

WHEN I was playing I was a slave to the instrument and I was a slave to my compulsive need for perfection. That can kill you, and I recognized it in myself, fortunately, in time to get out of it before it did kill me, as it has killed so many other people we could name in this business.

Dialogues in Swing (1970)
Fred Hall

So Far, No Further

IT MUST be recognized that jazz is a confined musical idiom; attempts to develop it tend to turn it into something that is not jazz. Bix Beiderbecke wanted to develop jazz, and he told Mezzrow that he was interested in Delius and Holst. His 'experiments' can be heard in two piano recordings, and it is obvious that they could not have gone much farther. Beiderbecke was not a musical intelligence of a high order; he was simply a tremendously gifted trumpet player with a kind of personal directness and honesty that appears in his playing; for us, the greater part of his charm is that he catches the atmosphere of the 1920s more than any other jazz man of the time. But his attempts to develop jazz were obviously pushing it in the direction of a sophisticated cocktail music – impressionistic 'mood' music that would make an ideal background for upper-class couples taking dinner instead of for Chicago bootleggers out on a spree; in the 1950s and 1960s John Lewis, Dave Brubeck, and Don Shirley have all developed this part of Bix's legacy.

Colin Wilson on Music (1967)
Colin Wilson

A European Future?

A UNIVERSAL cultural idiom cannot be judged by the same criteria as a special kind of art-music, and there was and is no point in judging rock by the standards of good jazz. However, rock deprived jazz of most of its potential new listeners, because the young people who flocked to rock found in it, in a simplified and perhaps coarsened version, much, if not everything that had attracted their elders to jazz: rhythm, an immediately identifiable voice or 'sound', real (or faked) spontaneity and vitality, and a way of directly transferring human emotions into music. Moreover, they discovered all this in a music which was related to jazz. Why would they need jazz? With rare exceptions, the young who would have been converted to jazz now had an alternative.

What made that alternative increasingly attractive, and helped to reduce the space for an embattled and isolated jazz still further, was its own transformation. As the bebop revolutionaries rejoined the mainstream of jazz in the second half of the 1950s, the new avant-garde of 'free jazz', moving towards atonality and breaking down everything that had hitherto given jazz a structure – including the beat round which it was organized – widened the gap between the music and its public, including the jazz public. And it was not surprising that the avant-garde reacted to the desertion of the public by taking an even more extreme and embattled stance. At the start of the new revolution it was perfectly easy to recognize in, say, Ornette Coleman's saxophone the blues feeling of his native Texas, and the tradition of the great horn-players of the past was obvious in Coltrane. Yet those were not the things the innovators wanted the public to notice about them.

But the situation of the new avant-garde in the dark decades was paradoxical. The loosening of the traditional framework of jazz, its increasing shift towards something like avant-garde classical music developed from a jazz base, opened it to all manner of non-jazz influences, European, African, Islamic, Latin American and especially Indian. In the 1960s it went through a variety of exoticisms. In other words, it became less American than it had been, and far more cosmopolitan than before. Perhaps because the American jazz public became relatively less important in jazz, perhaps for other reasons, after 1962 free jazz became the first style of jazz whose history cannot be written without taking account of important developments in Europe and, one might add, of European musicians.

The Jazz Scene (1989)

Eric Hobsbawm

Part of History

SEEN IN historical retrospect, jazz will almost certainly appear to be a phase in the development of the American Negro, and will be connected with the first three decades of this century in the way that we connect the operettas of Offenbach with the Paris of the 1860s, or those of Gilbert and Sullivan with the London of the 1880s. It is doubtful whether most of the things that have been done since 1930 will be counted as of great importance. Since the early 1940s jazz has had two faces: experimentalism, and a nostalgic backward-looking at the 1920s. Today, 'traditionalism' (which means in practice a rather vapid re-creating of the jazz sounds of forty years ago) is far more popular than 'modern jazz'. This in itself seems to prove that jazz is a period, an historical phase and the sensibility connected with it, rather than a new development in pure music.

The main objection to be made against jazz is its narrowness, its limitedness. Duke Ellington has been playing for forty years now, and has issued numberless records. Jazz would not have suffered if Ellington had retired twenty years ago, and if all but fifty of his records were destroyed. Louis Armstrong has been in jazz even longer; but he played his best jazz in the last five years of the 1920s. Again, it would be no great loss to jazz if all his other recordings were destroyed – although this is not, of course, to maintain that he has not issued many records since that compare with the best of the Hot Five and Hot Seven. Jazz enthusiasts often say that it was a tragedy that so-and-so died so young – Bix Beiderbecke, Bunny Berigan, Fats Navarro, Clifford Brown; yet considering the careers of most of the 'great' jazz men, one can hardly agree with them. It is, indeed, a pity that Beiderbecke did not live on into the age of great soloists, so that we might have a few records of his playing with tolerable bands and taking long solos. But even so, no one can say that he died too young to fulfil his promise. What we have is a satisfying body of work, as self-complete in its way as that of Ellington or Armstrong. It is unlikely that he would have shown any interesting developments. No jazz man so far has displayed any development analogous to the development of many 'serious' composers; in fact, I can think of no case in jazz where it would have seriously mattered if the composer had died after ten years of making records. (With many of them the period could be reduced to five.) This means that jazz is a limited field – like, say, that of the operetta, or zarzuela, or the modern Broadway musical. It is an interesting minor branch of music, and deserves to be studied as such by serious musicians. Whether it has any future, apart from popular music, is open to doubt. The sensible attitude would be to be grateful for its past.

Colin Wilson on Music (1967)

Colin Wilson

Youth, Relived

NEVERTHELESS, A jazz revival means the recruitment to jazz of a new generation of the young, including the impecunious and the unestablished, and certainly those not content with things as they are. In Britain jazz venues are cheap and multiplying. It is unlikely that the music the young play or listen to can or will remain confined within the limits of what is culturally and institutionally recognized, or what can be bought with a middle-class income, or even of what Charlie Parker and the Miles Davis Quintet played. Jazz is unofficial, unestablished and unpredictable, or it is nothing. The only thing that can be safely said about it is that it has survived the most difficult years of its extraordinary career. New relays of men and women will once again hear its marvellous sounds for the first time in their lives, and fall in love with it as we did; generally at the age of first love, as we did. They will not know that, fifty years later, through it one can relive the miraculous revelations of youth, and if they knew, they would not care. But it is true.

The Jazz Scene (1989)
Eric Hobsbawm

Where Did It All Go?

I INTERVIEWED James Baldwin once in London and asked him what he missed most about America. 'The bars, the barbershops, the Saturday nights,' he replied. 'Well, really I guess I miss my youth.' I thought of that when I saw him again, looking so small and so vulnerable, but never imagining that he didn't have long to live. Now I miss my own youth as well.

I loved all those afternoon sessions with the musicians, the hours in the bar after the interview. To see the young players rushing in and out of the hotel, enthusing about what they'd discovered on their first trip to Europe, the oldtimers taking it in their stride but never missing a trick. For years I took it for granted there'd be a hotel to go to and musicians to hang with, never ceasing to get a rush of excitement when someone said, 'Let's go for a drink.' It could be a 'living legend' of jazz or someone who had just joined the band from the back of beyond; each encounter was part of my education. I'd watch how Black professionals conducted themselves in a world that was frequently hostile, and in doing so, discover ways of dealing in circles where women's presence was still very resented. That I'd constructed a part of my life around the sound of the music, the majesty of King Louis, the eloquence of Sidney Bechet, was no accident; the music itself had been constructed as a means of telling the story, a tool for survival.

In the dark days before women's liberation, I spent many a night getting drunk with a friend from the Gateways, digging Dylan and Dusty. In more sober, businesslike moments, I was playing Charlie Parker and Coltrane, but heterosexual values predominated in the outside world and threatened to swamp me, and when I needed to remind myself who I was I'd go and see Pam. 'Like a Rolling Stone' and 'Just Like a Woman' meshed with 'Some of Your Loving' in my mind as I drove across London, needful. I was sure of a welcome, confirmation as well, years before any of us became aware just how much such self-expression is necessary for spiritual survival. With *Dusty in Memphis* on the deck I felt safe. She was something of a lesbian icon, a singer we thought of as one of our own; when someone taped her old sides for me for a recent birthday, I was transported back to those nights round at Pam's. We'd gossip about our less fortunate sisters, laugh to disguise the strains of living 'the life', and I'd tell her all about my latest caper. It's so much easier now, light years away from the consuming self-oppression that characterized that period for many. It's a hard-won freedom that women fought for, whatever their differing conclusions and political philosophy, but there's something about those desperate days that I can't forget.

Really, it was all part of growing up, whatever our ages. The Flamingo and those nights with the Blue Flames, Ronnie Scott's with Vi Redd and Blossom and Rahsaan Roland Kirk blowing his heart out, and where all the pianists sounded like Wynton Kelly and Bill Evans just for a minute. In New York there was a group of gay men who would take us dancing, to exclusive loft parties with ticket admittance, where people popped amyl nitrates and we danced as if there was no tomorrow. I wish I could dance like that now; in those

Manhattan lofts, at Bonne and Clyde's. Oh, my youth. Like the song: 'The youth of the heart and the dew of the morning . . . ', where have you gone?

Mama Said There'd Be Days Like This (1989)
Val Wilmer

Index